D1386988

THE RUSSIANS IN ISRAEL

The Russians in Israel

The Ordeal of Freedom

—————— Naomi Shepherd ——————

S I M O N   &   S C H U S T E R

LONDON·SYDNEY·NEW YORK·TOKYO·SINGAPORE·TORONTO

First published in Great Britain by Simon & Schuster Ltd in 1993
A Paramount Communications Company

Copyright © Naomi Shepherd, 1993

This book is copyright under the Berne Convention
No reproduction without permission
All rights reserved

The right of Naomi Shepherd to be identified as author of this
work has been asserted in accordance with sections 77 and 78
of the Copyright, Designs and Patents Act 1988.

Simon & Schuster Ltd
West Garden Place
Kendal Street
London W2 2AQ

Simon & Schuster of Australia Pty Ltd
Sydney

A CIP catalogue record for this book is available from the
British Library.

ISBN 0–671–71251–9

Typeset in 11/13 Palatino
by Florencetype Ltd, Avon
Printed and bound in Great Britain by
Butler & Tanner Ltd, Frome and London

To Rachel Guedaliova

Contents

Foreword

'In Russia we were Jews; here we are Russians.'

Over the last four years, between the end of 1989 and the end of 1993, half a million people from what was the Soviet Union have emigrated to Israel – now over a tenth of the total population of Israel.

For years this exodus had been anticipated and idealised: the liberation of Jews who had suffered under tyranny, the reunion of brothers and sisters separated for generations. For years the world had watched, on television screens, little groups of courageous demonstrators dispersed brutally by the KGB; the wives of refuseniks comforted by liberal Western leaders; bewildered ex-prisoners of the Gulag exchanged for Soviet spies. There were rumours of trade deals, of currency ransoms for Jewish dissidents. Several books were published documenting the courage and steadfastness of the Prisoners of Zion – those imprisoned, demoted, or refused work only because they wished to emigrate to Israel.

Expectations ran high because of the success in integrating the 150,000 Russian Jews who, against great odds, had made their way to Israel during the preceding twenty years.

Once the exodus was under way, Israel eagerly welcomed Soviet Jewry as a boost for its problematic economy, hobbled by a huge defence budget and unhealthily dependent on injections of aid from the United States. Economists predicted that, at least for one generation, Israel would have the most highly educated population in the world. Israel had, from its establishment, taken in the survivors of the Holocaust, penniless refugees from every corner of the world, the artisans of North Africa and the small traders of the Middle East (the middle classes went elsewhere), the lost tribes of Israel from the Yemenites to the Ethiopians, according to an uniquely generous immigration policy. Now, for the first time, Israel hoped for immigrants who would swiftly prove an economic asset, easily integrated into a modern society.

What few people had taken into consideration was the history of the Jews under Communism since 1917. Cut off from world Jewry, unable to practise their own religion, their leadership dispersed by the Bolsheviks and their communities fragmented by the Second World War, with no opportunity to study their own history or traditions, Soviet Jews had gradually lost their identity. Intermarriage with non-Jews diluted their Jewishness still more; only in the less developed Asiatic republics were they able to preserve the remnants of their own culture. Russian Jews corresponded to Sartre's bleak definition of a Jew as someone thought of as a Jew: Jews defined by the state, marked by the stamp *Evrei* in their identity cards.

Many of the earlier immigrants from the Soviet Union had studied Hebrew in secret, formed underground groups of refuseniks, taught themselves Jewish history, and were highly motivated to become Israelis. Some left Israel eventually for more prosperous and secure havens, but those who stayed became part of the life of the country. Of the hundreds of Russian immigrants interviewed during the writing of this book, only a couple stated openly that they had been members of the Communist Party. Yet it is clear that the vast majority must have had Party affiliations, if only to safeguard their continuing employment. The tensions between the earlier and later arrivals are palpable.

Nor could the Russians prove an immediate asset, given Israel's limited resources and the immigrants' own background. But the experience of the Russians in Israel constitutes an unique social experiment in world terms. Penniless, but dazzled by credit cards and consumer goods; unused, in the main, to personal initiative, responsibility and competition; with skills and talents nurtured in the Soviet command economy; and carrying a culture of alienation from authority which gave its intellectuals dignity, the Russian immigrants are struggling to find their feet in the world of private enterprise and free choice. There is no such social laboratory elsewhere in the world. While a quarter of a million Russian Jews emigrated to the United States before more stringent immigration laws were introduced in October 1991, they were not tagged like some rare species transported for their survival, and very little is known about how they fare. In Israel, on the contrary, their ordeal is a public one.

In the streets, in the schools, in the workshops and on the campuses, the Russians are conspicuous. Economists, sociologists and psychologists track them everywhere. Statisticians document their progress. Tens of voluntary organisations have been set up to help them orientate themselves. They have aroused sympathy, hostility, envy and disillusionment. This book is a first progress report from the front line, based on interviews with hundreds of new immigrants and those Israelis – veteran Russian immigrants and native-born Israelis, officials and volunteers – who are trying to help them adjust.

I am grateful to Professor Michael Shepherd, who first suggested the idea of writing a book on the immigrants; and to Carol O'Brien, whose discerning editorial eye helped me shape the final draft – the third time I have benefited from her experience.

I am particularly indebted to two people whose pioneering efforts on behalf of the Jews of the Soviet Union have inspired me: Martin Gilbert, the historian who documented the plight of the refuseniks most graphically, and Enid Wertman, Director of the Jerusalem branch of the Israel Public Council for Soviet Jewry. When I was looking for a skilled interpreter to communicate with those immigrants who knew no other language but Russian, it was Enid who introduced me to Rachel Guedaliova, who not only translated simultaneously from Russian into Hebrew and English, but acted as my interpreter in the widest sense of the word, sensitive to nuances I could not hear, and was a constant source of knowledge about life in the former Soviet Union. This book is dedicated to Rachel, who said to me, during our travels together in Israel: 'We lost our fear, but we also lost our pride.' It is in the hope that this loss will soon be redressed that this book has been written.

CHAPTER ONE

On the Eve

In Minsk, in late April, it had been cold and rainy when the plane took off in the small hours; at Ben Gurion airport outside Tel Aviv, disembarking, the immigrants came down the steps into a heavy cloud of heat. It was the last morning of one of the spring *chamsins*, pockets of desert heat from Syria and Iraq which had settled over Israel the previous week. By the time the Russians left the airport a couple of hours later, the air had cleared and there was a fresh wind from the sea, a few miles to the west. This was the immigrants' first physical experience of Israel, reminding them where on the map of the world they now were.

One of the older immigrants, a man with a keen, lean face, wore a brown suit with several medals on the right lapel, one with a hammer and sickle, and on the left breast, four rows of campaign ribbons. This was Yefsi Turkov from Stolbey, six kilometres outside Minsk, who had fought with the artillery of the Red Army from Russia's entry into the war until the liberation of Prague. During all that time he had never been home. When he finally received permission to go on leave to his family, which had been evacuated east to Orenburg in the Volga Basin, he found that his mother had died the previous day.

Turkov had been decorated for valour several times during the fighting in the Crimea. From one pocket in the worn brown suit he produced a plastic bag with more medals in the shape of stars, and from an ancient pocketbook, a crumbling, typed list of his decorations, stamped and signed by General Vassilievsky, the Soviet head of the armed forces under Stalin. The brown outfit in which he had travelled was his best suit; he wore the

1

decorations, he said, only on public holidays and festivals – of which the day of his immigration to Israel was one.

As a veteran of the Great Patriotic War he had received a pension twice that of an ordinary old-age pensioner, which he was losing on emigration. He had also been entitled to free transportation on trains and buses in Russia. Would the medals earn him similar benefits in Israel? No. But he qualified for an invalid allowance from the National Insurance Institute, as other documents testified that he had suffered two heart attacks and was in poor health.

Turkov, like so many other men and women his age, was part of the baggage of his family, who had applied for exit visas the moment perestroika had taken hold. His eldest son, a car mechanic, had been living in Haifa for three years, working as a driver; his granddaughter was a saleswoman in a carpet store. They had a flat of their own, he said proudly, and a car. After the death of his wife, Turkov had lived with his younger son, also a former army officer, with whom he had now left Russia. Unlike the earlier immigrants from Russia who, until perestroika, might have waited up to twenty years to leave the Soviet Union, Turkov's soldier son had received exit visas for himself and his family a mere month after application. Now Turkov hoped to find accommodation for himself: 'It is not good for a father to live with his children,' he said.

Anatoly Kartsev from Pinsk, aged nineteen and all alone, was travelling light in every sense. Apart from the clothes packed in two suitcases, his only possessions were a cardboard box, a gaily coloured backpack and a guitar bearing the sticker of a dump truck. 'Tolya', who looked exactly like any Russian of his age, without the slightest physical sign of his Jewish descent, said that his father had approved of his courage in going off on his own.

Tolya was going to stay, during his first week in Israel, with an immigrant family in whose five-room apartment lived grandparents, a son and a daughter, the son-in-law and a baby. They could just fit Tolya into a corner. The son, Anatoly's friend, was cleaning the streets in Tel Aviv and earning £150 a month, which to Tolya seemed a lot of money. He had come to Israel, he said, to try his strength outside Russia. He had completed his schooling and had no desire to go on studying; what he wanted to do, he said with a grin, was 'bisnis', a word which as yet has no equivalent in Russian. With whatever he could save in Israel, during the time he would not be eligible for army service, he would return to Russia and buy himself an apartment. As a Jew from a completely Jewish family he would be eligible for citizenship, but he had no intention of serving in the army. Before the end of two years he would take off again, perhaps for Canada or Australia, to seek his fortune. Israel? 'If I do well here, maybe I'll stay,' he said. 'If not' . . . he shrugged his shoulders.

The new immigrants range in age and nature from Turkov, who had paid all his debts to Russia and wished only to find an honourable old age in Israel, to Tolya, whose aim is to do 'bisnis' and feels obliged to serve no country and no ideology. It is three and a half years since Gorbachev opened the gates to all those Jews wishing to leave. The newcomers had almost all been preceded by other members of the family, or friends, and had sized up their chances in the new country or 'homeland' very carefully. Neither refugees nor political émigrés, scarcely Jews in any sense and certainly not Zionists, they were people in search of a better life – wherever that might be.

The Zelikow family, parents, daughter and son-in-law, were on their way to friends in Herzliya, a comfortable suburb near Tel Aviv. The father was a doctor and physiotherapist, the mother a teacher, and the son-in-law, who was not Jewish, but who was eligible to become an Israeli citizen as a member of a Jewish family, was an electrician. By corresponding with friends in Israel, they knew exactly where and how they could fit in; Dr Zelikow knew that he would have to undergo retraining before he could practise in Israel.

The Fibusovitz family, from a small town near Bryansk, retired parents and a daughter who was a construction engineer, were going to Upper Nazareth to join their son who, after three years in Israel, had found work in a factory. The daughter's speciality had been designing machines for cutting metal, a profession in which women in Israel were rarely employed. But she had managed to study Hebrew for two months. They laughed when asked whether they were disturbed by Israel's security problems, the conflict with the Arabs, terrorism. Anarchy and crime in post-perestroika Russia had worried them far more.

The Fibusovitz family had almost lost their links with other Jews; and to find Israeli emissaries dealing with potential immigrants they had to travel to nearby Gomel, where the remains of a community still existed. But the grandparents of the family, left behind in the cemetery there, had spoken Yiddish, and somehow the family had retained the knowledge of two Jewish festivals: Passover, the celebration of the exodus from Egypt, and the Day of Atonement. One was a historical, the other a moral link with that Jewish tradition proscribed by Communism, and with other Jews from whom they had been physically separated since the descent of the Iron Curtain.

Sylvia, one of the officials of Russian origin who receive the immigrants on arrival, finding accommodation for those who had nowhere to go, confirmed that unlike the situation two years ago, when hundreds of thousands jammed the airways into Israel and it took six hours to get a planeload out of the airport, the rate of immigration had dropped to between four and seven thousand a month. There were far more old people like Turkov, and many youngsters on their own like Tolya, who knew little about Israel but had little hope of making a decent living in Russia. Many of the families were motivated by the fear of Russian anarchy, poverty and pollution. Chernobyl and the more recent accident at Tomsk was in everyone's mind, she said. People worried about their children.

Many, said Sylvia wryly, were people in transit, hoping that America would again relax its immigration laws, or that they would eventually get into English-speaking countries elsewhere. In Israel they would save money and perhaps learn English. Only the Lithuanians and the Latvians, Jews from the Baltic republics who had managed to retain some semblance of a Jewish identity because Communism had not penetrated so deeply there, were arriving with a little knowledge of Hebrew and some background in Jewish and Zionist history.

The monitor screen announced the arrival of planes from New York and St Petersburg. Outside the airport, black-clothed, bearded Hasidim, singing and dancing in circles, hands on one another's shoulders, were welcoming one of their leaders off a plane from New York. The usual crush of Israelis waiting for their relations or friends just outside the customs hall jabbered and jostled for place, a cry of welcome going up as each sheepish couple back from honeymoon, or family bearing presents, arrived. Apart from those tourists who do not come with package tours – a tiny minority of the arrivals at Ben Gurion airport – everyone has friends or relations waiting.

Only the Russians are different. The passengers from the El Al special immigrant charter from St Petersburg come down the steps from the plane hesitantly, as if feeling their way on to a different planet. Some wear fur hats on this warm morning, and do not remove them; they are carrying too much in both hands – holdalls, canvas sacks, bursting plastic bags; one man has a dog in a special container (Israel has no quarantine law for pets); a little boy nurses a small violin case, and several youths have guitars strung over their shoulders. Most are poorly dressed. But what marks them out most from returning Israelis is their silence and obedience. A hundred and fifty passengers, many of them old people or young men on their own, with a few families, are met by Russian-speaking ushers; the children are presented with bags of sweets, and some of the passengers with bunches of flowers. They are ushered along corridors to a special reception hall with rows of chairs, like an auditorium. Compared with the rest of the airport, this hall is an oasis of passivity.

Everything in this part of the airport, down to the lavatories and nurseries, is labelled solely in Russian. Messages in red are scrolled across neon screens, with information about retraining courses, the Hebrew language studios (the *ulpan*), and other advisory services for which immigrants are told to apply at the offices of the Ministry of Absorption in the town of their choice. Each head of family will be called in turn to the cubicles at the side of the hall and the rest of the family can remain seated. They should have their documents ready, and will immediately be given part of the government grant all immigrants receive, in cheques and in cash. Those who have no accommodation arranged for them by relatives or friends already in the country will be allotted rooms in special hotels requisitioned by the government, or sent to 'absorption centres' or caravan sites near the main towns.

Boris Hellman, the head of the reception committee, a tall, thin, sharp-featured man in his forties, hurries up and down the hall, calling orders to his 'girls', most of whom are women in the uniforms of airport hostesses, and who sit behind computers in the cubicles.

Hellman addresses the audience in Russian: 'Welcome to your home, and to ours', and immediately turns to practical matters. He reassures the many elderly and frail-looking men and women among the immigrants that they will receive free medical treatment for their first six months in the country from the largest of the country's health funds. For the young, he explains that army service is deferred for their first two years in the country. For those who have not been reading the neon signs, he repeats the information about money they will receive, for it is clear that most of the newcomers have arrived with no more than their skills, their clothes and a few possessions.

'It will take time for you to get used to life in this country,' Hellman warns them, when he has delivered all the essential information. 'For some it may take a year, for some three years; it depends very much on the individual. This is a very different country to the one you have come from, with different laws and a different way of life. But underneath we are all the same.' He does not say, 'we are all Jews.' They are not all Jews.

Scanning the families waiting in the hall immediately dispels the assumption that all Russian immigrants are academically qualified. In fact, on this planeload, from one of the greatest centres of the Russo–Jewish intelligentsia, there are more ordinary working people than engineers and scientists; it seems possible that the reservoir of skilled immigrants is already emptying.

The Kalika family is a middle-aged and well-dressed quartet, the father a driver, the mother a housepainter; they arrive with two daughters. Another daughter has stayed behind in St Petersburg – which they still, from habit, call Leningrad. Zena Kalika, the housepainter, is smartly dressed and made up, a smiling, handsome Russian woman in her fifties, blonde and well preserved. She has been painting walls of apartments with a building firm for thirty years. Only one of the family's grandparents, a retired factory worker, is still alive; he decided to stay behind, as he has a pension and his own one-room apartment. That makes him a privileged person; recently a widower, he would not risk the further disorientation involved in emigration.

All their lives, the Kalikas have shared apartments with other families. They and their two daughters recently occupied one room measuring twelve square metres, and Zena Kalika shared a seven-square metre kitchen, with one stove, with three other women in the apartment. She was surprised when asked whether a rota was necessary for the use of the kitchen. 'But we were friends,' she said, 'we had always shared the kitchen.'

Leningrad is among the most overcrowded cities in Russia. Nearly fifty years after the Second World War, and with a low birth rate, the Soviet administration had still not been able to cope with the destruction of much of the city by the Germans, and the fact that those who had fled Leningrad during the siege and returned to find their homes intact, also found that they had acquired other tenants.

The Kalikas knew quite well, of course, that such conditions did not exist in the West; indeed, the hope of having their own home at last was one of the main reasons prompting their emigration. Zena enquires whether women are employed in Israel in housepainting, as she would like to continue in her own job. This is unlikely – building labour in Israel is exclusively male – but she says she will work in any job she is given – domestic work, for instance. Like almost all the immigrants arriving in the last year or two, the Kalikas have friends in Israel, in the port city of Ashdod, where they are going; they heard that there is work there, and government apartments for which they can slowly pay off a mortgage. This family – perhaps because they are ordinary working people with no great expectations – look cheerful and optimistic. They also look as if they had been model Soviet citizens. The young daughter says that her favourite subject at school was 'labour' – that is, knitting and cooking; for boys, she says, it was carpentry or mechanics. What she likes doing in her spare time is embroidery. It seems that only the father is Jewish; but under the Israeli Law of Return, that is enough to ensure the immigration of the whole family.

★ ★ ★

The Bayenis family from Tichvin, a smaller town near Leningrad, lived in more spacious quarters. They are slightly younger, in their forties, and they have more specialised skills, though whether those skills are relevant in Israel is doubtful. Yosif Bayenis is a mechanic whose field of expertise is petrol pumps, and he attended technical (vocational) school. His wife, Marina, is a kindergarten teacher. Like many new immigrants, part of the Bayenis family is already in Israel – Yosif's brother and his family, who arrived in Israel two years earlier and whose reports home were positive. His brother comes from Berdychev, in the Ukraine, and had first begun working in Givatayim, near Tel Aviv, as a building labourer; now he had found work in a printing press, and felt secure enough to recommend Israel to Bayenis.

'Our reasons for coming to Israel were economic; nothing else. In Russia our lives were too hard. Our salaries were buying less all the time, and my wife lost her job as a kindergarten teacher,' says Bayenis. The kindergarten was run by a factory for the children of employees. When the factory, like many others today, closed down, the various facilities serving it also collapsed. Many immigrants have similar stories of the disintegration of the economy which had supported them.

The Bayenis family, too, had left their pensioner parents behind, but hoped that, once established, they could bring them over. The younger daughter, who was eleven and who liked singing and knitting, had already begun to learn Hebrew.

But the elder daughter, thirteen years old, was the only member of the family who looked not only sad, but desperate. She sat tight lipped and pale, as her parents spoke. As far as she was concerned, leaving Russia had meant leaving her home, her friends, her school and her language. Too old to fit in easily now into an Israeli school, too young to have made her own decisions, it was clearly she who was going to have the hardest time.

Sitting alone, twisted round in his seat, anxiously listening for his name to be called, was Yuri Reshkin, an artist. Unlike the members of the Kalika and the Bayenis families, Reshkin was very Jewish looking, with semitic features, his dark hair thin on top but long on the collar, with timid eyes behind thick glasses, and a look of intense anxiety. He wore what looked like his best suit, and had long, stained fingers, one of which he had cut while preparing his departure and hastily plastered. His only piece of hand luggage was a worn briefcase.

Reshkin had painted portraits and landscapes, and also taught art to children. He was a graduate of the Leningrad Academy of Arts and a member of the Soviet Union of Painters. Despite his appearance, Reshkin was not, in rabbinical terms, a Jew, as his mother, an art critic who had died in his infancy, had not been Jewish. He was going to Jerusalem where he knew two immigrants, a mother and daughter, both professionals. He had decided to emigrate two years ago but had waited all this time for the necessary official invitation from Israel. Single people inevitably fall to the back of the queue.

Reshkin, who, when talking, lost some of his anxious look and became shyly voluble, said that he knew very little about the history of his family and his Jewish antecedents. His Jewish grandfather, he knew, had come from Simferopol in the Crimea, and before the revolution had owned a pharmacy. That was all. Reshkin was brought up by his grandparents; his grandmother had painted fabrics, so that art, or at any rate decorative work, was in the family.

In the Soviet Union, he said, an artist's life was difficult if you did not like painting murals or enormous paintings for public buildings, in which case you could make a good living. Reshkin had never done this – 'I was faithful to myself' – and had made ends meet by selling portraits, by selling his landscapes to friends, and, when really in want, going to live in the artists' communities in *dachas* outside St Petersburg which were available to members of the artists' union. They were allowed to stay there for two years at a time.

He had been out of Russia once before, to Norway, in 1991, where he had painted and sold many landscapes. Today, of course, everything had changed. Now there were private galleries and a flourishing market in Leningrad and Moscow, but an artist needed some capital to have his work put on show, as often he had to pay for renting space in the galleries, as well as a commission on sales.

But it was not economic need, said Reshkin, or the difficulties of perestroika that had impelled him to leave. Nor was it anti-semitism. He had no family to worry about, and he was mobile.

He had not even thought of visiting Israel. But relatives of his had brought back photographs and videos of the country, and the sight had entranced him. He simply wanted to live in Israel, he said, to paint the landscapes of the country, and perhaps to teach children art. When he had made this decision, he went to the library and looked up all the books he could find on the art, architecture and landscape of Israel. He thought he would live in a kibbutz on the outskirts of the city, where they needed an art teacher.

Alexey Nikiforov and Oleg Dudin had met on the plane; two handsome young men travelling alone. Alexey was nineteen and was in transit; he had seized the opportunity offered by the Jewish Agency of an entrance visa to Israel because his mother, a successful engineer, had left Russia two years earlier for the United States as a tourist, had settled there and married. She was living in Berkeley, California, and Alexey's great ambition was to study there at the university. His grandparents had followed his mother, but it was taking a long time for his own American visa to come through. Meanwhile, he had been thrown out of the St Petersburg Technical University where he had been studying. 'If your mother's gone, you'll be going too, and we're not wasting any more state money on you,' he had been told.

Since his mother's departure, Alexey had lived on his own, in her apartment and with her car, but longing all the time to be gone. Then his chance came; a year earlier, his mother met an American woman who was immigrating to Israel, to a kibbutz on the sea shore called Sdot Yam, and she obtained an invitation for him to work at the kibbutz.

What had been the reaction of his friends in St Petersburg to his leaving the country? 'They said they wished they could leave too,' said the young man, displaying a bracelet with a name plate on his wrist. 'That was given me by my best friend,' he said emotionally. 'He said: don't take that off your wrist until we meet again abroad.'

Alexey said he anticipated civil war in Russia. There were many weapons in private hands, he said, and it was dangerous to be out in the streets in St Petersburg after dark these days. He produced a money belt with a few hundred dollars: 'I was afraid in the taxi all the way to the airport,' he said. 'They could have killed me for that. When you walk along the streets and you look at the faces, people look like hungry dogs struggling for food.'

Alexey had met Oleg on the plane and had asked the officials if he, too, could join him at Sdot Yam. The kibbutzim need young labour; they agreed readily. Oleg, from Voroshilov in the Ukraine, was far less condemnatory about the state of his native land, and looked somewhat embarrassed by Alexey's description. Oleg had been an ordinary worker in a gas company and had also worked for an electrical concern. He was an orphan, leaving Russia to seek his fortune. After the period in the kibbutz, which was free, he intended to go to the 'big cities', to Tel Aviv or Jerusalem, and, like Tolya, to do 'bisnis'.

Boris Hellman, who arrived from Russia twenty years ago and has worked all the intervening years as an official helping other Russians assimilate to Israel, confirmed that the arrival of so many young people on their own was a new development. That never happened in the early years of immigration but now, he said with a smile, quite a few are seizing the opportunity to get off on their own, get away from their parents. Most of them were sent for an initial period to the kibbutzim, if they agreed.

He did not want to be pinned down to any assessment as to how many of the new immigrants were actually Jewish. The arrival of so many non-Jews, the result of the very liberal provisions of the Law of Return, and of the high rate of intermarriage of Jews in the Soviet Union, was nonetheless something which had not been so obvious when Hellman began working in 'absorption' in the early 1970s, when the first thousands of Russian Jews began arriving. The families who came at that time were distinctly Jewish, and more homogeneous. Among them, there were the 'refuseniks', that small minority of Jews conscious of their heritage and culture who had struggled for years to leave the Soviet Union. There had also been many Jewish immigrants from the Asiatic republics – from Bukhara and Georgia and Uzbekhistan – who had found it easier to retain their own tradition in the Muslim environment of Eastern Russia, which was more tolerant of religion.

The Law of Return, which allows relations of any Jew within

11

three generations (whether on the father's or the mother's side) to immigrate to Israel, is in stark contradiction to the provisions of Halacha, or rabbinical law, which regards only the child of a Jewish mother as Jewish. According to rabbinical criteria, many of the immigrants arriving in the last three years are not Jewish at all and may even have difficulty in receiving the status of citizens, remaining 'permanent residents' of Israel. Since the laws relating to personal status – from the definition of 'nationality' in the Israeli identity cards issued by the Ministry of the Interior to the laws of marriage and divorce – are all governed by rabbinical law, many problems await the new arrivals from Russia of which perhaps they are only dimly aware, if at all.

There is no civil marriage or divorce in Israel, so many of the children off the planes from Minsk and St Petersburg will not be able to marry, if the rules are not changed, within the frontiers of Israel.

'Rabbinical law will not change,' says Hellman. 'But if some solution is not found to the status of these quasi-Jews, in addition to all the other problems of adjustment which they encounter, they will leave, and Israel will lose many talented individuals.' He thought the rabbis might make conversion easier, and the immigrants would agree to some kind of a ceremony. 'After all,' he said, 'very many of the men and boys go through circumcision in hospitals. Anything to belong. It's human nature to want to be like the rest.' He thought only the minority who are practising Christians would object.

The other possibility was that, faced with tens of thousands of new, young secular-minded immigrants who were not Jews in the rabbinical sense but who wanted to remain Israelis, the Knesset would pass laws allowing for civil marriage – something which has not happened hitherto, despite the fact that the majority of Israelis are not orthodox or even practising Jews. 'I don't see the rabbis insisting on any change in the Law of Return to bring it into line with rabbinical law,' said Hellman. 'It makes no sense to break up families, or to encourage official lies.'

The attitude of the immigrants off the planes from Minsk and St Petersburg, the fact that none of them had expressed any ideals about Jewishness or Zionism, and the willingness of the young to go anywhere, did not seem, to Hellman, a disadvantage. 'There's no direct correlation between feeling a strong sense of Jewish identity and deciding to come to Israel,' he said decisively. 'In fact, it may even be a handicap for the immigrant to be too strongly Zionist. The higher the expectations, the greater the disappointment. It's much better to come without too many illusions, for practical reasons.'

The flood of new immigrants from the former Soviet Union, and the benefits and problems it has brought both to Israel and the immigrants themselves, are the result of several changes which had nothing to do with Israel. The Russians now have passports allowing them to travel, whereas before they only had exit permits, and were stateless until they received Israeli passports. So today they are not dependent on Israel providing them with a nationality. On the other hand, while in the 1970s and 1980s those Russian Jews who succeeded in leaving the Soviet Union often opted for emigration to the United States and elsewhere in the West, from October 1991 the change in the American immigration laws made it almost impossible to enter the United States. Elsewhere in the West, tough immigration laws, and widespread unemployment, have made Israel more attractive. The 'drop-out rate' at Vienna or Budapest, which earlier caused some sharp conflicts between the Israeli government and American–Jewish organisations, when Soviet emigrants with Israeli visas opted for America instead, has disappeared. Perestroika and its discontents have impelled many Jews to leave, with no alternative, meanwhile, than for Israel.

Where Israel was concerned, the new policy of 'direct absorption' adopted in 1987 according to which immigrants themselves became responsible for finding, or choosing, accommodation and work, with only financial assistance from the government, meant that the incentive to work was, in Hellman's eyes, far greater. Previously, the government itself had assigned immigrants to 'development areas' and created relief schemes for their employment. This policy had been evolved to cope with the largely unskilled waves of immigration from North Africa and the Middle East reaching Israel in the 1950s and 1960s. It had become increasingly irrelevant to a highly skilled, and easily discontented, immigration from the Soviet Union – one which all too easily became dependent on 'the authorities'.

13

On the way down to the luggage hall, the Russians queued for their one free phone call back to Russia to reassure the relations left behind. Their plane tickets and cargo had been paid for by the Jewish Agency, the organisation which brings Jewish immigrants from those communities defined as 'in need', which can include Jews as far apart in culture, appearance and skills as the Jews of Western Russia and those from the villages of Ethiopia. Staring at some of the Ethiopian Israelis in the uniform of the border police, one of the immigrants confessed: 'It is hard for me to understand how they can be our brothers.'

Most families had several trolleyfuls of bulging suitcases, cartons and sacks, and the Agency had laid on minibuses and taxis. It was here, down in the arrivals hall, surrounded by Israelis chattering Hebrew, with elegant luggage (where in the West do people travel with burlap sacks?), waving to waiting friends and relations, that the Russians looked most isolated and forlorn.

'The Israelis respond well to new immigrants at moments of crisis, under pressure,' said Hellman. 'But they can't keep it up. No one seems to understand how important it is for Israel, strategically and politically, that these hundreds of thousands of people should be integrated as quickly as possible into the life of the country. That means that everyone has to be involved. At the beginning of this immigration, in 1990 and 1991, on the eve of Passover and the New Year – which for many of the immigrants was the first encounter with Jewish customs – many families volunteered to invite the Russians to their homes. Sometimes I'd have as many as ten Israelis inviting every Russian family.

'That's finished now. All they get now is a couple of smiles, a pat on the back. Everyone's tired of the Russians. The state does the minimum – proposing accommodation, providing unemployment benefits, and so on. Then they're on their own. The previous government thought it had to concentrate on getting those loan guarantees from the Americans, and that was the end of it.

'The kibbutzim are taking some of the young people for a limited period, but they've taken the easy way out too. They need the extra labour but in the long term they don't have much for the immigrants. There's nothing else on offer. There's no relationship between the talents these immigrants bring with them and the kind of work that is proposed for them.

'This emigration isn't going to end. The Russians are going to keep coming, and there's no other source of immigration of talented qualified labour, cheap, trained elsewhere. The Jews of the West aren't going to come to Israel in large numbers.

'To my mind, those who are responsible for immigration have failed. They haven't stressed that all these people need understanding and support. Of course there is a problem of balancing the claims of the veteran population with those of the immigrants – that's true, but too much is left to volunteers.

'In the schools, far more could be done to educate children about the importance of helping the immigrants and giving them encouragement to stay. But very few people are directly involved. Veteran Israelis have got to feel like parents with small children, because that's what the Russian immigrants are. You get annoyed with them, they're often a nuisance, but they're your responsibility, and you have to look after them.'

Hellman's criticism, and the restrained passion with which he expressed it, emerged as typical of all those involved, on a daily basis, with the immigrants from the former Soviet Union. Yet nowhere else in the world would people like the Russians off the planes from Minsk and St Petersburg be so easily granted entry, merely on the grounds that they were in some way – perhaps very tenuously – linked to Jewry.

CHAPTER TWO

The First Circle

The hotel had been going downhill even before the immigrants were quartered there. Situated on a southern promontory of Jerusalem which led only to a kibbutz and an Arab village, it had never attracted tourists. Its pretentious facade of black glass was smeared and dusty, and there was nothing to suggest it was a hotel turned hostel; it looked more like a factory or warehouse, with crates piled up near the entrance and workmen's vans parked outside.

Four elderly women sat on the shallow steps, taking the sun. One was fine featured, elegant, and wore a lace blouse and a comb in her hair. The second had the dumpy figure and stubborn features of a Russian peasant woman; she had a door key suspended from a string round her neck, like a schoolchild. The third looked scholarly, and the fourth, her face deeply lined and her beet-coloured hair pulled tight under a kerchief, wearing a long flowered dress, had bright blue, mad, unblinking eyes. 'Never, never would you have found these women together in Russia,' murmured Rachel, my interpreter.

Three were chatting amicably in Russian, the fourth laughing to herself, and they welcomed us as a dull day's diversion. They were all retired, and had come to Israel for the medical care, they said, and the old-age benefits. 'If you're really old, or a small child, Israel is good.' When I asked if they'd worked, there was an affirmative chant: '*Da, da, robote*': what else?

The elegant woman was an economist from Moscow. The peasant woman was no peasant, but a telephone operator from a factory in the Ukraine; she had spent four years in a concentration camp, she said proudly – a testimony to survival, perhaps, or

17

something which earned her special consideration, like the rows of ribbons on the coat of an old man who passed by on his way indoors. The scholarly woman was a librarian from Sverdlovsk, the madwoman with the hennaed hair from Tagikistan.

They preferred to sit outside, they said, because of what went on in the lobby. Their rooms were crowded. They all had other relatives with them, and there was no room to move about. 'We're frightened of the Moroccans who live here,' said the economist. 'They put us here together with the city homeless, the problem families, and sometimes there are fights. Outside is better.' In the evenings, they kept to their rooms. 'There is no television, no restaurant,' said the librarian. 'We hope to be moved to the caravans, but it will take a long time.' She had a son living with her, an engineer, she said, who had found work cleaning school-rooms. To save the bus fare, he walked to work half an hour away.

They disagreed about the quality of the health care. 'In emergencies, they are good here,' said the concentration camp survivor in a tone of some experience. 'The surgery is better than in Russia. But not the treatment. In Russia the doctor came to visit you at home, for no extra charge.'

'I was released from hospital here while I was still weak,' complained the librarian. 'It was very crowded.' 'But the insurance is good,' said the economist. 'Besides, since perestroika it is very expensive.' 'Oh, perestroika,' they chorused, with unmistakable revulsion. 'My doctor came to see me,' said the former economist. 'He said "how can you possibly all live together in one room?" – I share with my son and daughter and their child. As if we *choose* to live together,' she added sadly, and the others nodded.

What was going on in the lobby was clear. This was no hotel – there was no reception, no bellboys, no brochures on revolving stands; it was a public precinct, where on the one ramshackle sofa a sullen middle-aged whore sat waiting for clients. Near the stairs sat a guard with a revolver.

On the upper floors, the corridors were dark, the electric bulbs either broken or removed to save expense. No chambermaid had swept here in recent months. Discarded cartons and bottles littered the corners, and the only light came from a window at the corridor's end. A small child raced past on a tricycle and tugged experimentally at the tape recorder. No man's land. In the communal kitchen – there was one to each floor – a woman was watching a saucepan on a stove completely coated in black grease. The overpowering, rancid smell of frying sausage was everywhere.

We met Natalya on the second floor, as she was leaving her room. She could not close her door, as she had no door to close. It had been removed, and in its place was a checked rayon blanket. She said the ministry computer had malfunctioned and her rent had not been paid, so the man in charge had taken her door off its hinges. Each time she went out, she took her few valuables next door, to her friend.

Natalya was a pretty, perfectly groomed woman in her mid thirties, smartly dressed, demure. Her room was as neat as she was, and her possessions were minimal – standard Russian collectibles. They were bright ugly vases, prints of cool alien landscapes, mountain scenes and lakes; lace doilies; photographs of distant relations; solidly bound volumes of Russian classics; and a clock cum barometer, which told you when to go to work and how many layers of clothes to wear.

Natalya had been in Israel for nine months. A woman on her own, she had sought the cheapest possible accommodation, to make her 'absorption basket' – the grant all immigrants receive – last as long as she could. She was a radiotechnician, from Kiev, with a first degree, and she had a heart problem. (The documents she showed us, from an Israeli hospital, described a faulty valve, which had provoked a minor heart attack during her first months in the country.) She also suffered, she said, from a kidney ailment. It was, she thought, something to do with Chernobyl.

In Kiev, her apartment had reverted to the state when she left. There was nothing to go back to. The hotel, she said, was terrible. Prostitutes worked out of the lobby all night, and drugs were peddled openly. The police only came in when the knives came out. One of the Moroccan populist politicians had canvassed here at election time, four months previously, and there had been fist fights. But Natalya was hopeful. Within a few weeks, she would move to a caravan, the next step up for immigrants too poor to put down money for an apartment.

Natalya had not found work in her profession, but she was

making enough to live on by cutting the hair of other immigrants in the hotel. She had been offered domestic work at the labour exchange, but had refused because of her heart condition.

The loss of the door to her room was the least of her problems. After two months in Israel she had boarded a bus by the back door (an offence in Israel, where the driver takes fares at the entrance). The driver had shouted at her, and the passengers pushed her to the front, where she presented her season ticket – lent her by a man friend in the hotel. The driver noticed that the ticket was not her own, closed the bus doors, and drove to the nearest police station. By this time, Natalya was hysterical, and had to be pulled off the bus at the station, where she wrestled with the policewoman brought out to deal with her. Without understanding a word of anything that had been said, or the offences she had committed – she said tickets were regularly swapped in Kiev and no one cared if you got on at the back if the front was crowded – she acquired a police file. On the charge sheet Natalya was accused of defrauding the bus company, resisting arrest and attacking a police officer. She was to appear in court in a week's time.

Then there was her health insurance. Her heart attack had taken place during the first six months in the country, during which immigrants are automatically insured against illness. But later, when she had to choose a health fund to which she would contribute every month, she made a false declaration, claiming that she had never suffered from any chronic disease. 'It would cost me too much to pay what they were asking if I told them that,' she said innocently. Although she had already been hospitalised for a chronic heart problem, and her case was on record, she did not or would not recognise that the health fund might well refuse to pay her hospital charges next time.

We accompanied Natalya to the court, where I spoke to the prosecutor, a harassed young woman who couldn't make head or tail of the case, and Rachel acted as interpreter. The judge was puzzled by Natalya. Respectable in her suit with the velvet collar, not a hair out of place, her face impassive, she looked neither deranged nor one of those delinquents who bag free rides and attack the police. The judge decided to believe her, but he insisted that his every word was translated, frowning at the unfamiliar language as he studied Natalya's face. She would have to admit to the charge of travelling on a ticket not her own; the other charges against her would be dropped. She must understand that what she had done was against the law, that she would be referred to a probation officer who would examine her living conditions and report back to the police. It was unlikely that a penalty would be imposed, but she would have to perform some public service. Had she understood?

Natalya nodded and agreed. Docile, she accepted the verdict and thanked the judge. Once outside the court, she threw her arms round me, the first sign of emotion since we had encountered her.

But when we turned up for her next appearance in court, it emerged that she had not gone to see the probation officer. Under questioning, it became clear that neither she nor Rachel had known what a probation officer was. There was no equivalent in the Soviet Union. Sighing, the judge once more adjourned the case, and Rachel took Natalya straight to the city probation office, with whom the case now rested.

Some weeks later, Natalya moved into a caravan on a hilltop site which city planners had originally destined for a residential suburb, but which had become a temporary home for other Russians in transit and homeless Israelis. There, Natalya, who insisted on having a Russian translation of her contract, put down £5,000 (20,000 shekels – 4 shekels is roughly £1.00) as leasehold for nine square metres of living space. The room had muslin curtains, Natalya's possessions, and a set of paper lampshades which, Rachel noticed, had been removed from the hotel. She had applied to a different health fund for membership, assuming that in this way she could hide her chronic illness. Demure and self-contained as ever, she had become the caravan dwellers' unisex hairdresser, undercutting all the barbers in town.

Immigrants who have friends or family in Israel to advise them, or invite them to share their apartments for the first weeks or months, or who have a job waiting, do not need government help. Those who do, or who prefer to save the initial government grant for later, are put up 'temporarily' in the run-down hotels or the caravan sites which have mushroomed all over the country.

The largest caravan site in the country is at Nahal Beka, just south of Beersheba, past the old city and the industrial zone, off the main road to the southern desert. Although it is only a couple of kilometres from Beersheba, capital of the Negev, it looks like a ghost town, or perhaps, in Russian terms, a Potemkin village, set up to convince some visiting dignitary that there is immigrant life in the desert, but ready to be dismantled the day he leaves. The problem is that these stage sets for social disaster look likely to remain in place.

Row on row of caravans – prefabricated rooms on platforms, not on wheels – have been set down in a grid pattern with huge bare avenues between them, wider than the main streets of Moscow. The desert climate, blazing hot in summer but with wadis which flood rapidly in winter, means that immigrants on their way to and from town are totally exposed. They have used the wood from the crates they brought to build porches, or frames for awnings, over which canvas or netting is stretched to keep out the sun. Some have even planted shrubs. As the caravans are 'temporary' there is no shopping centre, no cinema or recreation hall – only fenced-in kindergartens, an *ulpan* or Hebrew class, synagogues (separate ones for Russians and their fellow immigrants of the nineties, the Ethiopians, who worship differently), a chess club (Russian valium) and a place where the elderly can meet. There are few public telephones, and no letter boxes – so for people who depend on contact with their relations in Russia for emotional support, and for the offices in Beersheba for work, life is one long trek to the camp's post office.

The administrative office can only be located in this huge complex because an Israeli flag is flying there. Leonid, an ex-aircraft engineer and restaurant owner, in Israel for nine years, is the coordinator for the 6,000 Russian immigrants in the camp; another official looks after the 700 Ethiopians.

Leonid was afraid that the caravan camps, like the transit camps of the fifties and sixties, might become permanent quarters. One year should be the maximum stay for any family, he said; the conditions were hard, and the climate bad for old people. There were many chronically sick, many one-parent families – most of them women – and the camp had already had its first deaths, one a suicide. Like every dedicated official we were to meet, he said that all Russian families needed an Israeli social worker to explain to them the way the country functioned, the immigrants' rights and opportunities.

The main reason people stayed in the caravans was because they did not find work; but without permanent work they would never be eligible for mortgages to buy one of the thousands of flats the government had built in the suburbs of Beersheba in anticipation of mass immigration – now standing almost empty. Most of the Russians were engineers whose qualifications were not suitable for Israeli industry. The problem was not official policy, but the structure of the economy and work standards. Even if the immigrants picked up enough Hebrew at the local *ulpan*, it was difficult placing them, and few knew how to find jobs for themselves. Most of the immigrants, he said, wanted to set up little businesses, but – having run a restaurant himself – he knew that they knew nothing about taxation, about VAT, or even about how to make a profit. If they rented a shop and started that way, they were bound to lose whatever they had.

Moving them out in order of arrival didn't work; those few who had money to spare got out as soon as possible. The others stagnated, trudging in to pick up unemployment benefits, going once a week to Beersheba to stare into the shop windows at goods they couldn't afford to buy. There were shops which sold goods to immigrants at a twenty per cent discount; the flood of immigrant custom made it worth the shopkeepers' while. But most of the tenants of Nahal Beka were using this first period to save money, and for them the caravans were a lifeline.

Batya Waldman was one such immigrant. Single, in her early forties, she had come from Riga to Beersheba, where she had relations, some time earlier, and had spent a week in an apartment in town before deciding that the caravans were a good first option. With the money she saved she had bought a fridge and gas range, in addition to the inevitable vases, doilies, water colours and books. Like most of the caravans, hers displayed an outside thermometer capable of recording temperatures far below Middle East levels.

Batya was a philologist with a special interest in French literature and its influence on Turgenev. This, she said smiling, had been no good for earning a living, as she had not taken a doctorate, so in Riga she had worked as an editor of technical publications to do with irrigation techniques and automation. Such a career was far from rare in the Soviet Union, where arts graduates often ended up in factory offices as editors or translators.

In Nahal Beka, Batya had become unofficial spokeswoman for the caravan population, as a journalist for the local Russian newspaper in Beersheba: she was the caravan correspondent. Leonid found her a good spokeswoman for the immigrants: more public telephones had been installed, music and drawing classes added to the chess clubs. The bus service had been improved (a bus every half an hour – scarcely frequent on a burning summer or freezing winter day). Batya said that there were all kinds of advantages to living in the caravans if you were reasonably young and fit. Even if there was no shopping centre, the site was near the Beersheba open-air market, cheaper than shopping in town. If a couple had children, they could rent an entire caravan, with two rooms. There were local hairdressers who charged rock bottom prices (like Natalya), Russian dentists, and a host of homeopathic doctors – a profession popular in Russia, where medical supplies were short. From cobblers to cosmeticians, every service was cheaper than in town.

Nahal Beka was little Russia, but for those condemned to live there indefinitely, Batya said, it was becoming an immigrant ghetto. For a while, a handful of students from Beersheba, under one of the myriad volunteer schemes, had been sent to live among the immigrants. But without a knowledge of the language they were of little use, and soon shut themselves away into their agreeably cheap new housing, absorbed in their studies.

The man who had committed suicide was a locksmith, aged fifty-two – the worst age for an immigrant. Alone, without work (few break-ins, nothing to steal), afraid of the passing months which brought him closer to destitution, he gave up. Many of the newcomers were single people, who spent much of their allowances on drink; Jews, who everyone said never drank in Russia, took to the bottle. Russians didn't know how to organise, both fearing and obeying authority, and were slow to protest. The Beersheba municipality and the building authority disagreed over who was responsible for maintenance. The winter following our visit, the site, in a desert wadi, flooded at the first winter rains.

Near Batya's caravan lived a Russian father with a paraplegic son, Misha. Their caravan has a ramp leading up from the road to the entrance, built by Misha's father to get the wheelchair up to the door. Misha qualified for a pension from National Insurance, but not for the fifty per cent reduction on telephone calls which was essential for him to reach doctors in an emergency while enabling his father to balance his budget. For that he needed another six per cent disability rating. Without any knowledge of Hebrew, or of the labyrinth of Israeli bureaucracy, father and son would have been lost without Ya'akov, one of the many Israeli volunteers who step in when the system breaks down. Ya'akov besieged the local hospital until he got Misha's rating raised.

Ya'akov had come to Nahal Beka the day we visited not only to check up on progress, but to collect the product of Misha's working week, a sackful of spare parts for electric kettles. Like other disabled immigrants, Misha earns £3.50 for every thousand kettle plugs he manages to assemble. If he worked twenty hours a day, he would earn the Israeli minimum wage, but the work is provided not for a living, but to give Misha something to do. The work alone would be pointless if Ya'akov didn't turn up to drag the sack, with its thousands of kettle plugs, into the back of his beat-up Peugeot.

Ya'akov is a spare, energetic man in his sixties, forty years with the Israel arms industry, pensioned off early in the framework of current cuts in manpower – Israel no longer sells as many weapons abroad as it would like to do. Ya'akov belongs to that generation which remembers austerity, the volunteering spirit, the mass immigration of the fifties and sixties. He bridles at any criticism of Nahal Beka, insisting that the conditions are far superior to those of the transit camps provided for north African immigrants in the 1950s – asbestos huts with no plumbing in unpaved waste lots.

His chief concern is to help those disabled or sick Russians who, while they receive help from the welfare and health authorities, are in danger of losing their self esteem as they cannot work. The social services are hopelessly overstrained, so Ya'akov is the only link between housebound immigrants and the local workshop for the disabled. Handling three cases at a time is all Ya'akov can manage. He pays for the petrol himself. The immigrants are scattered across the length and breadth of Beersheba, not only in the caravans but in the poorer quarters of the town.

His second case is Felix, a sixty-two-year-old ex-coal mining engineer with thirty years experience from Karaganda, the infamous Gulag site in Kazakhstan. Felix arrived in Israel three years ago with an eighty per cent disability; he lives in a wheelchair, with only part of one leg in place. The amputations are the result of thromboses following complications from diabetes – all medical treatment performed in Israel at the taxpayers' expense. Felix, left with a powerful torso, works five to eight hours a day. He is married, with a daughter, and is cared for by his wife, who runs a nearby lottery kiosk. Amidar, the immigrant housing organisation has found him a cottage for which he pays £12.00 a month. The National Insurance Institute hires students to lift him and help him around, and the only bureaucratic puzzle still to be solved (with Ya'akov's help) is his tax file: immigrants begin to pay tax after three years in the country.

Venya, once a baker from the Ukraine, living in another Amidar cottage in a suburb of ill repute, is Ya'akov's third protégé. He arrived in Israel in November 1990, totally paralysed from the waist down. When Ya'akov arrived at Venya's cottage, he used a huge bunch of keys at his belt to get in – one to unlock the garden gate, the second an inner gate, and the third the front door. This was, he explained, because Venya had been robbed several times; money was even taken from the refrigerator where he had hidden it. Since the Six Days War, Beersheba has been one of the main drug centres in Israel, on the smuggling route from Egypt to the north, and there are all too many addicts in the town who would kill, let alone rob, an invalid for his money.

Venya was still assembling the last plugs of his weekly quota. His fingers are nimbler than those of Felix, for in Russia, once disabled, he was a typist, a skill much in demand in Russian factories where computers were in short supply. He had worked in many institutions and offices in Moscow, and students would give him their doctorates to type, as private typewriters were rare and expensive.

After re-locking Venya into his cottage, Ya'akov raced to get to the workshop in the factory area on the edge of Beersheba in time for his scheduled delivery. The workshop, subsidised by government and private funds, is entirely manned by the disabled, many of whom are Russians, those sufficiently mobile to come in from the surrounding Negev towns. On one wall a poster says ISRAEL NEEDS A FLOURISHING ECONOMY. Most of the disabled workers were connecting pipes and other spare parts for various machines. Igor, a fifty-three-year-old clocksmith from Kishinev in Moldava, was self-educated. He was a spastic, in his spare time learning to be a gardener. Sasha, whose only disability was a semi-paralysed leg, commuted every day from a nearby desert town, near Israel's sole nuclear facility; wary of a Chernobyl repeat, few Russians want to live there, so Sasha had a two-room, ground-floor flat. Luxury. In Russia, he said, he had worked in a military plant where he was paid 'more than a teacher'.

In six months travelling around the country, we were to meet few Russians with as few complaints as the old women on the steps of the Jerusalem hotel and Ya'akov's protégés in Beersheba.

A high-ranking official in the Ministry of Labour had this to say: 'The Jewish Agency [the Zionist organisation], people active in Russia, are doing Israel a disservice by encouraging the immigration of the old and sick; they're an unnecessary burden on the National Insurance and health facilities of the country. Successful absorption and retraining can only apply to the young.'

'I would never have dreamed of being a policeman in the Soviet Union,' said Muni, a burly middle-aged Russian Israeli in charge of security at the Napoleon's Hill caravan site near Acre, in Western Galilee. 'That would have been a real social stigma. Jews weren't policemen in Russia.' He still didn't admit to being a regular policeman, but a police 'community officer in charge of relations between new immigrants and the police'. 'I don't actually make arrests; and I try not to involve the Acre police in caravan quarrels.'

Muni is a veteran immigrant, one of hundreds of ex-Russians working with the newcomers. When he arrived in 1973, one of many engineers who had to downgrade their professional skills, he found work in a fruit-packing factory in Acre. There, Muni learned that there was a retraining course for police work, and having joined up first as a tracker and then as a detective, he became the natural choice for handling immigrants in transit sites. What he tries to do now is to keep the peace between Russians and Ethiopians, and to keep criminal elements in Acre, both Jewish and Arab, away from the newcomers.

Napoleon's Hill is smaller than Nahal Beka, and the sea is nearby, but the general prospect is the same. Little crowds of Russians and Ethiopians gather at street corners. There are separate though equal areas, the Russians to the north of the site, the Ethiopians to the south. Just beyond the site, in a large pool of rain water, two small Russian children have built a raft from the crates which held the immigrants' possessions and are happily punting up and down, covered with mud.

In Nahal Beka, there were two playgrounds; one for Russians, one for Ethiopians. In Napoleon's Hill, with its much smaller population, one kindergarten suffices, but a fence down the middle of the area divides it in half. No one planned it that way, Friedman hastened to explain, it just evolved. The Russians wanted secular education for their children, the Ethiopians sent them to the state religious schools. There is little contact. Language difficulties alone would make problems, but the question of faith is more important. The Ethiopians meet up at school with religious Israelis, not with the Russians.

'There's hardly any crime here, but a lot of problems between the two groups,' said Muni, 'Even between families, petty thefts between neighbours who don't get on. I had a case of two Ethiopian families who belonged to separate clans. Back in Ethiopia the feud between them went back years; in one clan, there was an army officer – many of these Jews held high-ranking positions in the Ethiopian army, they were real fighters. He recognised a man in another clan who had killed his cousin. In Ethiopia, he hadn't the chance to take revenge, they'd have executed him, but here, with no death penalty . . . I got to hear of it and I talked to both clans through an Amharic interpreter. The thing fizzled out. All that happened was that one clan member stole a bicycle from the others. That threatened to start the feud up again, but I went and bought a second-hand bicycle and that settled it.'

At the centre of the caravan site is a circular, thatch-roofed building which is obviously Ethiopian, topped with a Star of

David. A plaque announces that the synagogue was built with the help of the Jewish National Fund and American Jewry. There is no corresponding Russian building.

'The two groups are fairly apathetic about one another,' Muni went on. As far as the Russians here are concerned, living in the caravans meant being what they called in 'internal exile', alienated from their surroundings. Acre has a large Arab population and here there are the Ethiopians; both are equally 'oriental' in Russian eyes. 'The Russians will move out the moment they can afford it, but it's less clear what the Ethiopians will do. The Russians save money living here, but the Ethiopians are content with very little. The living conditions which seem primitive to the Russians are much better than those in the Ethiopian villages. Ethiopians don't worry so much about not working. Most of the Russians here have found work in Acre or Haifa, even if the pay is low. The Ethiopians manage on relief: no work ethic. On the other hand, unlike the Russians, they're very keen to go into the army, as they were in Ethiopia; they love to be in uniform and they see it as the quickest way to acquire status and prestige. In the Soviet Union, you did anything you could to keep out of the army.

'The main problem I have is to keep the criminals from Acre away from the immigrants. Particularly the pimps.' Muni put the blame on the press, which had run so many stories about Russian prostitutes. 'The pimps get in to the site at night and wander round looking for Russian women to work for them for two dollars a trick. They even accost married women. And sometimes the immigrants are so desperate that they're tempted. I can't touch the women [prostitution is legal in Israel, unlike procuring] but I try to get rid of the pimps and drug pushers on the files in the Acre police.'

As I left the site, two blonde girls waiting at the bus stop confirm the pestering at night. 'You can't wait here for more than a minute without someone driving up and making an offer,' says one indignantly. 'You just have to be fair haired and speak with a Russian accent.'

'You know, Tanya, at the beginning, those Sabbaths infuriated me. Imagine, you sit there at home like an idiot, for two days, not

29

knowing what to do with yourself. One day someone I knew came by, and we decided to go for a walk; he promised to show me something wonderful . . . We wandered through narrow streets, not many street lamps but bright light coming through the windows. Music coming from somewhere. We looked in and saw a corner with a table, covered with a white cloth, with candles burning, people in their best clothes, white shirts, and they were all singing . . . and you know, at that moment I was crying with envy. We don't know about something very important, we don't understand and we don't feel it, and because of that, we can't value it. Something very important is going on so near us, but it's nothing to do with us, we're blocked in, we're shut off.'

In school halls, in the evenings after school hours, a little group of immigrant actors read out letters they have collected from their friends, to and from families left behind in Russia. An American writer, Joyce Klein, has worked the letters into a forty-minute play about the Jewish Sabbath, showing the lighting of the candles, the blessings over the bread and wine, the family gathered round the table. Alternating with such domestic scenes are folk tales from eastern Europe, many taken from the Yiddish classics of Shalom Aleichem and Mendel Mocher Seforim – tales about bullying Cossacks and wily, humble Jews. The Russians respond to this. It is something from a distant but recognisable past, like the Yiddish of some of their grandparents. Otherwise Jewish culture – the festivals that have become the Israeli national holidays, the Sabbaths on which public transport stops, the Day of Atonement when even the radio is silent – is as alien to them as the probation service or the tax laws. Klein, and her little group of actors, are taking the play to Minsk and to Novosibirsk.

In Russia the buses and trams ran on weekends and you didn't need a car to get out of town, or if you were lucky, to the *dacha*. Sunday was a chance to buy whatever food could be found for the working week. There were no bibles in Soviet homes. There were no circumcisions, and no barmitzvahs. It is estimated that before perestroika there were about 10,000 Russian refuseniks, people who wanted to be reunited with other Jews and who worked and studied with that aim in mind. The others knew nothing about Judaism, and very little about Israel.

But while every family in Israel, and every Jew associated with a community in the non-Communist Diaspora, sits down to read through the Haggadah at the Passover Seder, Russians do not know how to do so alone. The Seder or Passover ritual tells the story of the Exodus in the words of the rabbis, a procedure with a thousand permutations, a text of rabbinical homiletic interspersed with liturgical chants and even nonsense rhymes, with an interval for a traditional meal. At Passover many of the participants of this new exodus sit at home twiddling their thumbs and listening to the singing coming from their neighbours' apartments 'feeling like idiots'. Community and absorption centres try to fill the gap with group or even 'mock' Seders, where many of the new initiates are old Bolsheviks in their seventies, who sit, looking puzzled, over the symbolic bitter herbs and unleavened bread on their plastic plates. The lucky immigrants invited to take part in an Israeli Seder sometimes read, in turn with the others, from Russian translations.

There are other initiations. In hospitals and private clinics, white-faced men and their adolescent sons sit waiting nervously for circumcisions done on an out-patient basis under anaesthetic, hoping that having a restructured penis will turn them into authentic Jews. Babies born to non-Jewish Russian women with Jewish husbands cannot receive the attention of the hospital *mohel*, or circumciser, and have to find a private doctor who will perform the operation, at a price, at the usual age of eight days after birth.

Mevasseret Yerushalayim absorption centre is one of the oldest established hostels for new immigrants in Israel. A suburb of stone cottages on a hill near Jerusalem, fifteen years ago it was the home for immigrants from North and South America, as well as of the Russians released under grudging quotas by the Soviet authorities. When I visited them then, the cashier at the grocer's said that the Russians could be identified not only by their cloth caps and baggy trousers, but the fact that they stocked up straight away on carbohydrates – unused to proteins and fresh foods – while the house mother said they were tidier and cleaner than the Americans, as they were used to making the best of close quarters. In the 1970s the big clans from the southern and Asiatic parts of the USSR were headed by merchants with loads of furs, carpets, or whatever else they could get out of the Soviet Union for a hefty bribe at the frontier. The educated Jews from Western Russia had to 'ransom' their diplomas from abroad. But the numbers arriving then were small enough for most of the academic and professional people to enjoy what sociologists called a 'soft landing'. With the absorption centres providing language courses, advice on employment, and a transitional phase for adjustment, most of them soon found work, even if some voiced the same complaints you hear today – about the 'oriental' dirty streets, rude behaviour, vulgar TV programmes and 'uncultured' behaviour.

Over the last few years the vast majority of the ex-Soviet immigrants have been engineers, architects, or possess other academic professions or technical skills. The absorption centres are still open despite the new policy of 'direct absorption'. But Israel, like the immigrants, has changed. In the seventies, Mevasseret was undeveloped. Today, well-off Jerusalemites have covered another part of the hill with elegant villas and gardens, a suburb perfect for the thousands who commute in fast new cars to Jerusalem or even to Tel Aviv. There is little contact between the two populations – one in transit, the other veteran.

Gidi Zar and Emma Griver, respectively Israeli and Russian born, are both officials with long experience of absorption. Zar, a nervous man who suffers from attacks of asthma, complains: 'People don't like the Russians. The sabras are aggressive to them and it rubs off on me. In Russia they were Jews, here they are Russians. The old, in particular, suffer.'

Russians were not the only immigrants currently in the centre. There were Ethiopians, and some new, religious, French immigrants. The advantage of the centre is that there is an *ulpan* on the spot, where the immigrants can learn Hebrew immediately. Zar puts the Russians in touch with the Encouragement Bank (Bank Idud) where immigrants who are studying, either Hebrew or at a retraining course, can get a loan of 3,000 shekels (about £700) if they agree to return it after six months. Many immigrants attend retraining courses in the morning, in Jerusalem, and study Hebrew in the evening. After six months, they are sent to the labour exchange.

The turnover in the centre is rapid. 'After one year here,' Zar

32

said, 'The immigrant becomes a parasite. This is why direct immigration is encouraged. Unfortunately there are some who have been here for four years. Particularly those with large families.'

They are also introduced to Israel on special trips round the country. But, he said, rather irritably, all too few Russians take advantage of the cultural programmes the centre provides. Sure enough, all the immigrants waiting outside the centre for the big tourist bus and guide to arrive were Ethiopians.

Emma Griver is the cultural director at Mevasseret. She came to Israel from Samarkand twenty-two years ago, with a group of Hasidic Jews. The Jews from the Asiatic republics, far from the Soviet centres, had retained their customs far more easily. Her father, from Western Russia, was orthodox and observant and was left to practise his religion as he wished. Thus, well equipped for life in Israel, Griver studied linguistics at the university, and for some years was employed at an institute which researches the history of the Jews of Palestine before statehood.

Griver had worked with immigrants during the 1970s, when the first group of Russians arrived, and so she was able to provide a comparison between the two waves of immigration. Like most officials who identify strongly with the immigrants they work with, she was highly critical of Israel's methods of absorption, feeling that they had changed little since the 1960s, despite the huge change in the kind of immigrants the country was getting.

'The main difference between the Russians who came in the seventies and those arriving now is the quality of the "human material."' (a nasty but familiar expression which jarred with the concern she expressed for the immigrants) 'There is no ideological motive behind the current immigration; they came for social and economic reasons. The seventies immigrants could cope with culture shock better because they were motivated. They thought they were coming to a desert, but they were prepared for material difficulties. The new immigrants see the new prosperity and want a share immediately.

'Israel in the 1990s is very highly developed technologically, and that is where the Russians' skills could be much better used. Instead, the politicians either leave them to the National

Insurance Institute or talk about "relief works" as if we were still in the 1960s and could send people out to plant bushes and sweep the streets.

'What we're seeing now is a glorified form of state charity, a corruption of the welfare state. On the one hand, the state can't direct the immigrants to work which fits their skills, and on the other, it provides handouts. The immigration chiefs are still thinking in terms of the mass immigration of the 1960s who brought very few skills with them, artisans and labourers.'

Griver thought that Israel's inability to place immigrants according to their potential and training would lead to the best among them leaving and the weakest, those who would become dependent on Israel's welfare services, remaining as a burden on the Israeli economy. 'They aren't prepared for life in Israel, and we aren't helping them.'

The housing Israel was offering them, too, she thought was inadequate. Public housing was standing empty while the immigrants were put into temporary housing where they might waste all their allocation, eventually, on rent. The caravans, said Griver, were a disaster, a repetition of the 'transit camps' or *ma'abarot* of the fifties and sixties which became instant slums. Direct absorption, she said, leaving the immigrants to their own devices, simply did not work. They were better off in the smaller towns, where people helped one another, but most of them headed for the big cities, where they were lost. As for employment, the welfare state was again responsible for the older immigrants' plight; people over fifty couldn't be employed, since employers were wary of involving themselves in providing pensions for people whose time with them would be short. No one thought of the possibilities of part-time work. The more the immigrants' dependence on the state, the easier it was for them to despair, become apathetic.

There were no follow-up studies of those passing through the Mevasseret centre. It was impossible to trace them all individually. In general, she commented, the Russians were worse off than the Ethiopians – who stuck up for themselves, organised marches and demonstrations and had a high level of internal solidarity. This community, a tenth that of the Russian immigrants in numbers, had both a religious and a political leadership and had over forty voluntary organisations. The Russians had problems no one understood or could solve.

Five Russian immigrant engineers, none of whom speaks more than a few words of Hebrew, were working with the Jewish National Fund project rebuilding a village at Sataf, in the Jerusalem hills. Ora Namir, Minister of Labour and Welfare in the Rabin government, had appeared on television a few days earlier to recommend that immigrants be referred to the JNF – Israel's forestry authority – and to the Department of Antiquities to do relief manual labour, rather than sitting at home idly, getting unemployment benefits. These Russians were doing just what she suggested.

Sataf is the site of an Arab village abandoned in 1948, to the western (Jewish) side of Jerusalem, among the forests overlooking the (previously Arab) village of Eyn Karem, according to Christian teaching allegedly the birth place of John the Baptist. There are numerous monasteries and convents surrounding Eyn Karem, with its old Arab houses and winding paths; it is now the home of Israeli professionals looking for a picturesque place to live; and, paradoxically, of hard-core drug addicts and criminals, left behind from the settlement drive of the 1950s, when immigrants from Arab countries were put into former Arab villages as well as into new state housing in 'development towns'.

So, on the face of it, Sataf is a curious place to choose to introduce former Soviet citizens to Israel. This of course was not the primary motive, which was to find people willing to work on a windswept hillside eight hours a day moving rocks; their co-workers are Ethiopian immigrants and Arabs from the West Bank. They are paid £1.50 an hour, well inside the minimum Israeli wage of £7.00 a day; but transportation is deducted from their wages.

Sataf was carefully chosen as the site of an experimental farm and model village, where tourists and Israelis alike could see how ancient agriculture flourished in biblical times. Here, it is possible to see the traces of agriculture going back to the Chalcolithic era. Primitive agriculture depended on spring water channelled downhill into small reservoirs, and terrace agriculture for vines and fruit trees. The terraces revived, a spring inside a cave is being rechannelled into a small reservoir. The velvety forests carpeting the surrounding hillsides, most of them pines – the vista is splendid in the early morning haze – are the work of the forestry commission. Despite the fact that hordes of tourists are already visiting the site, there is a shortage of manpower to do the basic restructuring – hence the cheap labour. Donkeys loaded with baskets of earth are being used for local transportation of materials.

It was easy to identify the little group of five Russians working at the site from their caps, their faces and their apparent indifference to the chill of the Jerusalem winter morning. The eldest, who wore glasses, was in his shirt sleeves. They were all totally unaware of the history of the site and the purpose of the project, under the impression that they were rebuilding an ancient *Jewish* site. As the people in charge know no Russian, and they only a few words of Hebrew, it could not have been otherwise.

They had been in Israel from periods varying between nine months and two years. None of them had been able to find other work. There was Alexander Rabin, an electronics engineer from Moscow, who had rented a flat in Jerusalem and was struggling to pay the rent – £300 a month for three rooms. The 'absorption basket' did not cover the family's food and lodgings. Evgeny S. (he would not give his full name, as he felt the work demeaned him) was a mechanical engineer who had helped build many war memorials and monuments in his native Kiev; Ya'akov Greenberg, from Tashkent, a 'driver of the first class' seemed gratified to be in the company of Michael Reiter, a mathematician and engineer from northern Russia. The fifth man was absent on this morning – he had a third degree in physics and mathematics. The Ethiopians who hovered shyly in the background with their asbestos buckets were, the Russians told us, not simple villagers either. One had been an officer in the Sudanese army, and another was an educated man who had visited Canada.

Reiter, the man in shirt sleeves, was in his sixties, and could hope for no better work than hauling stones on a hillside. His son was studying in university here. Alexander's elder son was in secondary school and his daughter was a secretary. Evgeny had a married daughter, one son studying law and another preparing for university. Talk about the dignity of labour and the indignity of receiving handouts from the National Insurance Institute made them angry. In the Soviet Union, no educated man became a manual labourer, they said, even if a teacher might earn less than a factory worker. Their wives were without work, though they were all qualified professional women, as is usual in such families. To have one wage earner in a family disqualifies the family from receiving help. Alexander knew other electronics engineers who had given up and left Israel. Greenberg said that all the Russian immigrants were qualified people, not like the Moroccans. 'They didn't have the problems we have when they arrived,' he said.

Why had they come to Israel? Not for economic reasons, they all stressed. They came hoping for a better future for their children. Times were changing in Russia, much of the land and resources were badly damaged ecologically; 'everything is poisoned,' said one. They didn't want to wait for another revolution, which they were sure was on the way. 'We didn't expect professional success,' said another, 'just proper employment.' Evgeny, the Kiev engineer, said that he had found a job in his field on arriving, with a firm needing precisely the kind of experience he had with the use of steel in construction. A handsome, grey-eyed man with an imposing presence, he said that when he told them he was fifty, they immediately withdrew the offer. 'That was my mistake, telling them my age,' he said ruefully.

So Evgeny S., who helped construct the massive monument entitled 'Motherland' in Kiev, and who is an expert in his field, hauls stones on the hillside at Sataf, rebuilding what, a hundred years ago, was an Arab village. All were disappointed to hear that their work, theoretically interesting though the project was, was not exactly the reconstruction of an ancient Jewish site, as they had thought. 'If that's so,' one asked, 'why do the religious Jews come here so often to collect the water?' It seemed unkind to tell him that some orientals, like some 'born again' Jews, are not too particular about the origins of 'holy' places.

CHAPTER THREE

The Noise of Time

'Every day, exactly at four o'clock in the afternoon, the engines of the crematoria started up. We knew that people were being burned, but we did not know about the gassings. We thought that they were probably burned alive.'

Tsila Guedaliova is a slight woman with a shock of white hair and intense dark eyes; in telling her story most of her smiles are bitter, her face is furious, though sad in repose. She has a curvature of the spine, the result of beatings by German soldiers, and other ailments which she attributes to malnutrition in Russia during the early part of the war and imprisonment in military camps, slave camps in Germany, and finally, in the political prisoners' section of Ravensbrueck, the women's concentration camp in Germany. Guedaliova survived interrogations by the *Wehrmacht*, the Gestapo, and – after the war – the KGB. She arrived at Ravensbrueck only at the end of 1944, just after the gassings of women had begun at this camp, and even then was not identified as a Jew, as throughout most of her captivity and interrogations she had managed to preserve a false identity as an ordinary Russian prisoner, a Kabardinian native of the Caucasus.

Guedaliova speaks Yiddish, Russian and German. Each of her languages represents a generation of suffering, and her terrible life story is the story of the Jews of Russia during the first half of the twentieth century.

After 1917, the Jews of the Soviet Union were freed of the restrictions regarding residence in the Russian empire and Czarist discriminatory laws were repealed. However, their identity was recognised and legitimised only selectively. Once the Bolshevik regime got into its stride, Jewish religious practices, like those of the Christians, were mercilessly put down by Jewish commissars as well as others. Jews could no longer study in their own seminaries, and the rabbis were regarded as the representatives of an obsolete and backward culture. Moreover, since as community leaders, they and the wealthy merchants had supported the Czarist regime, they were persecuted, driven out, or forced to abandon open observance of their religion and customs.

Well before the Nazi period, Russian Jewish awareness of the separate culture the Jews had preserved over centuries was on the wane. For their part, the younger generations, even if they spoke Yiddish at home, were fluent in Russian and regarded their culture increasingly as that of the Russian intelligentsia. However, the Soviet regime decided to regard the Jews as a separate ethnic group like the inhabitants of the various republics, with their own language – Yiddish. Many of the older generation of the current immigration to Israel still speak fluent Yiddish, and it is they, the generation of the grandparents, who have passed on some Jewish knowledge to their children and grandchildren – however sparse, however fragmentary – and a pride in their Jewishness.

From 1927 onwards, the Bolsheviks, with the support of the Jewish section (Evsektsia) of the Communist party, and the financial help of Jewish groups in the Diaspora, attempted to set up a separate Jewish autonomous territorial entity in Birobidjan, in the Soviet Far East. The experiment failed; at no time were more than 30,000 of three million or so Soviet Jews (many of whom perished in the Holocaust) attracted to this unpromising and infertile region. No more than a handful of Jews now remain there, and several hundred have come to Israel. In addition, the Evsektsia set up Yiddish schools in many Jewish townships and *shtetls* – like that which Tsila's mother attended – as well as in towns like Minsk or Vilna where the Jews constituted a major part of the population. These schools survived well into the Stalinist period, until the Evsektsia itself was dismantled, and the rabidly anti-semitic campaign of the Stalinists got under way.

Guedaliova speaks Yiddish because that was literally her mother tongue; her mother, Rachel, was the eldest of ten children of a Jewish tailor in the tiny Ukrainian Jewish *shtetl* of Geissin, sent to work at the age of ten in a tobacco factory despite the pleas of relations and her own burning desire for an education.

Every morning at seven, before she went to work, the young girl studied with a teacher who visited her home, but she never mastered Russian. Rachel waited nine years, from the age of twenty, to marry Hirsch, the local boy she loved; he served three years as a soldier in the Czar's army; captured by the Germans during the First World War, he spent another three years as a prisoner-of-war. After he was released, with the Revolution over and Russia out of the war, it took time for him to return home and save for the marriage. In 1919, when Rachel was three months pregnant with Tsila, Hirsch was gunned down in a pogrom in the *shtetl* by the followers of Petliura, the notorious Ukrainian anti-semite.

Rachel never remarried. She sent Tsila to the local school where, according to the Bolshevik dispensations for the Jews, the curriculum was taught entirely in Yiddish. Her mother encouraged her studies and she excelled in mathematics and natural sciences; when the Second World War broke out, she was studying at the Technological Institute of Leningrad.

The teachers and students endured the terrible winter and starvation rations of 1941–42 together: 'Sometimes we would be out in the street and, suddenly, one of the older people, or the weaker, would simply drop dead by our side.' Tsila, a slight, pretty girl, had a hardy constitution, and helped hack trenches out of the frozen earth on the outskirts of the city. But by the time the siege was lifted, she had lost a large patch of hair at the front of her head, was covered with sores, and had feet too swollen to get into her shoes.

Though she did not know it until after the war, by the time the siege of Leningrad ended, her mother was already dead in a massacre which had taken place on 16 September 1941, when one of the SS special divisions detailed to kill Jews rounded up the inhabitants of the *shtetl*, took them to the nearby town of Vinnitsa, and shot them down in the public park. Tsila found one of the handful of survivors living in Israel, in Ashdod, after her arrival in 1991.

After the siege ended, teachers and students of the Institute were sent south to the Caucasus to work on a *kolkhoz* or collective farm near Kidslovodsk. There Tsila regained her strength, eating fresh food and working in the fields. But the German army

41

was approaching, and the news of the massacres of Jews carried out by the SS was well known. On 7 September 1942, the Jews of the whole area were summoned for 'evacuation to work camps' to the railway station in nearby Piatigorsk, and two days later, they were massacred at Kidslovodsk.

Just before this happened, Tsila, who had witnessed the entry of the German soldiers into the city and memorised the numbers of their tanks and equipment, set out, like a small number of other students, to try to reach the partisans in the mountains. None reached their destination. Tsila was picked up by German soldiers after walking for seven days, begging food in villages, and interrogated. Her 'passport' or Soviet identity card, which bore the incriminating word '*Evrei*' (Jew) was hidden in her under-wear. But at first she was not stripped, though beaten black and blue. The *Wehrmacht* were looking for partisans, whose guerrilla attacks they feared, and not for Jews. Tsila was transported to a military camp in Piatigorsk where she was the only woman among a thousand Russian prisoners-of-war.

Here, again, she was interrogated, this time by the camp com-mander, an Ukrainian doctor, and a Jewish interpreter, a gradu-ate of a Berlin university from the Ukrainian town of Vinnitsa. The doctor, ordered to examine her, found the passport and closed it immediately when he saw her nationality; but the inter-preter had glimpsed it and told the commander. Though the German officer was inclined to free Tsila, saying that she was an educated girl, the interpreter warned him 'She is dangerous.' 'It is terrible,' said Tsila, 'that it was a Jew who betrayed me.'

Tsila was soon joined in the camp by a number of other Russian girls captured on their way to join the partisans. That night, with Tsila keeping watch, one of them made a swift and expert escape under the camp fence. 'After the war,' she told Tsila, 'ask for Klara in Kishinev'; and so she did, but 'Klara' had long since disappeared.

Sent with the suspected partisan girls to another, large camp which housed an ex-Soviet prison, Tsila, the only Jewess, was kept in a separate cell; soldiers brought her bread and matches as they were sure that she was soon to die. Together with six Jewish men, she was put into a lorry to be sent to Gestapo headquarters in the town. One of the men, fearful, asked her where they were going. 'To be shot, of course,' she said. 'Don't show you are afraid!'

But at the last moment, another German officer in charge had second thoughts. As the lorry pulled out of the camp gates, there was a shout 'Let the woman go!' and Tsila was sent back while the men went on to their deaths.

This last-second reprieve proved to be Tsila's salvation. The other girls, believing that she had gone for good, had taken her photograph out of the passport she had left with them, and torn the document to pieces. Tsila now had no papers to incriminate her; her appearance was not typically Jewish, and she was thousands of miles away from her home town. Everything now depended on her courage and presence of mind. On her return to camp, for the first time her hair began to grow where it had fallen out because of malnutrition; it was white.

The girl prisoners were sent north to the Ukraine, to a camp where the prisoners were covered with lice and a typhus epidemic was raging. Here, Tsila acquired a new friend, Natasha. Though until the war was over she did not know it, Natasha was also Jewish, a fact she did not reveal even to Tsila, who was always at risk that one of the other girls would betray her.

Natasha told her that she must change her identity altogether. Henceforth, and until the end of the war, Tsila was to be Fatima, or Tamara Afaunova, a name typical of the Kabardinian inhabitants of the Caucasus. She was one of eleven girls sent on to Germany, to serve as slave labour for the Nazis, quartered in a labour camp but sent out to work and sometimes living with German employers. It was in a suburb of Berlin that Tsila acquired her knowledge of German, working as a domestic servant in Berlin homes. In the camp where she was first quartered, she had her third narrow escape from the Nazis. While Tsila lay ill with typhus, one of the Caucasian girls told the camp commander that there was a Jewish girl among them, and the Gestapo was called. This time Tsila was saved by the camp doctor, a prisoner-of-war from Leningrad, Giorgi Krupovitch, who first argued that she was not Jewish, and then, when the Gestapo officer who arrived at the camp insisted that she accompany him for interrogation, warned him 'You'll shoot me tomorrow if you take her, because she's got typhus and she'll infect the lot of you.'

After the war, said Tsila, when all Russian prisoners-of-war were interrogated by the KGB and many accused of spying and shot, Krupovich received a twenty-year prison sentence. The girl who tried to betray her, and told Krupovich 'Let her die, she's only a Jew', received a twenty-five-year sentence. Tsila herself was repeatedly interrogated by the KGB, but was spared imprisonment because she belonged to an information network among the Russians in the camp, a network which was many-faceted and which had links with other Russian prisoners in Germany. When Tsila cleaned house for a German family, she managed to tune in on her employers' radio to Radio Moscow (it was then 1943) and spread the news of Allied victories to other prisoners in the camp.

Tsila remained in this camp until mid June 1944. Shaven headed after typhus, in constant fear of detection, Tsila's obvious education, and her now fluent German, stood her in good stead with the camp commander. When the house she worked in was bombed and the family evacuated from Berlin in February 1944, Tsila was sent out of the city to work in a series of villages, then – when she protested about conditions there – in a shop and a factory. But her luck had now run out. In June 1944 two Gestapo officers arrived in the camp to take prisoners suspected of political activity to prison. Tsila was put in solitary confinement, beaten and interrogated repeatedly about her 'underground activities'. But she stuck to her original story of being a Caucasian girl who had studied in Leningrad, denied all political involvement, and after some time, was sent to Ravensbrueck.

Tsila knew that the Jews in the camp were being massacred, but she never had any contact with them. Her worst memory was of the SS women warders, who, she said 'beat the prisoners as their daily exercise -- beating them unconscious, reviving them with cold water, and beating them again'. When, one morning, the prisoners found the guards gone and the gates open, they realised that the Russian army was near. Tsila, with the other prisoners, was taken back into the Soviet Union in army trucks.

'It was the chance of my life,' she said, 'I might have reached the West then. I had relations in the United States, I might have remade my life. But I could only think of my mother and the rest of my family, in Geissin; I had to find out what had happened to them.' What she found was the little town, the houses and the streets. Not one member of her family had survived.

Tsila returned to Leningrad, and to the studies which had been interrupted in 1941. She qualified as a chemical engineer, and was sent to work in Tashkent in a tractor plant. There, a beautiful young woman in her early thirties, she met a young Armenian, a non-Jew, and married him. But she soon regretted the marriage, left him when she was pregnant, and they were later divorced.

Tsila called her daughter Rachel after her murdered mother, and, like her mother, she never married again. The second Rachel, a talented linguist and a singer, was my interpreter during the writing of this book.

'The Russian intelligentsia has one feature which is probably not known in the West. Among the teachers of modern languages I encountered during all my years in provincial colleges, I only once met a true intellectual, a woman called Marta from Chernovitsy. She once asked me in great surprise why all those students who thirst after truth and righteousness are always so keen on poetry. This is so, and it is peculiar to Russia.' Nadezhda Mandelstam wrote these words towards the end of her great memoir *Hope Against Hope*; she could not answer Marta's question, yet her own friendship with 'Marta from Chernovitsy' was based on a shared love of poetry. When both women were exiled in Ulianovsk, Lenin's birthplace, to which many intellectuals were sent in the post Second World War period, it was Marta's ability to recite from Goethe which convinced Mandelstam that she was a kindred spirit; Goethe's portrait, hanging between the bookcases in Marta's little apartment in southern Jerusalem, is placed where, in most Russian immigrants' homes, there is a snowbound landscape.

Marta loves the Russian language, but knows little Yiddish. 'Marta from Chernovitsy' was not given her full name in the memoir because, when it was written, Mandelstam still feared that it might incriminate Marta with the Soviet regime. Nor would Marta allow me to use her full name here, for a very different reason. 'I am ashamed,' she said. 'I betrayed my parents; my father was a good Jew and a Zionist – I found his name in the archives here, as he attended the 10th Zionist congress in 1911.

I could have left and come to Israel in 1948. But as a young woman I was a fervent Communist, and I did not understand my mistake until after Stalin's death.' I had known Marta for ten years, and only now was she telling me that she was once a Communist.

Chernovitsy, or Czernowitz, is in the Bukovina, that northern part of Romania which was once part of the Austro–Hungarian empire. Marta's family were not deported by the Germans; her father was a teacher who remained at his post under the German occupation. Fifty-seven per cent of Romanian Jews survived, despite notorious Romanian anti-semitism. Yet they all lived in constant fear of deportation, and Marta, like so many young Jews of her generation, saw the invading Russians as liberators, and Communism as an utopian future. 'When the German army left,' said Marta, 'many of the young Jews were so happy that they tore the epaulettes off the shoulders of the Romanian soldiers who had been the Germans' allies – and they had to pay for that later.' In Czernowitz, she said, Jewish Communists, artisans, cobblers and seamstresses, were able to take their revenge on university professors who had sided with the Nazis.

Jewish intellectuals from Bukovina and Bessarabia were recruited by the Soviets to the Jewish Anti-Fascist Committee (the *Komitet*) in Moscow, where there were poets, actors and directors. The most celebrated actor was Mikhoels of the Moscow Yiddish theatre, said to be Russia's greatest Lear. That was at a time, said Marta, when the Soviet Union was looking for Western help for reconstruction and believed that the Jewish influence was important. The *Komitet* was later to be an easy target for Stalin's anti-Jewish purges. Mikhoels was shot in 1948, and his death was the signal for persecution of the Jewish Communists everywhere in the USSR.

In 1949, Marta, who was teaching English at Czernowitz University, went one day to check her class schedules on a notice board and found that they had disappeared. When she went in to ask the dean what had happened, he said: 'What, don't you know that you have been dismissed for bourgeois nationalism?' Her students, young Ukrainians, Moldavians, and Russians, many still in uniform, were as shocked as she at her dismissal. They attempted to demonstrate, and wrote letters of protest; at that time there were few teachers who knew and could teach English and German and also spoke Russian. Nadezhda Mandelstam told Marta later that she was lucky not to have been arrested on suspicion of having organised the students' protest.

Marta found herself unemployable. Writing to one Russian provincial university after another, she finally received a response from Ulianovsk. 'I came to the conclusion that this was the place where they were sending all those who were out of favour.' This remote Siberian town had become, like Gorki in the Volga basin, to which she was later sent, a centre for some of the most brilliant minds in Russia. It was there that she met not only Mandelstam, but the Russian professor of biology Lubischev, the grandson of a serf, who was in disgrace for his opposition to the theories of Lysenko – the geneticist notorious for perverting science to serve Communist theory.

None of those in exile in Ulianovsk and Gorki could be sure whom they could trust, who was listening. Eyes were watching. One of Marta's colleagues, seeing that she had a copy of Murillo's 'Gipsy Madonna' on the wall of her room, asked suspiciously 'Is that an ikon?' which was forbidden. Even Mandelstam was cautious with Marta. One day she was ill, and when Marta visited her, she found her reciting poetry which, to Marta, was clearly modern, and unknown to her. When Marta asked who the author was, Mandelstam quickly responded 'Pushkin'. It was, of course, one of Osip Mandelstam's unpublished poems.

From Ulianovsk, Marta was sent to Tbilisi, where she taught school. Among her pupils was the present President of Georgia, then five years old. Even after Stalin's death, when the threat to Jews lessened, Marta was still unable to compete on equal terms with her non-Jewish colleagues. In 1956, to apply for a new posting, she went to Moscow with a Russian colleague, who had been a student of hers; the man in charge at the Education Ministry told her that all positions were filled until 1963. Then he turned to Marta's non-Jewish colleague and said, in front of her, 'Bring us your documents and we will send you wherever you like.' Nearly forty years later, Marta winced as she told the story; 'Imagine the humiliation – in front of my own student.' It was not until she was fifty that Marta was able to take her doctorate.

By the 1960s, Marta was longing to leave for Israel. Yet it was only in 1981 that she finally arrived in Jerusalem and began to teach in the Hebrew University. A gentle, courteous, sad-faced woman, whose every comment is laced with irony, she takes a sardonic view of the new mass of immigrants who have arrived in the last three years. 'We call them "sausage immigrants",' she said. 'Finally they have the chance to eat *meat*.'

'In Russia,' she said, 'the Jews went out and waved flags on Lenin's birthday, on the anniversary of the revolution. Every year the same routine. But I have heard them speaking about the religious Jews with contempt; they say that religious Jews read the Torah over and over each year; how *boring* that is. They are the tragic result of Communist indoctrination, because they have no pride in their own identity as Jews, no respect for their heritage.'

When I remarked that many of the younger immigrants seemed to regard their clashes with the KGB as a game of wits, a challenge, she said, 'Yes, they have no sense of what it was to live as a Jew under the Stalinist regime, the fear and the humiliation.

'What all generations of Russian Jews have in common is the love of Russia, which does not like or want them. It is true that the Jews played a very important part in the Bolshevik revolution, so now that things have changed they are blamed for all that went wrong. Yet many of them today talk about how good it was in Russia, and they can even bring themselves to leave Israel for Germany. But many Russians today regard the Jews who leave as traitors, and at the same time envy them for having somewhere to find refuge from the terrible anarchy that is Russia today.'

The Yiddish language, which had been the lingua franca of the vast majority of Jews under the Czars, was abandoned by most Jews, who knew that Russian was the language they needed for advancement; but in many parts of what had been the Jewish Pale of Settlement writers, poets, and other members of the Jewish intelligentsia saw it as a lifeline to preserve some form of Jewish culture under Communism. Eventually, as the worst excesses of Stalinism culminated in show trials, exile to Siberia, and the murder of many prominent Jewish intellectuals, even this form of Jewish culture was stamped out.

Most of those writers who managed to escape the Stalinist

scourge were murdered when the Nazis stormed into the *shtetls* of Western Russia and the Ukraine; only a handful of Yiddish poets survived, almost all broken men after long periods of persecution and imprisonment.

But even today, there are those from the former Soviet Union who try to perpetuate Yiddish culture, in the face of neglect and of the competition from Hebrew as the national language of Israel, and of the disappearance of the generation for which Yiddish was a living and versatile expression of Jewish identity. One of these dedicated men is Boris Sandler, who is also trying, in his painstaking work in the KGB archives, to document the sufferings and lives of Yiddish poets imprisoned by the Communists under Stalin.

A vigorous man who looks younger than his fifty years, wearing a sweater and jeans, Sandler lives in the Mevasseret absorption centre. Like a small number of Russian intellectuals, he went in and out of Israel several times, testing the water, before deciding recently to settle here. He is a Yiddish writer in an age when there is no longer any solely Yiddish-speaking Jewish community, anywhere in the world.

Sandler was born after the end of the Second World War in Beltsy, Bessarabia, east of the Bukovina from which Marta came, an area lying between Romania and Russia which has changed hands a number of times over the last two hundred years. He belongs to the generation born under Stalinism but whose formative years were mercifully free of its excesses, in the age of Khruschev's reforms.

In 1940, Bessarabia came under Russian rule, but this was only a short interlude. German troops entered the area in the summer of 1941, the Jews were deported and massacred, and when the Russians reoccupied the area in 1944, only a few Jews were still alive. Most of Bessarabia now became the Moldavian Soviet Republic, but the ordeal of the Jews there was not over. Many of those who had survived Hitler, revived their culture, their language, and begun writing in Yiddish, were persecuted afresh by Stalinist Communists after the war, and only began to publish openly during the Khruschev era.

Sandler grew up surrounded by the survivors of the Holocaust who had filtered back into the devastated towns and townships. While Marta grew up in a German-speaking home – her mother knew no Romanian – Sandler grew up, he said, in a 'Yiddish atmosphere'. There was no Yiddish school in the 1950s, but Yiddish was spoken in the rebuilt synagogue, and Jewish children spoke Yiddish when they played together. Boris Sandler's generation was bilingual; Yiddish was spoken at home, Russian outside, at school and in the streets. They were all the children of survivors.

In his autobiographical novella, *A Ladder to Heaven*, Sandler sketches his post-war childhood in a little township called Tsigania (Gypsyland) inhabited by Jews and Gypsies, the two main Bessarabian victims of the Nazis. It is a vivid and impressionistic portrait of a Jewish family which miraculously remained almost intact after the Nazi invasion and 'the evacuation', the period during which many Jews fled eastwards, deeper into Russia: an exodus which, however, shattered Jewish community life, and as Sandler's grandmother describes it 'scattered people like stones on the road'.

The novella is peopled by characters who might have come straight out of the pages of the great Yiddish writers of the nineteenth century: Uncle Kopl, the shoeshine man, the two blacksmiths Reuvin and Ya'akov, Uncle Aaron the cabinet maker and glazier – all Jewish artisans in the *shtetl*. But they are all angry men with terrible memories, Red Army veterans; Sandler himself is called after an uncle, Boris, who died at the front. The only traditionally Jewish characters are the boy's grandparents: the grandmother who lights candles on the Sabbath 'as her mother had taught her', and the grandfather whom Sandler follows secretly to synagogue – attended only by old and bearded men. Only at the very end of the novella is there mention of his parents – his father, the engineer, and his mother, who works at the fur combine: Soviet citizens.

But perhaps the most revealing line in the novella, indicating when it was written, is when the grandfather, praying at home, 'took out a white ram's horn called a *shofar*'. In no Yiddish work of the past would there have been the need to *explain* a *shofar*, which is sounded in synagogue on the Jewish New Year, and at the end of the Day of Atonement. There is an element of the didactic in the novella; too much of Jewish tradition is explained, nothing is casual, and yet the picture is incomplete. An entire dimension, that in which daily life and religious practice were inseparable, is missing.

Sandler began life as a violinist and, after graduating from the Moldavian State Conservatory, studied Russian literature in Gorki. However, when he began to write it was in Yiddish. With the weakening of the Communist regime, and particularly after glasnost, he began to carry out research in the Soviet archives. Sandler referred cuttingly to the rush by the brigades of foreign scholars to publish incomplete or only partially understood material, particularly Americans, who have rushed into eastern Europe trying to 'buy up' documents and archives. His own scrupulously documented work on the fate of Romanian Yiddish poets whose lives had been destroyed by Stalin has been published, in Yiddish, in Jerusalem.

In Bessarabia, said Sandler, a rich Jewish life had continued right up to 1940, when the Soviets took power. There were Jewish schools, Hebrew teaching and a hundred synagogues. Some of these were closed after 1940, others only after the war. After the establishment of Israel, the Soviet regime recognised it as the Jewish state, but all other manifestations of Jewishness were discouraged. In Beltsy, none the less, there was a Yiddish theatre directed by Ya'akov Steinberg, and a number of gifted Yiddish writers and poets. Many were imprisoned and broken, or died, during the Stalinist post-war period.

Sandler's mother was from northern Bessarabia, which had remained in Romania; his father, from Moldova, Soviet territory, was a survivor of the death camps. The township he came from was totally destroyed, but Sandler's father, then a boy in his early teens, escaped deportation.

Immediately after the war, Sandler ascertained, many Jews from this area had tried to escape from Bessarabia to Poland and thence to Israel. In his research in the KGB archives, he found records of the arrest of these would-be fugitives. Too many people had talked. Henceforth, all Zionist organisations in the area were totally eliminated.

However, there was a revival of Yiddish literature. There was a paradox here: the Evsektsia, the Jewish section of the Communist

51

Party after 1917, had been against Jewish tradition, and Soviet power had liberated the younger generation from the domination of their orthodox families. '*Shtetl*, disappear!' one Yiddish poet had written. But the 'ethnic' character of Soviet Jewry could only be expressed in the language of the orthodox elders.

After the war, Jewish education had been attacked simultaneously on two fronts. In post-war Soviet Russia, there were no more Jewish schools; moreover, the evolution of one Communist culture, the would-be assimilation of all nationalities, encouraged many Jews to adopt Soviet identity.

A handful of Jewish writers, however, emerged after 1961. The Soviet Jewish magazine *Sovietish Heimland* has often been regarded as a Communist propaganda magazine; but nevertheless it published the first work of many young post-war Yiddish writers, including Sandler.

Deeply versed in the history of Yiddish literature, motivated by the sense of the tragedy and waste of so much talent under Communism, and the persecution of Russian Yiddish poets, Sandler will not and cannot accept that the era of Yiddish is over, or that the study of Yiddish is now confined to the university campus, like that of ancient Greek or Latin. To hear him talk is to hear echoes of the battles within the pre-Soviet and early Soviet Jewish intelligentsia, fiercely debating the comparative virtues of Hebrew and Yiddish. Hebrew – the revived language of the Jewish state; Yiddish – the language spoken by the Jews of the Central and Eastern European Diaspora over hundreds of years.

'I believe in the future of Yiddish literature. Yiddish is a continuous culture; there was no 2,000-year break in its existence. There is now no reason why it should not co-exist with Hebrew literature.' When I asked whom he had read in Hebrew, Sandler quoted Bartov and Shamir, Israeli writers of the War of Independence generation. Israeli literature has changed greatly since those days.

Sandler has found a cultural home in Bet Levitt, an institution devoted to the encouragement of Yiddish literature. He gives lessons in Yiddish in religious schools, though he himself is not an observant Jew. He has also made a film on Bessarabian Jewry for the Museum of the Diaspora, Bet HaTfutsot, in Tel Aviv. There are some Yiddish journals, run by survivors of the Yiddish-speaking Israeli community of the pre-war era; 'They say they want younger writers, but when I and other Yiddish speakers try to get jobs, we are discouraged.' There has also been a revival of the Yiddish theatre, moribund for the last thirty years in Israel for want of an audience.

Sandler has written numerous short stories, published in Yiddish magazines in several countries, and he is now writing a historical novel. The central figure in the narrative is a Russian, but Sandler is using real documents from the archives in which he has done research. The novel is constructed using the framework of diaries, and he experiments with various techniques to suggest that other languages are being spoken by characters in the novel, 'Like Hemingway's use of Spanish in *For Whom the Bell Tolls*,' he explains.

Wasn't it frustrating to write a book in a language which no one now speaks, apart from the older generation among the Russian Jews? 'No. A writer writes for himself. It is not professional to consider whether your language is spoken or not. But I would like to be translated, first into Hebrew, because I live here and my audience is here, and in Russia.'

He did not expect to be easily accepted by the Israeli literary world, which centres on Hebrew writing. But just as the Russians of the 1970s had been accepted and gradually integrated into Israeli society, he hoped the current immigration would follow suit. The Israelis, he said, would have to understand that Hebrew was only one of many Jewish languages. 'If you count all the dialects of Yiddish, there are twenty other Jewish languages, apart from Hebrew.'

CHAPTER FOUR

Nervous People

In the labour exchange of the Jewish Agency, which handles immigrants in trouble during their initial year in Israel, there is an atmosphere of improvisation. The signs are all hand written and the directions are confusing. The women crowd round the booth where Levana, herself an immigrant from Mexico, two years in Israel, sits behind a computer. Most of the women, young or old, are well dressed, carefully manicured and coiffeured, and with high heels of the kind few working women wear in the West. Their make-up is elaborate, vermilion and orange lipstick, thick black mascara; quite young women have gold and silver teeth which flash when they smile.

We are engineers, chemists, teachers, they say. Levana offers them housework, cashiers' jobs, reception work. No one wants housework, save as a last resort. Offers of work as cashiers make them apprehensive of impatient customers, of making a mistake and having to make up the difference from their own pockets. Reception work in a 'hotel' turned out to be in hostels for immigrants, like the place where Natalya had lived.

'Job descriptions' from Russia correspond in most cases to nothing in the West. Many people had worked in factories in production line jobs which were repetitive and limited, however grand their qualifications sounded. Engineers were people with any kind of mechanical or technological training. Even in the case of 'engineers' in the Western sense of the term, contractors would take no one over thirty-five, and certainly not women. Levana handed out as many chits for unemployment benefits as she did addresses of employers. If the women were retraining for other jobs, or studying Hebrew, they received benefits automatically.

The procedure took place in a language most of them could barely speak; and the idea of working outside the job you were trained for, like the idea of unemployment, was unheard of in the pre-perestroika Soviet Union. Work was provided, even if it meant no more than checking in and checking out again at the end of the day. To be unemployed was a crime punished by fines, if not worse. What was happening to these people in Israel, therefore, was only familiar to the very young, those who had looked for work during perestroika.

One woman, speaking so quietly that she was scarcely audible, said that she could not study Hebrew as her husband had cancer and needed constant care. When she had left, with her chit, Levana said, 'I can't bear cases like that.'

She had work in a restaurant for Bella, a cook from the Ukraine, who had years of experience in a Kharkov factory kitchen. Bella had two children of thirteen and eight and when asked who would care for them on evening shifts she laughed. Like almost all immigrant families, everyone lived crammed in together – parents, children, grandparents.

Levana said only about twenty to thirty per cent of the applicants found work through her, and practically none in work they were trained for. Many came with medical certificates testifying that they were unable to work. She was sceptical. Young people only qualified for three months' unemployment benefits, and three refusals of work disqualified even the older women.

Men came on a different day, to be received by another young woman, Valentina, who had grown up in Israel. There was a barber who wanted work as a watchman. But security firms wanted people with security clearance, hard for a new immigrant who hadn't done army service. You didn't need much Hebrew to stand guard at a factory gate, but in Russia few people had permits to carry arms, unless it was for hunting rifles.

Another man said he had worked in Russia as a factory 'expeditor'. This apparently was a forwarding clerk, a specialised job, but one which no longer existed in the computerised modern industry of the West. A cook from St Petersburg, when asked his speciality, smiled, aware of the incongruity, and said 'Pork dishes, mostly'. Amazingly, he was sent to Jerusalem's most orthodox hospital. Valentina said casually: 'They'll explain the dietary laws to him.' We warned him that if he wanted the job he had better make no jokes about pork, or mention that he had handled it.

Just as none of the women wanted cleaning work, building work was not acceptable to the men. While the Israelis grumble that the Russians don't want to use their hands, the Russians explain in private that in the Soviet Union, even if a labourer was paid more than a teacher, he was not respected. Russian Jews see manual work as relegation to the despised proletariat, not as pioneering.

While the women had dressed up to present themselves at the office, the men looked neglected, all far older than the age they declared. A man in his forties, who had worked mainly in the warmer and southern parts of Russia, said he was an expert on refrigeration of all kinds; he had expected this to help him find work in the sultry climate of Israel, but the head of a firm, consulted on the telephone, said he had twenty such 'experts' on his books already.

Valentina has seven years' experience as an official in the labour exchange, and in her local community centre. A good-humoured, relaxed girl, she is a reassuring presence.

'When I was at school, in the 1970s, I read about the new immigrants and I volunteered to go and visit immigrant families. I always liked reading, and I liked meeting older people. I think there's some connection between this and being interested in the immigrants.

'From what I remember of the Russians who came in the seventies, and the way we received them, I think the atmosphere was better, we accepted them more easily as equals. Of course the numbers were less, and there were many immigrants from other countries, South America for instance.

'Where the work is concerned, the Russians are quite choosy about what they want and don't want to do. They've worked out how they can get unemployment pay without doing domestic work; you saw for yourself the face they make. There are all kinds of ways of getting unemployment benefits; you say you're ill, that you aren't strong enough for that kind of work. I don't argue with them.

'The first two years you have to be patient. After that, they have to learn to conform to life here. I've a lot of sympathy with the young women. They're so gentle, so refined compared to our girls, they haven't been in the army, they're good at languages. But Israelis don't accept them easily. I know one girl who has an Israeli boyfriend. His friends don't want her, and her family objects too. Some girls get jealous. Lots of the Russians are beautiful, blonde, they don't look like Israelis, they're very attractive sexually to our boys, who like to show them off.

'They're much less materialistic than our people. They're interested in music, in ideas, in books, much more than we are. And the Russians respect independent women, not like us. I have to think about what my father and mother will say, but they're often alone. There are lots of single mothers, women living without men. They dress very provocatively, even at work, see-through blouses and short skirts.

'In our society there's no equality between men and women, here there are far more women who stay at home. The Russian women are used to going out to work. Sexually they're much more permissive. The Russians have cornered the market in call girls, that's for sure.

'Russian girls sell sex all the time, even single mothers, it's a source of income for them, they tell me that. As for Aids, I don't know, Israeli men don't think about that yet, but if there's an epidemic the Russian women will be blamed.

'There's no doubt the Russians are exploited at work. A woman who works five days a week cleaning and cooking gets rock-bottom wages and sometimes they're paid below the legal rate, but they don't know what it is. Among immigrants, there are phoney employment services, Russian 'helpers' who say that they can get jobs for other people and then ask for a fee.

'The Russians don't understand all the government services here, and sometimes those who are in transit, who're poor, fall into the hands of the Russian mafia, who charge them for getting accommodation, or cheat them by lending money at crazy rates, all kinds of criminal deals like that. The problem is that they're frightened of authority, they can't see that the authorities are there to help them. On the other hand they think they can get round the rules as they did in Russia.

'We Israelis aren't very patient with the Russians. In the 1970s we were all told to accept immigrants and help them. Today the country's richer, more materialistic, children are ambitious, and immigrants are just a nuisance; there's no ideology, no feeling that they are necessary, that taking them in is what the state was founded for.

'They don't react like Israelis when they don't get what they want. Israelis easily turn violent, aggressive. The Russians are never like that, they're just passive and depressed when you can't find jobs for them. But they lie like mad. They're endlessly devious. I get handed documents I don't think are genuine, or out of date. Lying is their way of getting out of trouble. Not banging on the table.'

Devorah Sindorf, the experienced Jewish Agency official who runs one service in conjunction with the Jerusalem municipality, says: 'During the first two years, practically every immigrant needs a representative between himself or herself and the authorities.' Sindorf has worked with Russians, Argentinians, and Ethiopians, and has travelled to most parts of the world to brief prospective immigrants. In her view there is insufficient liaison between the various government departments and the voluntary organisations, of which there are many. The Russians, with all their demands, show up the weakest links in the Israeli welfare services.

'There are virtually no dental services in the USSR, and those which existed were backward. That is quite clear when you see men and women in their thirties and forties with gold teeth, which went out in the West about fifty years ago. But the Israeli dental services anyway are the poorest branch of the Israeli medical health funds. Private practices flourish, and are extremely expensive. The Russian immigrants need special advisory aid and treatment and clinics are few and far between, some of them sponsored from abroad. There are special insurance schemes, but an immigrant who gets a salary of 500 shekels [about £125 a month] cannot possibly afford dental treatment costing half this sum. He also needs a reference from his place of work to get health fund assistance. Dental services, he will find, are not included. Nor are orthopaedic services like hip replacement.'

'When the Ethiopians arrived, they underwent massive health screening and tests as it was known that they carried TB and Aids with them, hence public hazards. But there was little or no information about the Russians, so they were generally not given health check-ups. As for mental or psychological problems, which the Russians have in plenty, there is no provision for therapy under any of the health fund systems.' Sindorf complains that precisely at the time when mass immigration began (in the early 1990s) the government cut back on welfare services, including social workers handling immigrants. No one was concerned with people over forty-five, who were practically unemployable. Sindorf, unlike many Israeli officials, is against trying to put doctors and musicians into street sweeping and cleaning jobs. She thinks budgets could be diverted from unemployment benefits to retraining schemes or attempts to employ people in their own professions. Sindorf says that she was already doing this where benefits were concerned, on an individual basis, with the Labour Ministry. Every time the telephone in her office rang, she was handling another problem ad hoc; each time, she shook her head, and said 'I *really* shouldn't have to be doing this, it isn't my job.'

The retraining courses run by the Ministry of Education were, she thought, geared to the needs of an earlier immigration of artisans – courses for jewellers, builders and plumbers. There were many handicapped people at present unemployed whose skills could be used. People over fifty with varicose veins and scoliosis could not do manual labour, or stay on their feet as waitresses. However, they often had brought other skills which could be used. Cottage industries could be set up if the administrators could be found. But all this needed a guiding hand.

Compassionate, troubled, Sindorf has the view of someone who deals every day with the casualties of the Russian immigration. Ron Bar-Yosef, head of retraining in the Ministry of Labour, a sardonic man with a clipped manner, has the attitude of a surgeon who sees no point in lying to the patient. Sitting in his office in the government complex near the Knesset, he obviously does not share the views of those who saw the Russian immigration as Israel's chance to move into the big league where skilled manpower was concerned. He took a critical view of Israel's 'welcome' of so many middle-aged, old and disabled people.

'The Russian immigration has come at the worst possible time for Israel. In 1983–84 Israel went through wild inflationary spirals, and it also had to reorganise, after the Conference of Rome, for entry into the European market. Economic priorities have changed. As the economy became modernised, automated and brought into line with the West, this involved sacking those unable to fit into a modern production line, and by 1989 there was a four to seven per cent unemployment rate. [Today it has risen to over ten per cent.] When the first Russians began arriving in 1989–90, they interrupted this development and put more pressure on the system than it could contend with. The labour force grew by eight per cent in three years. Moreover, this was just the time when the post-war baby boom of 68–69, those born after the Six Day War, began injecting new Israeli job seekers into the market after their army service.'

Retraining, in Bar-Yosef's view, was the only solution. He said that forty per cent of those immigrants who entered the work force had to be, and were, retrained, many of them in special five to six week retraining courses set up by Israel in the ex USSR with the agreement of the authorities there. Israel rents premises and equipment, and prepares technologically qualified immigrants for the rather different Western systems. This was the most efficient and least wasteful way of preparing for their entry into Israeli society. There was also liaison between the teachers at these courses and the immigrants' future employers in Israel, matching supply and demand. Where women were concerned, it was true that they had a far wider range of experience at work than women in Israel, who were usually segregated in specific professions like teaching and nursing. In the ex USSR, women had competed at all levels. Bar-Yosef proposed no immediate answer to this problem. But he also qualified his remark about women's skills: 'In Russia I visited a *kolkoz* where one woman's job was to clean out the muck in the cowshed. She described herself as a 'cowshed engineer' who had studied agronomy.' As to the calibre of the immigrants, there was a vast difference between highly trained personnel from the big cities, sometimes better qualified than Israelis, and many Jews from the periphery and the Asiatic republics who, even if they had studied, had done so in correspondence courses.

He was not against government-sponsored labour projects which would keep the immigrants out of the job market for another six to eight months. But the bottom line was clear. There was very little hope of a future in Israel for any immigrant over forty.

Many disgruntled, disorientated people, in their first months in Israel, flood into the offices of 'the Zionist Forum', or just Forum, situated conveniently near Jerusalem's central bus station, for people continually wandering from place to place looking for homes, work, or both. This Russian immigrant association, headed by Anatoly Sharansky, is funded from abroad. On the board are twin notices to new arrivals: one giving advice on how to write official letters asking for work, and the other giving the address of a psychologist's counselling service. The forms given to immigrants to fill in when looking for employment include 'lists of patents' (most Russian CVs are rich in these).

Natalya, a first-time immigrant offender, told us that she had not had much help from Forum. The Russian-speaking Israeli lawyer who works there on a part-time volunteer basis, Jonathan Livne, a curt, brash young man, said that a lawyer, for the Russians, represented the state even if he was a private practitioner. There had been few Jewish lawyers in the Soviet Union and they did not understand the significance of a private law practice – in the USSR, said Rachel, only criminals had lawyers – and assumed he was exploiting them if he later took the statutory fee for a power of attorney or to represent them in court. Volunteer activity was something they didn't understand, and was accepted as part of the establishment's handouts. It was a rude shock when they were later asked to pay for various services.

First in line outside Livne's office was a father of a man soon to be married. He was puzzled and concerned with the Israeli marriage procedure which was still entirely in the hands of the rabbinate. Why was his son having to put down money for the bride? Livne explained that this was an archaic formality linked with the ancient Jewish marriage ceremony and that the money was purely symbolic and didn't have to amount to more than a few dollars. The father went away not entirely reassured.

The next distressed immigrant had bought a new Japanese car

with a chunk of his government grant and had now been told that he didn't qualify for unemployment benefits. This is Israel's Catch 22. All immigrants are offered tax-free consumer goods – cars, televisions – within three years of arrival, while veteran Israelis pay crippling import taxes which make such goods almost twice as expensive as elsewhere. Ironically, the original rationale of this tax break was to attract immigrants from the prosperous countries of the West, who could not be expected to accept the (once spartan) lifestyle of the Israelis and had to be bribed with cars and refrigerators at their real cost. The desired immigration from the West had never materialised, but the concession, bureaucratically fossilised, had remained, and the temptation for the Russians to take advantage of it was overwhelming. They would have had to have worked twenty years in the Soviet Union to buy the glittering new private cars with power steering and electric windows which were now within their grasp. Hence the incongruous sight of so many Mitsubishis and Subarus, for which the Russians had no money for petrol, standing outside nine-square-metre caravan homes or shabby rented flats. Now Livne was explaining to the despairing owner of one such car that he was not eligible to receive unemployment benefits unless he sold his car; in other cases, it was the television, or the video the immigrant had bought.

A third immigrant came in complaining that he had bought an electric oven which did not work properly. The shop where he bought it had meanwhile closed down. Could the authorities get the money back? When he had gone, Livne said, 'The state is Daddy. They don't understand the difference between state and private responsibility. If the shop owner has gone bankrupt, he probably can't get his money back. But he expects the state to reimburse him.'

An old lady came in haltingly, leaning on a stick. For a while she simply looked at Livne, and then, after fumbling in a huge shabby handbag, she brought out a letter, which she read aloud. It was addressed 'To Anybody'. It outlined her life story. She was from Belarus. During the rule of Stalin, all her family had suffered. One brother had died, all had been refused work, another had died of a heart attack. She was alone, suffering from many illnesses, including asthma, and the landlady at the flat she had found no longer wanted to be responsible for her sick tenant, and threatened to evict her.

Livne interrupted her and asked: 'What about an old age home?' The old lady said she had been offered a place in such a home, but, she insisted, she would not go there. 'How much more should I pay? I have so little. I want to stay in my own place. I want to spend my last days without the eyes of strangers staring at me.'

For as long as the old lady continued to pay her rent, Livne told her, the landlady would have to keep her. Usually, tenants were protected, judges did not throw people on to the street or repossess property even when the tenants defaulted on payment. In the Soviet Union, he later told us, bribery would do the trick. The larger the sum offered, the more believable was the protection the immigrants thought it afforded.

A stream of immigrants followed, all in need of legal help. A young woman injured in a car accident had lost a month's salary and the employers didn't want to pay, confident she would not take them to court. A divorced man had been told he had to pay for the maintenance of the son of his wife by a previous marriage – many such families had arrived and then divorced. The National Insurance Institute had sent investigators round (spies, said the immigrants) to check on the circumstances of a family applying for assistance. Livne explained that they had a perfect right to do so. The immigrants nodded at one another; they knew all about the long arm of the State.

Another elderly woman on the verge of tears was claiming reparations from the West Germans for all her possessions lost when she was interned in a ghetto during the Second World War. She had been listed for deportation to a death camp but was sent back due to a clerical error. At the offices in Israel, she had been told she was lying and not a candidate for compensation; she had waited too long. But now she had a letter from an eye witness still in Russia. 'Authorisation costs 30 shekels [£7.00],' Livne said automatically. He had heard too many such stories to waste time. There was a problem with the East German reparations, introduced only since German reunion; all kinds of offices advertising in the Russian papers were claiming to take on clients, for a fee, but the details had not yet been worked out between governments. Too many organisations were waiting to prey on the new arrivals.

Finally, Livne had to explain to the immigrants the Israeli concept of a 'guarantor'. To buy a flat, to take out a mortgage, to obtain a loan from a bank, anyone without collateral needs the famous Israeli *arev* or guarantor. This practice goes back to the time of the pre-state and early state Jewish community, when everyone knew everyone and people lent money on the basis of personal agreements. Over the years it has solidified into an Israeli institution. People sign on the dotted line for friends, which can sometimes be a risky procedure. If the money wasn't paid, the guarantor could be arrested for a civil debt. In the West, a bank examined a man's bank account, or his salary chit. Here, it was the signature of friends and acquaintances that counted. This was particularly hard on the Russians, who rarely knew anyone solvent enough to sign, and who were easy prey for money-lenders promising loans at exorbitant rates. Often groups of Russian friends were bailing one another out in relays, the same money going round and round like the pawned 'second' candlestick in Chekhov's great story 'A Work of Art'.

The Technion in Haifa is Israel's leading institution of technology; it has trained most of the country's engineers and architects, and today is one of the country's foremost research centres in everything from aeronautics to computer sciences. Founded in the early years of the century at the initiative of German Jews, it was the centre of a controversy over the language of the future Jewish state, and the opening of the institution was delayed while scholars and teachers argued as to whether it should be called Technikum (the German word) or another, Hebrew word, and whether the language of instruction there should be German or Hebrew. By the time the Technion became a university campus, Hebrew was firmly established. So it is ironic that today so much Russian is spoken there by emigrant engineers that many complain that they have no opportunity to speak Hebrew. Engineers and architects make up twelve per cent of the immigrant population, the largest single group.

Chariana Sokolinsky is a research professor specialising in heat absorption systems in cooling and air-conditioning apparatus. In

Leningrad, as a graduate of the prestigious Technical Institute, she worked in the state cement industry, more in applied engineering than in theoretical work. With a group of other Russian engineers, she now works in the aeronautics building of the Technion, a vast conglomeration of buildings on the campus stretching over the wooded hills behind the Haifa bay. Both she and the colleagues I met at the Technion were desperately uncertain about their future. They are all approaching, or over, fifty.

Unlike the situation with Russians trained in so many other fields – for instance teachers or doctors – Russian technologists and scientists are more than qualified to compete with, and work with, Israel's trained either here or in the West. But the question is whether Israelis institutions of higher education can find room for them indefinitely. Sokolinsky and her colleagues are all working on temporary contracts, valid for two years, and their salaries are paid by the Technion only because they are heavily subsidised by the Ministry of Absorption, which pays up to eighty per cent of the cost. Whether the contracts would be renewed was a source of constant worry, like the uncertainty as to whether they would be given tenure. Most private firms hesitate to employ Russians of this age because of future obligations. Will institutions like the Technion want to keep them on when, in another fifteen years or so, they will have to contribute to their pensions?

Another source of concern was that while the equipment provided by Israeli research institutions was much superior to that available in Russia, and the potential for theoretical research was thus splendid, the actual money available was restricted.

Sokolinsky's immediate colleages are all distinguished ex-Soviet scientists: Dr Valery Rosenband, of Moscow, an expert on aeronautics and formerly head of the laboratory at the Institute of Chemical Physics at Chernogolovka, a branch of the Moscow Institute of Physics, financed by the Soviet Academy of Sciences; Dr Alex Osharov, an expert in military rockets who had waited fifteen years for his exit visa; Dr Yura Nehamkin, an expert in air hydrodynamics and thermodynamics; and Dr Michael Dvinyaminov, an expert in chemistry and in the dynamics of shock waves, who had worked in simulation projects in nuclear reactors. Before perestroika, it would have been inconceivable that scientists of this calibre, privy to so many Soviet research projects needing high security clearance, would have been allowed to leave the Soviet Union.

All the scientists thought that Israel had not exploited the possibilities opened by scientific research in engineering technology in the West. In their field, said Sokolinsky, Israel had really forged ahead only in solar energy. In other respects, they all thought, there was a five-year lag behind the West.

Clearly, wealthier countries in the West were attractive to scientists from Russia. Not only could other countries pay higher salaries, but under present circumstances, these scientists were not eligible to receive the benefits available to veteran Israelis in academic institutions, such as funds for further studies and sabbatical leave. What was holding the Russians back from emigrating to the United States was their poor English. Sokolinsky said that only in the big Russian centres was there adequate teaching of English. The Communists had not encouraged the study of foreign languages (perhaps, as some immigrants suggest, to discourage contacts with the West). Few scientists had travelled, or read journals in foreign languages.

The scientists' only option, meanwhile, approaching the time when their subsidised contracts came to an end, was to apply for work in industry – nationalised or private. In the Soviet Union, they explained, research facilities were seconded to state industries, as everything was on a much larger scale, so that theoretical scientists were not limited to work on the campus.

Why had they left? Sokolinsky said that she had known virtually nothing about Israel, had never been out of Russia, and thought Israel was more or less like Europe. All the scientists agreed heartily that Israel was not really the West. But Sokolinsky had been worried about what would happen to her career in post-Communist Russia. Many of the research institutions were closing down. Perhaps there had been too many, but the future for scientists was now grim. It would take decades for Russia to catch up with the West under the new dispensation, perhaps twenty or thirty years. People of her age did not have that kind of time.

She complained of 'the lack of cultural facilities' in Israel and the 'oriental' atmosphere though the Israel–Arab conflict was less alarming than the rising crime wave in Russia. Compared with the fear in the Russian streets, the scientists agreed, the poverty, alcoholism, and violence, Israel's security problems seemed a minor concern. Sokolinsky had arrived during the Gulf War, but it had made little impression on her.

Osharov, the military rockets expert, said that he appreciated the challenge of more research and development projects in Israel. Perhaps this was because he had sent his CV to the aircraft industry and immediately received a recommendation to the Technion. He would not say much about his work, save that the field he worked in now was similar to that in the Soviet Union. Of the little group, he seemed most likely to get permanent work, as the Israel defence industry would always need scientists of his calibre.

Osharov had no specific political or ideological ties to Israel, but he was practical about the opportunities it offered. It was true, he said, that the cultural level in Israel was lower than that of Moscow, but he thought things were little better elsewhere in the West.

He had a son who had done two electronics courses in the Russian army, had studied in Bar Ilan university near Tel Aviv (a university with a religious foundation), and now was working with Scitex, one of Israel's foremost electronics companies. For all these reasons he seemed likelier to stay than the others.

During the entire conversation, none of the immigrant scientists expressed the slightest interest in Israel as the Jewish state, the least hint of any ideological or emotional commitment (Sokolinsky had voted for a left-wing party in protest against the last government's treatment of immigrants but said she was 'disappointed in democracy'). It seems likely that if they can, with the possible exception of Osharov, they will re-emigrate to the West.

The Wingate Institute, on the coast north of Tel Aviv, is the main sports training centre in Israel, and boasts magnificent facilities, gardens, and in addition to the ordinary training gyms and stadia for physical training instructors, it has laboratories for research into the physiological and technical aspects of sport. Three Russian scientists are working here under the same kind of agreement as the engineers at the Technion; the Institute is a non-profit organisation subsidised by the Ministry of Education but, for research and development, dependent on donations from sponsors. M.A. Trakhimovich, of the All Union Institute of Sports and Tourists Equipment, Moscow, had been chief researcher at its Laboratory for over twenty years; V.B. Issurin, a graduate of the State Institute of Physical Culture in Leningrad had been, from 1988, professor at the Central State Institute of Physical Culture in Moscow; and J.N. Dobrov, an engineer with a PhD, in cybernetics, served between 1986 and 1990 as assistant professor in the biomechanical faculty of the Moscow Institute for Physical Education and Sport.

The first two were in their late forties, Dobrov in his late fifties, and they had left Russia at the height of their careers, having published tens of learned papers, in a country whose sporting achievements were among the highest in the world and where outstanding sportsmen were coddled from early youth to represent the glories of Soviet power – in space or at the Olympics.

Trakhimovich's speciality was the methodology and theory of athletic training, particularly that of the sporting elite, and the biomechanics of water sports. At the Wingate research branch he was working on stress measurement apparatus, seeing how far the body can sustain the kind of stresses involved in sport. Issurin was working on similar experiments, and Dobrov was assessing what particular sport was best suited to individual athletic abilities, and how best to use the natural rhythms of the sportsman's body. Only in the physiology department of the Weizmann Institute, Israel's foremost research facility, was any comparable work being done.

One of the scientists said of their situation that 'we are floating, like Alice in Wonderland'. They were not sure of their future, or if there would be money to keep them going. Obviously, in a small country the potential for producing great sportsmen was less, as the catchment area was so small. It had taken two centuries, they said understandingly, for the United States to achieve primacy.

The trio were considerably more appreciative of the facilities they were getting than the engineers in the Technion. What Israel had given them, they all agreed, was access to first-class equipment and the technology to work out some of their theories and ideas. While Dobrov worked with familiar equipment, the other two had much better instruments than those placed at their disposal in the Soviet Union.

The Wonderland aspect of their work was whether what they were doing, under the benevolent aegis of their sponsors, had any function beyond keeping them busy. Talking to the immigrant students at the Institute revealed very quickly that the kind of sophisticated research the Russian scientists were doing was about as relevant to Israeli sports as the Lobster Quadrille. It seemed to Dobrov that, given Israel's scientific talents and resources, it should be doing better.

The scientists had been in Israel less than two years, and they could not possibly have realised the contrast between the magnificent facilities of Wingate and the run-down state of sports facilities in the vast majority of Israeli schools, to say nothing of the average Israeli's attitude to sport.

Israeli children do not grow up with sports as a serious part of the curriculum. Few schools have fully equipped gymnasiums or their own football fields, PT is a joke, and children can be seen panting round streets near the school on a practice run from which, by the end, many of them will have dropped out or gone off to buy ice lollies before rejoining the run at the finishing line. Swimming lessons are not usually provided at school.

It has long been established that Israeli kids reach the army in very poor physical shape. They are then during basic training submitted to a wickedly tough regime of physical endurance, carrying heavy backpacks over long route marches or, for a select handful whose 'medical profile' is high, going through commando training. This leaves most Israelis with the determination to avoid any further physical effort or interest in sports beyond betting on the results of football matches on television. Most swimming pools are only open to subscribers (at least £250 a season), and municipal pools are often insanitary and crowded. The climate in summer is not suited to any but water sports, but the seashore in Israel is particularly dangerous, subject to violent currents and undertow at the eastern extreme of the Mediterranean. A familiar sight is that of crowds *standing* in the water to keep cool, herded into a tiny area between two black flags, with coastguards with megaphones shouting at anyone venturing further than a few yards from the shore. Only for brief periods in

70

spring and autumn is the sea quiescent. The idea of sports as an integral part of life, as an enjoyable way of spending leisure time, is limited to a small and financially well-off sector of the population.

The students at Wingate were severely critical of the army, whose training methods, they said, could wreck any sportsman's body in a few weeks. They said that they were now extremely cautious about how far they were prepared to carry out instructions. One student they knew suffered seven stress fractures, simply from ordinary training, in his first months in the army. Most army health officers had no link whatever, they said, with basic training and combat training regimes. There was no gradual workout system to prepare the body for the kind of challenge the army offered.

The second problem facing sportsmen who wanted to go on to become PT instructors was the very low salary offered in the schools, 800 shekels after tax, or £200. Although all sports teachers in Israel study at Wingate, the immigrant students there, chosen at random, said they wanted to study stress physiology (like the scientists) and perhaps become private instructors in one of the many health clubs now springing up all over the country, or physiotherapists, or to teach children in private classes. Yet they all agreed that sporting heroes were important for any country, and that they needed the proper background and training to succeed.

The Russians at the Technion and the Wingate Institute represent fields in which the Soviet regime was prepared to invest heavily: weapons development and related technologies, and athletics. Each in its own way boosted Soviet status in the outside world. Soviet medicine, by contrast, was, according to Israeli experts, thirty years behind the West. Though basic science teaching was advanced, and theoretical work excellent, the general health of the population was a low priority, and this is reflected in the background of the doctors arriving in Israel.

The Hadassah medical complex functions as a university hospital and houses the country's foremost medical school, run in conjunction with the Hebrew University. Hadassah has provided training, via the medical school, for many immigrant

Russian doctors, preparing them for the examinations which would enable them to take out an Israeli licence to practise medicine – provided by the Ministry of Health. These examinations are conducted in *Russian*, not in Hebrew, in order to help those doctors who are medically qualified, and have undergone the necessary retraining, to enter the job market. This sets Israel apart from all other countries receiving Russian immigrants.

Yet Russian doctors and dentists probably have the worst prospects of all skilled immigrants today. This is because the doctor–patient ratio in Israel, already among the highest in the world, has risen with the arrival of the Russians to twenty-one doctors for every thousand patients – beyond saturation point. So although the Hadassah retraining system had a fifty per cent success rate (elsewhere in Israel only a tenth or less) it remains difficult to integrate the Russians into the Israeli health system unless they are prepared to work as medical technicians or in those medical fields which are not attractive to Israelis, such as radiotherapy, pathology and anaesthetics – all of which involve minimal contact with the patients. Hadassah has managed to employ a number of Russians in nursing jobs formerly occupied by Filippino nurses and Arabs from the occupied territories: the first were content to leave after saving a few thousand dollars, the second were branded as collaborators during the *intifada* and did not return to work. But these new Russian nurses are not only former doctors, but engineers, journalists, and even artists. So it is not surprising that Russian Jewish doctors, one of the most distinguished professional groups, make up little more than two per cent of the current immigration, and that their numbers are constantly dropping.

Even if the doctors manage to emigrate elsewhere, they will need complete retraining in order to function in the West. Hadassah had studied the Russian doctors closely, and Ze'ev Olstain, its deputy director general, said he had come to a number of conclusions about Russian medicine:

'Russian doctors had a totally different attitude to pain to that of Western doctors. In the West, the patient wants the doctor to stop the pain as soon as possible, and the doctor complies, having a huge range of pharmaceutical products at his disposal. For the Russian doctor, pain was "part of the sickness, and an aid to diagnosis" [an idea which is outdated in the West] and his answer to the complaining patient was: the pain comes from a sickness, I shall diagnose and try to cure that, and then the pain will go. Of course there were economic and social reasons for this attitude. The Russian pharmaceutical industry did not provide painkillers in any variety.'

'Where dentists were concerned, this attitude to pain affected treatment most notably. Russian dentists did not perform root canal treatment, as this is abominably painful without analgesics, and extracted the teeth instead. Abortions, too, were performed without anaesthetics. Where the dentists were concerned, they knew the substances to be used in their work but not the trade names, and they had to be taught all these.'

The Russians simply did not have the modern technology to help them make diagnoses, and relied on instinct and experience. 'They use their hands,' said Olstain. There were X-rays, but only a few CT scan machines in the Soviet Union, in the big centres, and no use whatever of ultrasound. In the US, by comparison, there are 20,000 CT scan machines to detect tumours; there was only one in the Moscow Institute of Medicine. Hence, the Russians resorted to surgery at a far earlier stage than surgeons in the West, and this is exploratory surgery in the main. Very often, they performed unnecessary operations.

There are many treatment procedures standard in the West which are unknown in Russia, such as the heart balloon pump used to dilate clogged arteries, and hence prevent heart attacks. The Russian doctors had been kept in almost total ignorance of what went on in Western medicine. The *Lancet* and the *New England Journal of Medicine*, for instance, were imported only by the Soviet Academy of Sciences, and articles were translated and distributed very selectively. Most doctors knew no English, and thus had no access to foreign material. Very few attended international congresses, and their political affiliations were often as important as their professional qualifications where visits abroad were concerned. While Western doctors take it for granted that they continually have to update their knowledge by reading medical journals, or taking courses, the Russians learned only from experience.

'In clinical and hospital work, there were in Russia no disposable items of equipment. There were no disposable diapers for babies, and no disposable plastic syringes or needles. When we introduced a Russian doctor to these in Hadassah, he did not believe his eyes. In Russia, every piece of equipment has to be sterilised. They also have to get used to the idea of patients' rights.' Doctors in Russia, said Olstain, as favoured members of Soviet society had much better food and clothing than their patients. Only in alternative medicine were the Russians, predictably, ahead of the field. From their skills in 'using their hands', they were particularly good at medical massage.

In Hadassah's experience, it would take three to five years to retrain a Russian doctor – in other words, almost as long as to train a doctor from scratch.

In a community centre in a Jerusalem suburb, at one of a number of pilot project workshops set up all round the country, a score of immigrants are leafing through telephone books, scanning newspapers, and, under the watchful eye of a burly, energetic man, carrying on their own negotiations with prospective employers. 'Don't do it for them,' he warns one of his helpers who is trying to hurry things along; 'They've got to learn how to confront employers on the phone.'

Dr Rafi Gelbart, formerly chief scientist at the Ministry of Labour, today head of his own agency, 'Self-Directed Job Search', said that the government's schematic approach – *ulpan* (language studio): retraining course: jobs – was much too rigid, and unsuited to the character of the Russian immigration. He believed that the Russians should start looking for work on arrival, even with the few words of Hebrew at their command. Gelbart sets up his special workshops all over the country, using local community centres as his premises. Pupils pay a modest fee. In these workshops, the immigrants are screened, instructed in local conditions, and almost immediately encouraged to start exploring and familiarising themselves with the Israeli employment market. This helps them acquire the unfamiliar skill of 'selling themselves', working out how to interest potential employers, and finding out how the skills they possess can be used in ways which are perhaps unorthodox, or experimental.

Liuba Gurevich, forty-one years old, a pleasant, round-faced woman with big blue eyes, comes from Zolnychnogorsk, near Moscow. Before she located the workshop, she had almost given up hope of finding work. She had a PhD from the Moscow Institute of Agricultural Production Engineering, and was an expert in the quality control of farm machinery. She had worked, in Russia, for ten years in a machine-testing station: 'In Russia your skills were decided at school, then you got a subsidy to study, and then you were "directed" to a job.' There was another factor in her choice of profession; her father had done the same work, had written books about it, and wanted his daughter to follow him.

Liuba came to Israel in September 1991, but she had spent one and a half years without work. Her husband, a gynaecologist, had found work in one of Israel's maternity hospitals, Misgav Ladach, where he was now employed as an ultrasound technician (a classic case of the necessary downgrading of Russian physicians).

In Russia, she said, checking the quality control of machinery was definitely women's work. Not so in Israel. She did not do the repairs recommended. Her parents had remained behind, in Kirov, where her father still worked in a local Institute of Engineering. He had not emigrated, fearing a loss of status. She and her husband had two children, a boy in a boarding school where he was getting vocational training in electronics, and a daughter of six who was in first grade and already spoke fluent Hebrew. Her husband was still hoping to work as a doctor again, but he needed to learn the medical system of Israel. He would be able to work as a GP if he took further examinations, and would be subsidised by the Ministry of Absorption during his studies; meanwhile, Liuba must be chief breadwinner.

She said her ignorance of English was a handicap. English teaching in the Soviet Union had been poor – she was making sure her daughter learnt English by sending her to a cultural centre. After some weeks in the workshop, she decided to work temporarily as a full-time children's help, and meanwhile to learn English herself.

Galina Suvolev, a slight, delicate brunette with carefully made-up dark eyes, a marine construction engineer, was an expert in light-weight aluminium craft. Her speciality was designing and repairing aluminium boats. The only firm which could give her this kind of work was one belonging to the Israel Aircraft Industry in Beersheba. But she was not accepted, and, pending a promised job with a tourist agency planning trips on the Volga, she was taking a computer course which would ensure her unemployment benefits.

Gelbart said that he had been inspired by the scheme introduced in the United States to cope with the influx of foreign immigrants entering the country in the 1970s. He was convinced that a correct interpretation of available statistics could help those assisting the immigrants to find work in the right sector – and that this was not done. Contrary to what was believed by officials, over fifty-seven per cent of the immigrants had found work in business enterprises, most of them small.

There were many jobs, Gelbart contended, waiting to be filled, but the immigrants simply did not know how to reach them. Within five weeks after completing his workshop training, he maintained, seventy-three per cent of the immigrants had found work. He thought his system could develop into a valid alternative to the conventional labour exchanges. Israeli immigration policy was 'the Zionism of kiosks', in that it had an ad hoc policy of getting immigrants any kind of work, however temporary and unsuitable. It was not true, he maintained, that immigrants had to be prepared to change their professions.

Engineers, technicians, doctors, usually had to work at a much lower level in a related field. Nevertheless, Gelbart stressed, the immigrants would eventually raise Israel's professional and technological level all round. In Israel, at present, only eighteen per cent of the population had a university education (compared with forty per cent in the US) and among the immigrants, the vast majority had some kind of higher education. Israel could use the immigrants, eventually, to enter the high-tech field in exports to Western countries on a far more extensive scale, if they received the correct updating and retraining courses. There was no absence of training facilities in Israel.

He agreed that there was a particular problem with the Russians' passive reliance on authority to find them work and keep them there. Once people had left the labour market there was a real danger that they would get used to a parasitic life, or drift to the margins.

The signs of dire poverty and need are there, for those who have eyes to see: in the street markets, on Sabbath eve, when the last greenish carrot or soggy orange is going at rock bottom prices, or abandoned to be picked up from the ground by neatly dressed senior citizens; at the warehouses to which Israelis send the scarcely worn clothes of the newly dead; at the charitable soup kitchen in a central meeting hall, where the tables are laid with cloths and flowers and the diners who buy a three-course meal for £1.00 are entertained by an immigrant musician playing *Moscow Nights* on a concertina; in the hallways of apartment blocks where bespectacled professorial gentlemen wearing rubber gloves swab the steps down (the Arab cleaner having been sent home in case he is carrying a kitchen knife). Just occasionally, women in fur jackets and peroxided hair can be seen scouting around the dustbin areas in elegant suburbs, looking for discarded armchairs and outmoded mixers. In one of the brand new shopping malls, far from the loudspeakers outside the cassette and video shops, in the centre of a tiled hallway, a young Russian music student sits at an upright Volga piano playing Chopin nocturnes, a cloth cap at her feet.

Russian buskers, most of them middle aged, throng the Jerusalem pedestrian mall in Ben Yehuda street, at the centre of the crowded triangle of the downtown commercial area of West Jerusalem. With one exception, they are like characters from *A Fiddler on the Roof:* the men in baggy trousers, the women in straw hats tied with ribbons, caricatures of Soviet ethnic Jewry, playing the tunes popular in Jewish immigrant quarters in Western cities fifty years ago – *My Yiddishe Mamma, Bei Mir Bist Du Scheine.* Among them strolls an ancient Yemenite, a genuine beggar, shaking a tin can in people's faces with no pretence at entertaining anyone ('I was here before anyone had heard of the Russians') and, further down the street, an up-to-the-minute ensemble of crew-cut Americans and long-haired North African Israelis from the popular 'Natural Choice' oriental music group, bonging and tootling on African instruments and contemptuous of the old-fashioned *kletzmer* combos up the street.

The exception among the Russian buskers is an odd figure who has been filmed by every lazy cameraman in the pay of Western television companies and cast by every cliché-prone journalist in the role of the persecuted Russian Jewish intellectual reduced to penury in the Promised Land. This curious figure – a middle-aged man in a suit and straw hat, his eyes fixed on the ground – sings unaccompanied operatic arias and Russian folk songs and 'romances' in a bass baritone almost totally inaudible over the noise of the traffic from the nearby main road. He looks almost autistically detached from his surroundings, but at home, in an elephantine grey multi-entrance apartment block far from the centre, which housed North African immigrants in the early 1960s, he is talkative enough.

David Hrishtein is a mathematics teacher from Leningrad with twenty-four years' teaching experience. His wife worked as a machine-tooling mechanic in an industrial plant. Hrishtein is of Polish parentage; his parents fled to Leningrad in 1939, nine years before his birth. The rest of his family was killed in the Holocaust. Like most Russian Jews, Hrishtein became aware of Israel's existence during the Six Days War, when it looked to them as if the Israelis were to suffer the same fate as European Jewry. But he was never a refusenik, never joined any Jewish organisation. It was only in the spring of 1991, when the right-wing, strongly anti-semitic Russian organisation 'Pamyat' began threatening a pogrom, that Hrishtein thought it was time to leave.

The Hrishteins rented their flat, which has three rooms, from a North African family, once the poorest of Israel's immigrants, people who had gone up in the world and had accommodation to spare. Hrishtein's wife took a retraining course in electrical engineering and now works for a firm producing dishwashers.

Hrishtein has taken to singing in the street, a gesture of defiance despite his meek exterior, rather than applying for unemployment benefits. He earns some 50 shekels (about £12.00 a day), and not a few jeers and requests from passers-by to move on. Hrishtein's view of Israel is unrelievedly grim: 'Israel is full of swindlers, liars, cheats and a bureaucracy worse than that in Russia. No one explains anything to you. Everyone is rude, religious people are intolerant. We expected difficulties but not as bad as this. Jews ought to be more good hearted.'

All this Hrishtein utters in a mournful drone, as his small daughter Natasha listens from a shabby leather armchair. 'The teachers have no knowledge. There is no discipline in the school.

In Russia, Natasha went to school with pleasure; here, she says they play with her hair. She's wasting her time, learning nothing.'

Asked to speak for herself, Natasha, a pretty child of eight with lively eyes and a long dark plait, looks warily at her parents, too shy, too obedient, to respond. She whispers something inaudible, stops in the middle. What is she to say to this catalogue of woes? But she agrees to explain the pictures she has drawn which, fixed with drawing pins to all the furniture in the room, are its sole decoration. Her friends (Israelis); the teacher (who looks suitably stern and disciplinarian); symbols of the festivals of Passover and Tabernacles, about which she has been learning for the first time, and a picture of the Dead Sea, where a skull and crossbones, on the further side, indicate the presence of the dreaded Arabs.

When requested, Natasha produces a surprisingly cheerful picture of herself. While Hrishtein has been casting himself in the roles of Amonasro and Fiesco, despairing parents both, in the shopping mall, Natasha has portrayed herself riding a red bicycle, with a bunch of balloons flying from the handlebars. She looks out at the spectator with a tentative smile. Beside her in the picture is a savagely lopped tree trunk, from whose unpromising bark some wispy, new green leaves are beginning to emerge.

CHAPTER FIVE

Das Kapital

'Under the Soviet regime, the first to acquire personal laptop computers were the gangsters; they were the only people who could afford them. The price of a computer was about $6000 and a monthly average salary was $20.'

What the gangsters did with their computers, the three computer scientists – Ilya Rotschanker, Misha Shoman and Moshe Wasserman, from Georgia, Tashkent and Kiev – were not sure. But they knew that the Mafia, especially in the Asiatic republics, where the long arm of Soviet law was overstretched, were more up to date than most Soviet citizens. Ilya Rotschanker had worked in the Soviet statistics industry, and knew the facts about crime in Uzbekhistan. He had some notion about the relative crime statistics in other parts of the Soviet Union – those which were official. He had not known how crime statistics in Israel, Britain, or the US compared with those of the USSR. The outside world was sealed off.

At the Hilton hotel in Tel Aviv, the three scientists were taking part in a trade fair. Israelis and Americans in identical smart suits were exchanging sales talk and glossy catalogues. They have all been 'absorbed' into the Israeli branch of John Bryce, a big American computer firm and are currently working on its most recent system, 'Oracle', which coordinates and updates obsolete or multiple information networks into one coherent and streamlined whole.

The main difference between Russia and the West, they said, was that here there were many sources of information, access to hundreds of foreign networks. But even without comparative data Rotschanker had disbelieved the Soviet authorities' claim that the

Soviet crime rate had been lower than elsewhere; while violent crime was curbed by a strong police state, the Uzbekh mafia, equipped with their laptops, creamed off the products of their fertile countryside for black market sales.

Couldn't the Soviet computer whizzes break into foreign networks to get access to information from elsewhere? Rotschanker and his colleagues said no, that there was no way. On the other hand, actual software was pirated from the West, in the same way that, today, consumers copy one another's programmes without paying royalties to the producers.

Misha Shoman: 'The difference was, in a word, markets. In Russia our work was commissioned by the Soviet hierarchy and was tailormade to the system, whatever field we worked in. Here there are many different markets, many different opportunities for development. But the basic knowhow is the same, the training (we all had academic training) is the same.'

Oracle is geared to programming, for instance, municipal bonds in US cities, systems of cellular phones in cars, competing insurance companies, and so on, and in keeping up to date with the international money market. Clearly there was nothing like that in the USSR.

Computers were not used, for instance, in banks (there was no banking system as we know it), in shops, in theatre bookings, or for the multiple other links between supplier and consumer; so far, only airline bookings were programmed by computer.

Misha worked in Tbilisi for one of the local ministries. His job was linked to the guidelines laid down by the minister for the distribution of information. The computer work was not geared to the real needs of the people, but to the current ideological line, or 'fashion' as he put it. During perestroika, of course, all these structures had been destroyed, and the programmes he had worked on were now useless.

'Computerisation can only really work as part of a healthy economy. It is part of capitalism – competition. We had the technology, but we couldn't put it to its proper use.'

Had the spread of information technology led to more political awareness in the Soviet public, and thus helped to hasten the end of the Communist regime? They all shook their heads. Ilya: 'Each programmer worked only within his narrow field. Only the head of a division had all the information. Our vision was very narrow; the results of our work went elsewhere.'

Anyway, they all agreed, computer technology would not have given them any extra awareness of the rottenness of the system. They knew things didn't work anyway, they knew the economy was falling to pieces. The problems of working in the computer industry grew less as perestroika advanced. But there were still other differences between working there and in Israel.

Moshe Wasserman, for instance, had worked in a textile firm. The difference in the cost of producing clothes in the USSR and the West was striking. In the USSR, ninety per cent of the cost of the final product was the actual material, and only ten per cent styling. In the West, the exact reverse was the situation.

But apart from such differences, which stemmed from the supply and demand system in the USSR (problems of getting raw materials to the plants, lack of choice by the consumer) there was the much larger question of whether a country like Russia could afford computerisation on a large scale in industry. Misha: 'The sheer computer power of a system like Oracle is equivalent to the entire computer power in the whole republic of Georgia. We'd never seen Japanese systems, but our impression is that only the USA is rich enough to develop a system like Oracle. The USSR was beyond the law, where computers were concerned; systems were pirated and used in a different way because the Soviet regime didn't want to be involved in any international network because of the rules of secrecy. The whole point about the computer industry in the West is the rapid diffusion of information. The Soviets weren't interested in that, of course.

'Russia is twenty to thirty years behind the times in computerisation, we can see that now. Take telephone communications, which are computerised all over the West. The infrastructure is in such a bad state, so expensive to repair, that now it will take years to introduce computerisation. A few years ago, when not everything was computerised in the West, we might have caught up. Now the gap has widened and it will take far longer.'

Ilya: 'If people are going hungry, they don't need advanced new programmes. So it won't be on the government's list of priorities.'

Misha, Ilya and Moshe all arrived in Israel two or three years ago. All admitted that initially they had considered going to the United States. Moshe was almost on his way, but his wife was going to give birth, and during the last period of her pregnancy, the Americans tightened the immigration laws.

'They got us very cheap,' said Misha. 'The Israelis didn't have to pay for our education.' But he also admitted: 'From letters I get from the States, the situation isn't all that good there, and Russian Jews feel isolated. Here, I must say, I do not feel lonely.'

Why had they come to Israel? Ilya couldn't remember. Misha said he felt his skills had not been fully exploited in the Soviet Union. His speciality had been demographic studies and employment. Another factor was the civil war in Georgia. Ilya's specialisation was programming, and the free market experience was important for him.

There was certainly no suggestion of an ideological upheaval in the motivation of these new immigrants. Just as they had made no real effort to widen those narrow telescopic sights they had had in their work in the USSR, they would have gone anywhere that offered them a better career.

In the industrial area of Herzliya, near Tel Aviv, a highly specialised firm deals with Measurement and Control Systems in industry, hence the name MACS. Measurement technology is connected with Israel's links with big international companies and the export of vital products such as fertilisers from the Dead Sea Works. All but one of its staff are Russians, even including the office cleaners.

The odd man out is Barry Swersky, MACS' PR man, an ex-South African who at one time ran the publicity for Bat Sheva, the Israeli dance company. Swersky had gone on from management of Bat Sheva to handling the Georgian national airline after perestroika. In this way he had met the present head of the firm, Serge Bomberg, from Azerbaijan, who had put in a request for an exit visa from the Soviet Union in the 1970s, but had only managed to emigrate in 1990.

Bomberg is fifty-three, a doctor of science from Baku with over twenty-six years' experience in measurement information and technology, having served during most of this period as head of the automation laboratory at the Scientific Research Institute of

Engineering in Kuibyshev, with eighty-six Russian patents to his name. He had helped create various systems for controlling and monitoring liquid mass, density, levels and leakage measurements in reservoirs and tanks, of importance in the oil, aircraft, marine and other industries.

MACS headquarters are in the US. They employ about 5,000 people in all in research and development, of whom about thirty to forty are Russian Jews, most based in Israel. Six of these were selected to head the Israeli branch of the firm. The Russian immigrants who make up the staff have shares in the company.

The immigrants went through a total metamorphosis where the organisation of their work, if not their expertise, was concerned. Firstly, the work is concentrated in a very few hands, and they had to get used to the idea that one hundred people working on a project could be more efficient than 500. The idea of sub contracting was new to them, and that of profit making. That 'size is not quality', said Swersky, was a new concept for the Russians, as a group of thirty people work in a firm with a $30 million turnover.

Soviet industry had been command orientated, with priorities given to heavy industry, though in the 1970s most Russian industries employed fewer than 200 workers. However, from 1973 onwards the trend was to larger and larger enterprises. Swersky described Russian industry as 'vertically orientated' which meant that decisions were taken far from the actual technicians in huge organisations, in the central political bureaux.

But the chief difference, of course, was the notion of competition. Trying to find out what other firms were doing looked to the Russians like spying. 'Contacts' and 'marketing' were also new concepts, or rather variations on something which in the USSR had been illegal. In the USSR there had been no competition, but much nepotism, and money changed hands to secure the monopoly on specific projects. The idea of taking initiative, alone, was strange to the Russians. Profits were irrelevant, and there were no risks. An industry could happily be run at a loss.

Alex Buchman was the youngest member of the team. He had been two and a half years in Israel, and just over a year in MACS. He had spent three months learning Hebrew, could read the local newspapers, but it was his knowledge of English that helped him with his contacts with the parent firm. He was the firm's chief liaison man with the US head office, as well as technician.

Buchman is an electronics engineer by profession. His job in the USSR was controlling how much residual material remained in a bottle after washing. Like the other members of the group, he was from Azerbaijan, but had studied at the Polytechnic in Leningrad. Subsequently he had worked in Baku for seven years, and then taken the train for the nearest airport, in Budapest, despite the risks en route, he said, of Palestinians threatening Russian emigrants to Israel. A bespectacled, reserved young man, Buchman said it was a huge advantage to work in a firm to which you belonged, and in which you had a share. Russian engineers, he said, had not known how to present themselves to potential employers; it was not only a question of language, but of initiative. In the USSR you did not have to sell yourself; either you got your job through 'connections' or you were chosen for your skills, by people far above you who just saw your academic record.

The main difference between his work in the USSR and in Israel was that the cost of the instrument he and his colleagues produced had to be competitive and worthwhile. 'In the West we take this for granted, but in Russia there was no incentive to make money.' The cost of the product was unimportant. Nevertheless, reliability and accuracy was important and money was allotted to scientists. Here, every move had to be calculated, every component carefully checked for cost and advantage. In Russia, he said, there was no information available about component parts for an instrument, and no choice of manufacturers. You took what was going.

But Buchman was not uncritical of Western standards. 'In Russia,' he said, 'the catalogues were bad but the products good. In the US, the catalogues are glossy but the products often of poor quality.' Still, in Soviet Russia, he said, such a high-tech, small company as MACS would have had problems surviving.

Right at the opposite end of the skills spectrum, among Russians who have found their way into private enterprise, is Igor Wissotsky, a skilled furniture restorer from Leningrad who worked in one of four teams, each including half a dozen people, who served the various museums, including the Hermitage. He also worked in the Rimsky-Korsakov Museum and the new Priyutino. Eighteenth-century furniture is on display in all such museums, and Wissotsky was one of the few experts who knew how to repair, preserve, and reproduce antique furniture.

On the face of it, no skills could be less adapted to Israel. There is very little antique furniture in Israel: inlaid Arab work originating in Damascus, or the few pieces imported from Europe by those immigrants who arrived in the twenties or the early years of Nazism, and were able to bring some of their belongings with them.

Wissotsky is a master craftsman, immensely proud of his experience. By training he is an electronics engineer, and thus one of the few who managed to buck the system and choose his own profession without state intervention. He was born in St Petersburg and was three years old during the siege. One married son remained behind in St Petersburg, one came with him and his wife to Israel.

From childhood, Wissotsky had loved carpentry. During the siege, many pieces of furniture were destroyed for firewood. As a small child, he found old furniture damaged by bombardment left in the street, and some he took from the rubbish bins, fascinated by the intricate work which remained. As he grew up, he began to collect books about restoring furniture. More than 3,000 books had been left behind in St Petersburg with his elder son. Most of his knowledge of restoration had been acquired from books, and from watching how veteran restorers worked.

Wissotsky's first place of work in Israel was a crammed junk shop in the Jerusalem city market, run by a wily Persian merchant. The furniture there was 'antique' only in the sense of being old, battered, and overpriced. The Persian was systematically exploiting new immigrants from Russia, many of whom were expert carpenters, paying them starvation wages. The phoney antiques market was to be Wissotsky's problem as his Israeli career progressed; would Israelis understand the skills he possessed, and be prepared to pay a genuine market price?

Wissotsky's next job was in a workshop in the Jewish Quarter of the Old City, working for someone who brought him broken furniture, doors with damaged hinges, and benches from synagogues and halls to mend. It was the most primitive kind of work possible, badly paid, work for an ordinary joiner, not for a master. He suggested that we talk outside, on a bench in the sunny piazza, and not in the workshop, which was chilly and uncomfortable. While we were sitting there, a young man with a skull-cap came up to Wissotsky and asked rudely what he was doing. When Wissotsky, a gentle, soft-voiced man, explained, the young man said 'Not in my time you don't. Get back to work.'

But such humiliations were not to last. Wissotsky made contact with a woman at the Israel Museum to whom he showed some of the work he had brought with him, and an album of photographs of his work in Russia. Wissotsky said that in Russia there had been no 'schools of carpentry' such as Chippendale, and it was only coincidental if one knew the name of the manufacturer of a piece of furniture. But he regarded himself as one of a long line of skilled craftsmen. Personal fame, he said, was unimportant.

In his tiny flat in a Jerusalem suburb was a superb period piece he had built of Carelian birch, which he had brought with him, a reproduction of an eighteenth-century writing bureau. On the basis of his albums and this one piece, he received a commission to work on a wooden synagogue shortly to be brought from India and to be incorporated into the Museum's collection of tiny ancient synagogues. The only other institution which had approached him was the Weizmann Institute, the scientific campus in Rehovot named after Zionism's greatest diplomat and the first president of the state, which wanted repairs to the furniture in Weizmann's old house. 'But most of it was not worth the expense.'

'There is no culture of hand-made furniture in Israel. Arab carpentry is very crude; they cut the heads off the nails, which is dangerous. But no one understands the complexity of restoration and they do not want to pay the real price of many days' work. Only the people at the Museum had some idea of the effort invested.'

Wissotsky had come to Israel because, in the post-perestroika period, he thought Jews should be together. He felt that anti-semitism was once more in the air, and the general atmosphere was depressing. But here everyone expected the Russians to work for a pittance, and to be satisfied if they had any work at all.

During the first two years in the country the rent of his flat had cost him his entire salary. His younger son had found work in an aluminium factory.

He found Israeli society puzzling as there were so many different groups. In Russia there was the educated class, the intelligentsia, and a huge gap between this and the rest. He thought the general culture in Israel was of a 'low level'. 'Either we don't meet the intellectuals here or we don't speak their language (in all senses).'

Wissotsky said he did not want to go on living just among Russian immigrants. 'That contradicts the entire purpose of our coming here.' None the less, both he and his wife Galia agreed that it was easier, if not desirable, to mix with those who spoke one's own language.

Wissotsky had a serious criticism of Israel. 'Here all artists want to make money. In Russia, the real masters were just masters, they didn't think of making money, but of their skills. They wanted to express themselves and improve their professional abilities.'

Meanwhile, however, Wissotsky was beginning to receive commissions from Israelis who had imported furniture from abroad which needed repair. Today, Wissotsky has established himself. He orders consignments of wood from Russia, and manufactures beautiful reproductions of antique furniture for discriminating – and wealthy – Israeli buyers. As few other Russians have done, he has created his own market.

Tatiana Kochergina is a theatre and film designer whose husband was Jewish, but who is not Jewish herself. She arrived in Israel in 1990 with her twenty-five-year-old son and was eligible for an entry visa because of her marriage to a Jew; but her husband remained in Leningrad. Kochergina's son had been disappointed by Israel, and returned to Russia after a year and a half. Kochergina remained, alone. She rents a room in a flat in the commercial district of Tel Aviv but does not speak Hebrew.

Kochergina has a high-cheekboned, slightly Mongolian face; extremely pale, she speaks with elegant gestures. She was born and brought up in Leningrad, and had eighteen years' experience in film and theatre, having worked as a costume designer with some of the most famous of Russian film directors – Aranovitz, Kanevsky and Heifitz. Her career flourished in the Brezhnev era.

During her first months in Israel, she spent three or four days a month packing cardboard boxes, eleven hours a day, for 200 shekels (£50) a month. Eventually she made herself known to the Russian theatre group, Gesher, who also performs in Hebrew for whom she designed costumes, and since then has worked in many other capacities, from knitting clothes, to restoring, with one other woman, Gobelin tapestries brought to Israel by a French millionaire. She also mends upholstery.

Working under the Soviet regime was not easy, Kochergina said, as it was difficult to get materials. The old costumes from before the revolutionary times were falling to pieces. She would advertise for materials kept from the pre-war period, such as velvet and lace. Sometimes she patched together one costume from three. Elderly people sold her materials they had kept, and even jewellery which they were afraid to wear. Hence, very often, where in the Western theatre all the glitter of royal jewellery was paste, in Soviet Russia what you saw on the stage was the genuine article, real jewels no woman could possibly wear under Communism.

Kochergina was now designing costumes for an Israeli children's TV programme, and when the Tel Aviv Museum recently put on an exhibition of the original Sleeping Beauty costumes designed by the great Leonid Bakst, it was she who made four of the puppets in the show. Kochergina, who lives very modestly, and does not even have her own home, voiced no criticism of Israel. As she is neither Jewish herself nor, any longer, a member of a Jewish family, she does not qualify for Israeli citizenship, and will probably always be a 'permanent resident', ineligible for state benefits, always a stranger. She is, quite simply, pleased to have work.

Three young women immigrants, all of whom have struck out on their own, live together in the unfashionable market area of Jerusalem. Anna Bernstein cleans schoolrooms, in shifts with other Russian girls, after the children go home and the chairs are piled on the desks. Anna is a gentle, slow-spoken girl who has been in Israel seven months. She came from Moscow, without her parents, at the time of the Gulf War. Her married brother, a computer scientist, had preceded her by a year. Like three-quarters of Russian women in Israel, Anna began as a domestic worker, cleaning private homes and then working as hired help for an invalid. Part-time cleaning work, late in the day, left her time to train for a new career.

Anna is a qualified sound technician, who learned her trade in Moscow and Leningrad. She had worked in a radio laboratory for six or seven years, editing music. In Russia, all the enterprises were enormous, and many people were employed in work which has been replaced by machines elsewhere. For instance, in Israel, as elsewhere in the West, the sound track for films, or incidental music in plays, is packaged by a laboratory. The work Anna did slowly, putting pieces together, comes ready-made in the West. In Israel, as she could find no work in television or radio, she is retraining to do montage work for publishers, fitting photographs and graphic artists' work together for a printer. The working hours are long and the pay, she says, is poor.

Anna shares a flat with Lena and Faina, acquaintances from Russia. The flat, with only basic furnishings but modern kitchen equipment the women have paid for themselves, is decorated with Faina's drawings and paintings, mostly landscapes of the market area seen from the window, and nudes for which her friends modelled. The fourth tenant, who does not pay rent, Alexander (Sasha), is two months old. No mention was made of his father, and I felt it would be improper to enquire. His mother, Lena, is a dentist in private practice with two other Russian immigrants. At present she is on maternity leave, but she said she had to work, and would take Alexander with her as she intended to continue breastfeeding as long as possible, and wanted to keep him with her all the time.

Lena, Anna and Faina, all in their mid twenties, have all found work; all are energetic and enterprising. That their set-up – three women and a baby living together – is unusual in Israel does not appear to worry them.

Lena had worked for seven years in Moscow as a dentist, and had retrained in Israel. She had been in Israel three years. Faina had just graduated from art school when she came, on a tourist's visa, just before the Gulf War, and decided to stay. She, like Lena, has been able to find work in her profession, and at present does the graphic work for a publisher producing illustrated rabbinical tracts. Her employers are North African, and French speaking.

Of the three, probably Faina was best qualified to find her feet in Israel. While still in Russia she had begun studying Hebrew, and though she, like her flat mates, is not religious, she acquired some knowledge of Jewish history and tradition from two rival religious groups which offered courses, and lodgings, to immigrants. The synagogue she and other people went to was a meeting place, somewhere she met other Jews and other would-be immigrants. Faina, who kept her options open for six months longer than is usual for a Russian to stay on a tourist visa, said that it was the Gulf War which made her decide to remain in Israel.

'I understood for the first time that the Israelis were a people, that they feel for one another; when there was an air raid warning, people in the street helped me and told me what to do. That would have been impossible in Russia.'

Her friends reminded her that during the Great War (the Second World War) Russians were supposed to have helped one another. 'Yes, but not now; every man is for himself. Friends help one another, but not strangers. Here I feel the potential for the future.'

Lena said that she came on the spur of the moment. 'I got up one morning and decided: that's it, I'm going to Israel.' After the mandatory retraining period, she and two dentist colleagues got a five year loan from the Jewish Agency, for those setting up in 'small businesses'. A dentist's surgery qualifies as a 'business', though she thought it a pity that they could not advertise. Most of their clientele were other Russians, who could not pay the high prices Israeli dentists charged and who liked to go to Russians with Israeli licences. They charged less than Israelis, Lena said, 'But not too little. If you charge very low fees the patients think you can't be any good.' She was very defensive about Soviet medicine, saying that although they did not have the benefit of sophisticated Western equipment, they had done a good job with what they had.

The young women had not managed to make friends among Israelis of their own kind and age. 'Only older people, no one of our own age. There's one contractor who rented a flat to friends of ours. He's a real Israeli, one of those who left Hebron after the 1929 massacre, and he more or less adopted us, brought us things when we needed them. A man in his sixties, very kind.' But otherwise? They know the people in the market, ordinary uneducated people, but not sabras, native-born Israelis, of their own age. 'The people I can be friends with, I don't really want as friends,' said Faina. 'The people I'd like to know, I just don't meet.'

Lena had shared a flat for a few months with an Israeli girl from a kibbutz who was studying at the university. 'All she ever said to me was "Shalom, good morning, how are you"; well, that was fine, we got on all right, but we didn't have much in common. I was pretty shocked that she decided after a few months at the university that studies were not for her; she just stopped going, after the kibbutz had sent her and paid for her. She said she wanted to travel before it was too late, before she had to settle down and marry and have children in the kibbutz. So she didn't study at all. We Russians couldn't possibly do that. For us, to study and qualify, to have a profession, was the most important thing of all. As Jews, we had to do well, otherwise we'd have been nothing.'

'Here we're all Jews, so not everyone can be a professor,' Lena went on. 'That I understand. But it's still surprising to us that there are Jews who say "I can make more money running a stall in the market, what do I need to study for?" In Russia, every Jewish child plays an instrument, and the parents take children to museums, to theatres and concerts. We never had time to play outside, we were always sent to special courses – music, English. But we hardly saw our parents: an hour and a half a day, that was all. All the children in Russia go to school with the doorkeys hanging round their necks. I'd like to spend more time with my son.'

How had their non-Jewish friends reacted to their leaving? That was an uncomfortable question. 'They couldn't understand how we could do it, just get up and go.' 'Jealousy?' 'Maybe.' Pause. 'Today in Russia they say it's a good thing to marry a Jewish husband or wife so you can get out of Russia. It's terrible for our parents. Their salaries barely keep them going, with the inflation rate in Russia. But they are too old to uproot themselves now and start over again; they're all people with professions and status. Older people here, especially the men, have a very hard time. They can't find work in their professions, they feel no one needs them – not their colleagues, and not their families, because the women are doing all the work. They sit around at home in a state of depression and make everyone miserable. I know one man in that situation who actually committed suicide.'

Sasha smiled contentedly in Lena's arms, where he had been held and rocked throughout the conversation. At his age, he was no threat to the wellbeing of these three independent young women, who expressed no need whatsoever for another man in the family.

Those who can, work. For those who cannot, the Hebrew University has set up a pilot training project for immigrant 'entrepreneurs' together with the Open University, the local business centre and the Ministries of Labour and Absorption at the Scopus campus, in the adult education centre. How to be a capitalist, in many uneasy lessons.

The Russian coordinator of the course, Dr Boris Bogoslavsky, the holder of three degrees in economics, dresses all in black and wears a gold chain round his neck; a neat black beard fringes his chin. He is soft spoken, and faintly threatening. The course was meant, he said, to discourage the fainthearted (nine out of thirty-five had dropped out by the third session). 'I don't want any favours,' he kept repeating. All the lecturers were people from the business world, not academics; they were not teaching economic subjects like inflation, stagnation, stagflation. These were all abstract Western notions and there was no point in talking about them.

Where he himself was concerned, he emphasised, he was running this course because his Hebrew was not yet up to coping with a more demanding job. He was extremely critical of the Israeli economy (which he said was not an economy at all) but said he was reluctant to express his opinions in poor Hebrew. In his view, the Israeli government had used the Russian immigration to get more money from the US: the Israelis were not prepared to handle the immigrants, and the only way it could be done efficiently was for a team of Americans to administer the loan funds themselves.

The Russian immigrants at his course went through a stiff screening process, and they constitute only about half of the class, in which there are also Americans (one with a second business degree) and new immigrants from France. This was supposed to be part of the Russians' initiation – to be thrust straight into the trials of a pluralist society. What they wanted to know is how businessmen do business, and all the lecturers were people who talked about marketing a product – an idea which had no equivalent in Soviet Russia. Some of those present had some experience of running a shop or business. Others were doctors, engineers or lawyers who were striking out afresh.

At the opening session, the Russians included Natasha, from a small town near Moscow, who described herself as an economist, had studied economics in a college in her home town, had run a shop there, and wanted to open a grocery shop in Jerusalem; Paulina, a veteran child minder and Anya, a music teacher, who both wanted to run classes in their homes; and Grigori, a law graduate from Sverdlovsk who would only say darkly that he had great plans for a large business but would not reveal what it was.

Paulina had worked caring for thirty babies in a crèche for working mothers in a Kharkov factory which was open from 7a.m. to 7p.m. She and another woman had worked six-hour shifts. No such institution exists in Israel, where the proportion of women in the work force is exactly half of that in the Soviet Union – forty-two per cent. No crèche is open after 4p.m., and no factories have facilities for babies.

One of the main reasons why young Israeli married women do not find it worth while to work is that all their salary goes to private child minders; but few Israeli mothers would want to see their children only an hour or two a day. Even in a kibbutz, the women working in the nurseries do not handle more than three or four babies each.

'*We* were the mothers,' said Paulina proudly. She was considering taking on twelve babies, with one helper, between the hours of eight and four; she was learning what foods, and diapers, were available in Israel, and what licences she needed to open such a crèche.

The course was held in a hall where a lecture on geriatrics had just taken place. DO NOT GO GENTLE INTO THAT GOOD-NIGHT was the notice on the wall. The lectures, it was explained, would be on banking, law, taxation, marketing and 'presentations'. A businessman from Jerusalem would give the immigrants a realistic picture of a tough and competitive society as an introduction. All students would be expected to 'present' their own programme of a projected business, and also be able to opt out of the course if the Hebrew, or the pace, was too rapid.

The professor in charge of adult education, Dov Friedlander, in his opening words, stressed the problem of the 'insider network'. The greatest problem for immigrants, he said, was going to be how to get *in*. The first lecturer, a businessman who was also a friend of Friedlander's (perhaps an initial illustration of the importance of the network) was a mechanical engineer, a graduate of the Technion, who had set up his own medium-sized business supplying air conditioning to hotels, contractors and factories.

He began by telling his own personal story: his education, and his subsequent years working for a large mechanical firm where there were about 3000 employees. He himself now employed about a tenth of that number, having started with a dozen or so.

Reducing overheads was all important, he said. Directors should not go for impressive front offices with nothing behind them, and it was more important to feed back all profits into the firm itself, its equipment. He said the manager should be responsible for everything, and should have good direct contact with his workers. He said in his case that 'the door is always open'. The Americans nodded rather impatiently; the Russians sat quietly baffled.

Only once did one of them ask a question: 'Where did you get the money to start with?' 'Oh, through the family,' he said airily. Banks, he said cheerily, only lent money to people who don't need it. Joke. The Americans asked about relations with works committees and trades unions, all of which was Greek to the Russians.

Friedlander intervened several times in slower, more careful and simplified Hebrew, pointing out that the student capitalists would start with only one or two workers, and with, at the most, a starting capital of £7,500. He, however, spoke of 'role definition' and warned the would-be bosses that they had to keep their hands on the reins, and that they must not identify overly with their employees. 'Remember your employee is not your colleague,' he told them.

The image of the businessman in Israel, said Friedlander, was negative, and suggested dishonesty. This rang a bell with the Russians, for whom most businessmen were *mafiosi*. The small entrepreneur in Soviet society was usually dishonest, and under perestroika, a rank profiteer.

There was a query from the Americans about fluctuations in the market due to inflation. This, again, puzzled the Russians. In the Soviet Union there had been no official inflation; prices simply rose overnight, without explanation. Supply and demand? Someone opens a restaurant in New York, the class was told. For eight weeks there would be no clients, and this is to be expected. But if *after* eight weeks there were still no clients, the proprietor might as well close. This caused the Russians to look round in consternation; several drew in their breath in dismay.

Noting this, Friedlander tried to be encouraging. There was no academic definition, he said, of what made a successful entrepreneur, but research showed that 'outsiders' or people on the margins of society often made good more easily, that the lack of roots was useful, that immigrants had new approaches, better ideas. Psychologically this might have helped the Russians, had it not been in total contradiction to what the lecturer had said, which was that knowing the ropes, having contacts, and having a good reputation based on past performance was all important. Immigrants, Friedlander added, had to take risks.

The second lecturer taught the immigrants how to prepare to open a business. He said that the prospective employers had first to contact the tax authorities and open a file. The accountant, he knew, had not existed in the Soviet Union, but he was very important in Israel, a key adviser to entrepreneurs. The most important initial step for the businessman was to get credit facilities, (more dismay), but, where income tax was concerned, the accountant could be adviser and therapist. The Russians asked one another how much an accountant had to be paid, but they did not raise their hands.

Natasha and Paulina made copious notes about zoning laws and the opening of different kinds of businesses. To open a business in your own home, they learned, was all right, but the police and fire authorities had to check out the premises. Locks, and alarms, were sometimes demanded. More expenses, they murmured.

Partnerships, VAT, oral and written agreements, dividends, ordinary and extraordinary shares, low and high risk businesses, all flowed on fast – the Americans nodding impatiently, the Russians scribbling diligently. What alarmed them particularly was the idea of the limited company with shareholders. The shareholder, it was explained, could not risk more than his investment. The owner risked all.

Grigori asked who was responsible, financially, for losses. The lecturer answered indirectly by saying that losing money was not a criminal offence, unless the money had been stolen, so that shareholders had no right to complain or go to court. First lesson in capitalism – risks and losses.

The banks only provided loans, said the lecturer, if the share-holders signed guarantees. What happened, he was asked, if the business folded? If any money remained, he said, mortgage holders on the property had first claim. Bond owners divided what was left, together with the employees and the various state authorities. If anything at all was left, it was divided among the shareholders.

The Russians looked horrified. Some said later that they were beginning to understand the benefits of Communism, with its cast iron guarantees of employment and payment, however low; of housing, however miserable; of annual holidays, and of all the benefits the state provided.

Progressive taxation, deductions, pension funds, allowances; the company paid forty per cent of profits in taxes. Here one of the Russian women asked: 'If I don't earn anything, does Income Tax pay *me*?' This raised a laugh from the Americans and the French. But the question was reasonable enough, from her point of view. The immigrants to Israel receive so many handouts, that it was difficult for an ex-Soviet citizen to distinguish one type of authority from another. The lecturer did explain, at this point, that there was no tax at all if the business sustained a loss, and that this loss was taken into consideration for the next seven years.

The women present were overwhelmed by all these details, their ambitions being far more limited. But Grigory, who had been in Israel for two years, complained that the lectures were all too slow. He could be learning more, he said, if he was already working. As far as risks were concerned, he said, they were much greater in Russia today.

'Salesmanship', something totally new to the Russians, came next, imparted by a Mr Dotan, a young man with a carefully clipped moustache, a well-cut grey suit and a James Bond brief-case who appeared on the scene after several weeks of the course. He was an expert on marketing and the first lecturer on the course to address himself immediately to the Russians.

The customer, in the Soviet Union, had no choice, he told them, and was not a 'player' in the business game. Now they were thinking of opening businesses, they had to learn not only how to set up a business but how to sell whatever it was they were producing. They had to work out for themselves reasons which would justify a customer spending his or her money on what they were selling, and first of all, the suitability of their product for the market. Does an Eskimo need a fridge? he asked. Alternatively: how did you sell shoes to the barefoot – on the face of it an easy task. He personally knew an Israeli firm which had sold shoes in Africa, or rather, sandals. 'You think that's easy?' he asked them. Not at all. The Africans in the tribes they were 'targeting' believed that the shoe salesmen had stolen their feet, because they could no longer see them. Answer? Transparent plastic sandals which enabled the tribesmen both to protect their feet from thorns and sharp objects and to see that their feet were still there. The firm had made a fortune.

'Difference between a *client* and a *consumer*: consumers have to be wooed.' Marketing skills came high up on the list of necessary qualifications in capitalist firms. There was no captive, passive consumer as in the Soviet Union. There was competition. There was invention, the need for new ideas. There was money to be spent.

What you had to sell were either services or products. Both needed marketing. What were services? He'd explain things simply. Supposing that you had a couple in which the husband was studying and the wife working. She was selling him her services in exchange for the higher social status she would achieve as his wife, later on. The Russian women looked surprised, but did not react. An American woman student asked, not very aggressively, whether marriage, in this sense, was a 'service'? Oh yes, said Dotan, shamelessly; take a rabbinical student who studied in order to be a great rabbi, and his wife who worked. There was an exchange here all right, of labour for status. Marriage brokers knew this and 'sold' the husband to the wife's family. The Russian women shook their heads, but as usual, asked no questions.

The lecturer went on to explain the 'selling of the president'. 'Image' was all important. Shimon Peres, for instance, was not Prime Minister of Israel because on TV interviews he was unable, because of a rare condition, to blink. His unwavering stare, said Dotan, gave him a shifty look, as the upper and lower parts of his face were out of synch, the lower part moving while the upper part remained static. This lost him credibility with the voters. These things were important.

The Russians were puzzled by this. They could not remember whether Brezhnev, Andropov, Chernenko, or even Gorbachev blinked or didn't blink. It seemed to them that what they did, or said, was more important. They had been shunted into power, one by one, that was all. Yeltsin had a flat-footed walk. Did that count with the Russian voter today? They doubted it.

The essential thing, the immigrants were told, was to try to identify with the Israeli customer. Price was important. The market changed all the time. Dotan asked for a definition of marketing, but of course no Russian could answer. An American came up with the correct answer: the marketing process is one whose object is to bring two or more sides into an exchange carried out of their own free will.

Dotan was delighted, but the Russians still looked puzzled. All right, said Dotan: a man with a cup of water met another who was dying of thirst, and asked one million dollars for the water. The man of course paid up. That was the exchange. No one, rather surprisingly, questioned whether the thirsty man had really exchanged his money for the water of his free will. At this stage, the Russians had given up taking notes.

'I'm scared,' Dotan said afterwards, 'for the immigrants from Eastern Europe. People can sell them anything. They don't know their way around.'

From the Jewish Agency pamphlet on Finance for Immigrants (in Russian only):

> The bank wants to be sure when loan is given that it is repaid in time. Therefore he who gets loans must give security.
>
> Guarantors may promise collateral for loans.
>
> Defaulting on payment can increase the cost of credit. If a person can't pay in time, it may be necessary for an additional loan or to try to solve the problem with the bank. Or to return the money over a longer period of time.

[Under the Soviet system, individuals could not get loans, which were reserved for state industries. Only among criminals was there a money-lending system. Loans with interest were criminal offences. In a big plant, workers might buy a television or car by taking loans from the government firm. Sometimes groups of workers had savings schemes. Glasnost revealed widespread debts.]

> Economists say money must work for you. Stagnant, it loses its value. Two reasons: one is inflation; two: you lose interest if it is left in the current account.
>
> If you have money you don't need to spend, try to invest it in a programe with good interest. Banks help you to save and maintain its value and gain interest. The State helps new immigrant with privileges and subsidies and good credit facilities and grants. Loans should be used.
>
> Don't fear getting into debt! Research shows us that after four to five years in Israel, the income of an average family from the USSR reaches a level eleven per cent higher than that of the average Israeli. That means that returning the loan you got via absorption is not a heavy burden on your budget. On the other hand, it is important to calculate how much you spend not only during your first months in the country but during your first three years. If you can, postpone non essential goods, or until the income of the family is stable. Goods are temptations for you on the Israeli market.

★ ★ ★

'How much simpler things were in Russia,' said one of the would-be capitalists. 'You queued – you bought whatever was on sale. As for marketing, in Russia, we could sell anything but buy nothing. In Israel, the situation is exactly the reverse.'

CHAPTER SIX

Resurrection

'At Passover 1987, the Lubavitcher Rebbe prophesied the mass wave of emigration from Russia which began two years later. God told him of it, and it was accomplished.'

The Lubavitcher Rebbe (rabbi in Yiddish) is the spiritual head of one of the most important sects in pietist Jewry – the Habad Hasidim. Lubavich was a small town in the Smolensk region of Byloerussia, an important centre of religious Jewry until the late nineteenth century, when many Hasidim emigrated to America and set up, among other communities, an imposing centre at Brooklyn Heights in New York. In 1941, most of the thousand Habad Jews who had remained in Smolensk after the mass exodus were shot by the Nazis.

The Habad Hasidim are not only learned Jews and, in the eyes of many secular Israelis, amiable or detestable eccentrics; in Russia, throughout the Communist era, they put up a determined resistance to the official campaign to wipe out the Jewish religion, going underground to do so. Those who escaped Nazism continued to observe their religion secretly during the remaining years of Communist rule.

How they did so is explained partly by the life story of Bezalel Schiff, an Israeli Hasid who described the Lubavicher's 'prophecy', and also provided a comprehensive picture of how effective was the Habad network in Soviet Russia, a network of information which extended far beyond the Iron Curtain because of the international character of the Habad institutions. Historians of the Holocaust have noted that very often it was Hasidic rabbis who alerted Jews outside Russia to the extermination of the Jews. Far less is known of their continued resistance to Communism, and the double life they led in order to preserve their faith – a life which often involved them deeply in the Communist regime. The Lubavitcher 'prophecy' was probably based on excellent sources of information within the Soviet Union.

The Habad have a large following in both the United States and in Israel, with their own communities, educational and welfare services. Not only is the Lubavitcher Rebbe, an ancient sage in failing health who appears to be continually, and miraculously, revived, a prophet; he is also, according to his followers, the Messiah in person. The elderly gentleman who bears such a heavy historical and theological burden was expected almost daily in Israel during 1992, when huge billboards beside the main eight-lane highway into Tel Aviv bore the news of the Messiah's imminent Coming. For years thousands of cars owned by Hasidim and their born-again disciples have carried stickers saying 'We want the Messiah now.'

Bezalel Schiff, a lawyer, is one of the heads of *Shamir*, an organisation set up to help observant Russian immigrant scientists find employment at SATEC, a 'science park' to the north of Jerusalem.

Schiff's father had studied in Rostov and at a *yeshiva*, or religious seminary, in Kharkov. He was both a high Communist official and, in secret, a Hasidic Jew. In 1940 all the seminaries were closed down by the Stalinist regime, but the Hasidim continued to keep the Sabbath at home, and remember the festivals even if they could not celebrate with ritual objects and public festivities.

Schiff senior had occupied many posts under the Communist regime, from railway ticket collector to owner of a restaurant in a circus and manager of a factory. During the Stalinist period, when merely to be a Jew was to be suspect of 'bourgeois nationalist' tendencies, he was arrested and imprisoned for seven years. During the war, he was drafted into the Red Army, while his wife took the children to Uzbekhistan, an 'evacuation' like that of so many Ukrainian Jews. Incidentally, though so many older immigrants speak of 'evacuation', this was not organised by any Soviet authority, but initiated by the Jews themselves. In Uzbekhistan, as in the other Muslim republics, the situation was easier for Jews than in Western Russia, and they were even able to perform circumcisions on their sons.

Schiff senior returned from the war in 1943 without a right hand, but with many medals on his chest. He became second secretary of the Communist Party in Tashkent. 'He couldn't refuse the offer,' said Schiff, half apologetically. At the same time, he remained a religious Jew at home, where the dietary laws were observed; prayed regularly with other trusted Hasidim, and taught his sons all the observances, including wearing a prayer shawl under his shirt and putting on phylacteries (the tapes binding small boxes with scriptural excerpts to forehead and arm) each morning as a part of the prayer ritual.

Bezalel Schiff studied law at the University of Tashkent, which also meant studying Latin. As the Latin lectures were held on Friday, the Sabbath eve, Schiff did not attend and thus was not able to complete this part of his legal studies. But his father, meanwhile, had become secretary of the Communist Party in Tashkent, a position of great authority and power, and the young Schiff managed to complete his course. He found work with the local police force because, he said, his father had issued a state pardon for the delinquent son of the head of police.

Schiff maintains now that he himself was never a Communist party member. He wore his prayer shawl at all times, which might have got him into trouble when, for instance, he went to the health centre for inoculations and had to undress. Fortunately, he said, the nurse giving injections was also Jewish. On another occasion, however, he was caught with the phylacteries around his arm at work; his colleagues suspected that they were some kind of electronic recording device. But his father's high ranking position, which meant that the Schiffs were wealthy as well as influential, kept him out of trouble – something particularly easy in Tashkent, where the local authorities were far less fanatical than in Western Russia.

The Habad Hasidim managed to keep up their links with the West through the occasional foreign visitors, communicating information via Habad escapees. One particularly wily survivor was a Habadnik called Rozenstein, who Schiff claimed went in and out of the KGB offices unscathed. From 1945 until 1971, he said, the Habad network in Russia was particularly active, unlike the earlier period when Stalin tracked down and punished the Hasidim mercilessly. In 1927, a death sentence had been pronounced against the Habad leader in Russia, who mysteriously was allowed to leave the Soviet Union alone.

Schiff said that between 1944 and 1948, several thousand Hasidic families, using forged Polish passports, managed to get into the United States and join the Brooklyn Heights community. In Tashkent, where he grew up, the synagogues remained open, and Hasidim in the congregation communicated with one another by singing liturgical melodies which only they knew, conveying by hints, news within the community. While officially no Jews were allowed out of the country, Habad Hasidim went in and out of Russia carrying Yiddish tracts, prayer books and even ritual objects like the *etroq*, the rare citrus fruit held during prayers at Tabernacles. During Schiff's time as a student, one of these fruits was passed to him in the university lavatory; he carried it out in his trouser pocket.

The numbers of observant Jews in the Soviet Union dwindled steadily, until only the communities in the Asiatic republics retained some notion of their traditions and culture. But with the immigration to Israel during perestroika, many immigrants from Russia have become converts to the Habad sect in Israel who, like some of the Christian communities in the country, are energetic missionaries for their faith.

Mark and Sonya Lotkin, two musicians from Kharkov, arrived in Israel recently and – unfamiliar with the educational system of Israel, which includes both state secular and state religious schools and the private institutions run by religious groups like the Habad – they sent their only son, Yigal, to the nearby Habad school where, they had heard, the mathematics teaching was excellent. There, Yigal acquired far more than good marks in mathematics.

Yigal is ten years old. He wears a skullcap secured with something that looks like a large paper clip, the system used by observant Jews in Israel to keep their heads reverentially covered. In Israel the degree and kind of religious orthodoxy is noted by dress. Ordinary observant Jews, those who keep the Sabbath, festivals, and dietary laws, will simply wear the (usually knitted) skullcap. The extreme orthodox, who are far more rigorous and spend the larger part of their lives in study, let their earlocks grow and their beards, and wear fur-brimmed hats (the *streimel*) and Edwardian frock coats, under which they wear a shirt but usually no tie; peeping over their trousers is a fringe which demonstrates the presence of a *tallit* or prayer shawl worn at all times.

Yigal does not have sidelocks – something which indicates that he was not born into a religious community. But he wears his *tallit*, and plays constantly with the fringes which are visible under his sweater, as well as with an additional talisman, a doorkey on a chain. His nervous, slender fingers are busy all the time. Two or three times the key breaks loose from the chain and is reattached by his worried, slightly irritated father. Yigal eats in my home without enquiring about the ingredients of his food, whereas an orthodox Jew like those with whom he now studies would not even drink a glass of water there.

The absence of sidelocks yet the presence of the fringes, the lack of interest in dietary laws and the willingness to converse with a woman, all indicate that Yigal, though a born-again Jew and a boy who attends a single sex, extreme orthodox school, does not come from an orthodox or even an observant home, and began life as Yega, who until two years ago was a miserable small boy tormented by his Russian fellow pupils at school for his very Jewish, nervous and frail appearance. Yigal, in appearance, is the epitome of the over-bright, over-zealous, ultra-religious Jewish male child, the product of hundreds of years of Jewish scholarship in the ghetto. Three generations separate Yigal from the last Jews in his family who knew anything of Jewish history and Talmudic study (his grandparents spoke Yiddish but the Soviet Jewish Yiddish schools of the early Communist era were secular institutions). In Israel, in an extreme orthodox school, his religious antecedents have reasserted themselves with a vengeance.

His parents are not particularly Jewish either in appearance or in manner, though his father has a long arched nose. His mother looks like any Ukrainian woman, blunt featured and fair skinned. Yigal is emphatically Ashkenazi Jewish: dark haired, pale skinned, dark eyed, full lipped, with a curved semitic nose. But more strikingly Jewish are the nervous gestures, the speech which is so rapid that it frequently becomes a babble, the rushing, searching mind tugging at the reins of orthodoxy, the constantly roving, curious eyes. As soon as he entered my living room he made a beeline for the bookcase and pulled out three or four volumes of the Hebrew Encyclopaedia, under whose weight he staggered slightly.

His parents are out of their depth in handling him; they barely speak Hebrew (as usual, the woman is better at languages, but then she also teaches) and when Mark Lotkin converses with me in Hebrew, he continually has to ask his ten-year-old son for words.

When I said I was a historian, Yigal was immediately interested: what books had I written, on what subjects? He told me that Jewish history was central to world history, and that Jewish history could not be separated from the history of the Jewish religion, that they were one and the same, and that the Jewish religion, and Hasidism in particular, had an answer to all the problems of history. We talked about Zionism, but he resisted the suggestion that it was both the outcome of secular historical forces (nineteenth-century nationalism, the persecution of the Jews in Europe) and of an ancient tradition which had its roots in religion. He immediately insisted that the secular forces, while they had certainly had an impact on the return to Zion, were in the service, however unwittingly, of religious forces.

One of the most striking things about Yigal was that his manner, his way of talking, and his constant reference to Hasidic lore, a quote a minute, might have been a brilliant take-off of his elders, almost a parody. But he is perfectly serious, and beneath it all, somewhat frightened and superstitious. He told me that it had been a 'sign' that the day before the family left Russia, his father had bought a Jewish book on Hasidic mysticism. 'It was accidental,' his father protested. 'No,' said Yigal, 'not an accident at all.' Another indication of Yigal's transformation from terrified little Russian Jew to defiant religious Jew in a secular environment was his social behaviour – so unlike the careful, almost old-worldly politeness of most immigrants. He slurped tea from his cup bent almost double and gobbled bananas (rarely seen in Russia). Above all, there was his posture – the hurried, twitching, boneless movements of an embryonic Hasid with his contempt for physical grace.

108

All this made his parents redden: 'Yigal, your behaviour is not cultured,' his parents frequently remonstrated. To no avail. He was influenced by the school to which they had sent him, they said, clearly deploring every moment of it.

The Lotkins were a gentle, cultivated couple, proud of their Jewishness while knowing nothing of Jewish learning or tradition, who had come to Israel solely for their son's benefit, afraid of his inability to defend himself at school. But Yigal may well become an extreme orthodox Jew who will ultimately turn against them and demand their conformity to every Jewish law. Otherwise, in the end, he will not be able to live in their house, eat their food, or allow them contact with his children. At the moment, at ten years old, he is still under their tutelage, lives under their roof. When I asked him where he wanted to study at secondary school, he immediately said in a *yeshiva* (rabbinical seminary). Here his parents intervened: 'We want him to know other things apart from Jewish learning; we want him to go to secondary school' (there are orthodox secondary schools in which Jewish learning is taught more intensively). But Yigal's choice will cut him off from the mass of Israeli Jews: he will be exempted from army service, and unless he resists the proselytising Hasidim, he will be one of a marginal sect on the fringes of Israeli society, locked into a sanctuary away from modern life, learning and culture.

The Lotkins' life in Kharkov was a good one; they had a three-room apartment, permanent jobs in the theatre orchestra, which performed a different work every night for thirty days (opera and ballet), eight months of the year.

After a struggle of nearly two years, Mark Lotkin now has a job as viola player in Tel Aviv chamber orchestra, and Sonya, a violinist, teaches music in four Jerusalem schools and also gives private lessons at home. The Lotkins are doing well by Russian immigrant standards; they both work in their own professions, and may in fact soon form part of a string quartet. But they had also brought with them from the Soviet Union, together with crates of books and their musical instruments, a political culture acquired in the Soviet Union. They could not understand how Israel could make concessions to the Palestinians or return any of the territory conquered in 1967. Mark Lotkin, and Yigal, both thought that Israel would show weakness if it gave an inch. Sonya said that the answer to the Palestinian problem was 'transfer' – deporting all the Palestinians to Arab countries. Yigal suggested that there might be a repeat of 1948 and '67 when they did leave 'on their own initiative'. There were bad Arabs who made trouble, and Arabs who were passive. The first should be expelled. The older Lotkins agreed that Israel depended on aid from abroad, and that the Americans might not countenance such a policy, and the nonplussed Yigal found himself outvoted.

But his father had a better suggestion. Israel, he said, should show more 'Jewish intelligence'. No Arab from the territories should be permitted to enter Israel, they should not be given work; once they were unable to feed their families, they would understand that they had to leave. 'We were "transferred" from Russia to here, why shouldn't they be too?' In his view, each time a Jew was stabbed or shot, Israel should take an Arab *prisoner* out of jail (since Arabs in jail were, *ipso facto*, criminals) and shoot him.

Dina Brodsky, a political scientist working at the Hebrew University and herself a Russian immigrant who arrived in 1976, commented: 'Even if Jews in Russia were hostile to the regime, they were formed by it. In Russia they may have struggled for Jewish rights, but they can't admit that there are other groups here in Israel who are not equal: Israeli Arabs, Sefardi Jews, for instance. Certainly the Russians who come now do not see the Palestinian lack of rights as something wrong. They believe some people's rights have to be sacrificed to the interests of the state; a sign that deep down, they identified with the authoritarian regime.'

We came across Yefim Svirsky, an engineer, in the caravan town of Nahal Beka, on the outskirts of Beersheba. Both his reasons for coming to Israel, and his present accommodation with rabbinical Judaism, are closely linked with his experiences, and disappointments, in post-perestroika Russia.

Svirsky was not a Zionist, nor had he been particularly interested in Jewish tradition before arriving in Israel. In Israel he had become very interested in Judaism, and particularly (like many of the immigrants) in Kabbala.

Svirsky also comes from Kharkov, one of the larger towns in

the Ukraine, and was largely ignorant of Jewish tradition until the Hasidim in Israel began seeking recruits among the immigrants. This is a curious twist of history; modern Hasidism originated in the mid eighteenth century in the Ukraine, bringing rabbinical Judaism and the mystic tradition, in particular, during a period of great persecution, to the largely uneducated Jews of this area. Its message is apparently equally attractive to those with a Soviet education.

Svirsky's caravan consisted of two rooms (the family allocation). He shares it with his wife and their fifteen-year-old daughter, who attends a religious secondary school. In Kharkov, he admitted, he had not followed Jewish tradition, but had always believed in God. He knew Yiddish, having studied in one of the Communist Yiddish-language schools. A man of about fifty-five, strongly built, he looked, like so many other Russian Jews, exactly like a non-Jewish Ukrainian; fair skinned, blue eyed, with blunt features and a straight short nose. His early biography was that of the luckier Russian Jews of his age: a small boy when the Nazis entered the Ukraine, who with his family fled to Samarkand in Uzbekhistan. But this meant that when, after the war, they returned to Kharkov, they felt like outsiders, as they had not shared the experience of their fellow Ukrainians. From the third grade, he said, he had sensed their hostility.

After attending vocational secondary school, Svirsky became a skilled mechanic. His wife was a nurse. Both were now having problems with work, as they did not want to work in menial jobs, but their Hebrew was not good enough for them to work in their professions. Svirsky had been a teacher in a vocational high school for twenty-five years in Kharkov.

Svirsky was a candidate for membership of the Kharkov regional soviet (Council) in 1988–89. His rival was a man called a 'simple worker', a member of the Communist party who had a fourteen-hour working day. However, the 'simple worker' was elected by a big majority. Svirsky had not identified himself as a Jew during the elections, he said, but his second name 'gave him away'. He had enjoyed a comfortable life in Kharkov, but the 'angry faces' in the street during his election campaign had alarmed him and he attributed his defeat to anti-semitism; he decided to emigrate.

111

Svirsky told me that they had known there were difficulties in Israel, that the economy would make it hard for them to find work, but he said he and his wife had not been interested in that, or influenced by letters from dissatisfied immigrants. They had suffered so much from anti-semitism in the Ukraine that they sought and found a new homeland in Israel.

His conversion to orthodoxy was more complex. Like all Jews, he said, in Russia he had grown up under the totalitarian system, but he personally had not forgotten that he was a Jew. The synagogues of the Ukraine were closed in Kharkov under Communism, but reopened under perestroika. He was, he said, 'the first' to re-enter the synagogue. After perestroika, more young people took an interest, but many were still afraid to enter the synagogue. He himself began to wear a skullcap in synagogue. He said that his wife now keeps a kosher kitchen, and they follow the various observances re-taught them by their daughter, such as switching off lights as the Sabbath appears. They did not buy meat from Arabs in the Beersheba market, only fruit. His daughter attended Bnei Akiva, the religious youth movement.

Svirsky's 'return' to Judaism had begun when he saw an advertisement on the notice board in the caravan centre, in Russian, for a course open to all. It cost £2.50 for the whole family, half that for single persons. Most new immigrants did not regard such lectures as useful, especially if they had to pay, he said caustically. About a hundred immigrants in all had attended the lecture, including many old women. There was free food for new immigrants, and those who showed an interest were offered accommodation for the duration of the course.

What had impressed Svirsky about the Hasidic lectures was that he thought they offered a 'scientific' vindication of the existence of God. The Hasidim, for him, had 'proved' that the Torah could only have been written by God. There was a 'code', he said, like a genetic code, in fifty letters. The Hasidic *gematria*, or hermeneutic correlation of letters with numbers, was used most frequently by the rabbis to provide various interpretations of scriptural texts. Now, he said, it was being used to indicate that human hands could not possibly have written the sacred texts. God dictated the letters which appeared on a rock in the desert, he said, and Moses copied them without understanding their significance.

Evolution according to Darwin is anathema to the religious and is not taught in Israeli religious secondary schools. Svirsky, graduate of the Soviet system and with a scientific education, insisted that Darwin, at the end of his life, had disowned his own theory. Whereas the bible provides continuity, he said, there were 'missing links' in Darwin's theories.

Svirsky repeated the Hasidic view that the Torah is only understood literally by little children, and needed symbolic interpretation. He did not feel that this contradicted his earlier statements about 'authentication'. Secular cosmology could be scientifically confirmed by religious dogma. How, for instance, could there have been primeval 'darkness' on the face of the earth if the notion of darkness and light were not known? The Hasidic answer was that we still did not understand the 'code', the 'real' meaning of Genesis. Philosophers were correct in saying that there is no proof that God does not exist. The primal explosion which cosmologists say produced the planet earth also produced light. Yefim Svirsky from Kharkov, ex-engineer, penitent believer, in his caravan outside Beersheba, has a new ideology.

Boris and Tatiana are Jews from Moscow who have become Christians. Tatiana was involved in the conversion process in Russia, possibly because she was suffering, and still is, from cancer, and needed a faith stronger than dialectical materialism. Boris, who in Russia did not hear the call, was recruited by the International Christian Embassy, which supports the return of the Jews to Zion as a prelude to the coming of the Messiah – a rather different Messiah to that of Bezalel Schiff and Yefim Svirsky – and holds a big conference in the Israeli capital every autumn.

Boris was a drummer in a Moscow band. A large colour photograph of him at his drums is on one wall. His wife played the piano. At present he is employed as a cleaner, pausing occasionally to read from the bible which accompanies him everywhere. In Russia, he said, he was Jewish by nationality, but not religious. In Israel, he was baptised in Tiberias, at the Church of the Loaves and the Fishes. He belongs to a forty-strong congregation in Jerusalem, and the bible has become his handbook in which he seeks for and finds, inevitably, an answer to every problem in his life. During the conversation he opens the bible a score of times, finding the passages he wants easily; the whole book is scored with marker pencil, entire verses blocked out on each page.

Boris is a large, childlike man with protuberant large brown eyes and a receding hairline. He has a bad stutter but this does not prevent him from talking volubly about his new faith, in a wondering, dreamy way. The usual immigrant troubles – his future, how to make a living, what will happen when the immigrant grant runs out, his wife's illness – do not crop up once during the conversation, or rather Boris's monologue, as he scarcely listens to questions. God will provide. Most of his answers are quotations from the bible – rather like Yigal's quotations from the rabbinical commentaries. When I asked him how he would manage if he did not find work, he said 'Ask and ye will receive.'

'I never saw a bible before in my life. You could buy them in churches, but I wasn't interested. I wasn't looking for God, or a religion, but now I think it is natural. "My thoughts are not your thoughts, or my ways, your ways."'

The fact that he, of all people, became a convert, says Boris, showed that anything is possible. Like Yigal and Svirsky, he saw divine guidance in the events that had brought him to religious belief. His wife had read in a newspaper advertisement that anyone wanting a copy of the bible could call a number. She said that she wanted a bible in Russian. After a few days, not only the bible arrived, but representatives of the Christian Embassy, Baptists. Boris offered them vodka, which they declined, saying all they wanted was to speak to him. (He drank and smoked, he added parenthetically in his pre-Baptist days. Now he had given up both.) His old life had died; he was reborn, like Christ in the Resurrection. Converting was a sign he was different. If he had not believed in it, it would not have worked: 'But I say unto you that every idle word that men shall speak, they shall give account thereof in the day of judgment.'

'God loved the world so much that he gave them his Son, so all who have faith never die, but live eternally,' he had told Tatiana. Having begun with these words of comfort for his wife, together they went back to the Creation and the concept of original sin, the crime of knowledge and the appearance of death.

Boris was astonished to hear that the Jews had made the serious mistake of failing to recognise that Jesus was the Messiah, despite Isaiah's prophecies. All this was completely new to him: like most of those who had been born and grown up under Communism, he had never read a bible, either the Old or New Testaments, and was startled to discover that Isaiah had apparently, seven hundred years earlier, predicted the coming of Christ. He was equally struck by the fact that God had foretold the Jews would regather in Zion.

Did he then connect Zionism with prophecy, and if so, was that why he felt he had come to Israel? Boris shook his great head. He had left Russia because he was 'disgusted with the system' (this meant perestroika, not Communism). Yet he saw a connection between his own return and a predestined fate for the Jews.

All his family had gone to America, but God, and the Chosen People, had led him to Israel. He felt proud at having rejoined his own people. But as a Christian, he said that God had told us that all men were God's creatures, and would become citizens of heaven.

The Baptists told him he was free to visit them or not to do so. But within a week, he was drawn back to them. They had meetings in Hebrew translated into Russian, and also some with other Russians. At first Boris had thought the Baptists merely exotic, but after three or four meetings he was expectant, and looked forward to his conversion. He began learning about Christianity and saw videos of masses. At the next Pentecost, he began praying, though at first he did not know how.

Unlike Yefim, he was not looking for scientific explanations of miracles, but for miracles which might have scientific results. Boris suffers from psoriasis, visible on one of his hands, and had been for some weeks in hospital. While he was there, he tried to explain his faith to the Jews in his ward. And what did he think of other religious Jews, orthodox Jews? 'I feel sorry for them, as God tells us "Love ye your enemies, and do good, and lend." '

In hospital, the other patients had asked what was the book he was reading so assiduously all day, all the time. He told them it was the bible. 'Then why aren't you wearing a skullcap?' they asked, taking him for an orthodox Jew, since only they read the bible demonstratively in public. He had his answer ready: 'Tell

115

me where it is written in the bible that you have to cover your head to read the Holy Book.' When they were nonplussed, he pressed his advantage home. 'Tell me, what is more important, a man or a skullcap?' The patients, embarrassed, said 'the skullcap.'

There was however an observant Jew in the ward, who alarmed Boris at first though he did his best to pass on the Word. He couldn't tell, he said, whether or not the other patients were interested. He got hold of a Hebrew Russian bible to try to make his points more accurately. Tatiana had brought him sweets and chocolates, and he handed them round. The observant man asked whether the chocolates were milk or not, a question Boris did not understand, as he knew nothing of the Jewish dietary laws. It was explained to him that milk and meat could not be eaten together, and that the patient would have to wait several hours after a dinner containing meat before he could eat the milk chocolate, which he took away.

Boris found an appropriate comment in Mark: 'Do ye not perceive, that whatsoever thing from without entereth into the man, it cannot defile him? because it entereth not into his heart, but into the belly . . . that which cometh out of the man, that defileth the man.'

On a more prosaic level, Boris, no fool, had not changed the 'nationality' clause in his documents from Jewish to Christian. He knew perfectly well that he would not be automatically accepted as a citizen of the state, if he were to tell the authorities that he was a Christian. 'All men are brothers', after all. It distressed him, he said, that Israel was seeking to deport some of those Christians who had settled in Israel.

Boris certainly would not want to return to Russia. He had encountered 'vulgar anti-semitism' at school, and in the army. When he had played in a band in a restaurant, Jewish songs were prohibited. When he played the Israeli tune *Hava Nagila* he was thrown out of his job. When I asked him how he expected to continue in Israel, he shrugged his shoulders. God would provide. 'Spiritual food is more important than physical,' he said. Meanwhile, he had contacts in a nearby town, where he hoped to find work as a music teacher.

Russian immigrants don't like to work as building labourers, and it is rare to see one willingly scrambling about on the scaffolding with the Arabs from the territories. It is still rarer to find one who actually says that he was proud to find his first job in Israel swabbing the floors in the local supermarket. But this is the claim of Alexander Belousov, who arrived in Israel two years ago and ever since has lived in Maalei Adumim, the satellite town in the desert overlooking the Judean desert, to the east of Jerusalem. Belousov is everything an Israeli official could desire in an immigrant from Russia; he began life here by accepting any work available; he has found his niche in the new country; he speaks fluent Hebrew and is happily settled in permanent lodgings; and he is a fervent Zionist and Israeli patriot.

Alexander Belousov is not Jewish.

A bearded man with a bold, impressive face reminiscent of the old photographs of the early Russian populists and revolutionaries in the history books, Belousov was born in Samara (formerly Kuibyshev, in the Volga basin) in 1948 – 'ten days after the declaration of the State of Israel', he emphasises. Another prophetic coincidence.

Nothing distinguished the schoolboy Belousov from millions of other budding Soviet citizens until, at the age of fifteen, an incident with his teacher at school changed his life. Belousov, like all his schoolfriends, had grown up as an atheist, ready to declaim the Marxist line on religion as the opium of the people. But the teacher, a woman who discerned an unusual intellect in the making in the boy, and whose professional conscience prevailed over her Communist training, (perhaps because, coincidentally, the era of Stalinism had recently ended) told him that if he wanted to condemn the bible, he should study it carefully first.

This was not easy. The bible was proscribed reading, but Belousov not only decided to find a copy, but to seek out the heirs to the people who had written it: the Jews. He set out to find the local synagogue – as it happened, the only synagogue in the entire region which had escaped destruction during the Second World War and where old Jews still worshipped.

The Kuibyshev community was not a very old one. The region was well outside the Pale of Settlement, and only from 1872 had a handful of Jews been allowed to settle there, in recognition of their contribution to the construction of the Czarist railways. The synagogue dated from 1908, and the little Jewish community only stabilised there from the time of the revolution. After the Second World War, however, refugees from further west (the Nazi invasion had stopped just short of Samara) had swelled the community to 20,000 people.

Boldly, the young Belousov walked into the synagogue one Saturday and asked to talk to the rabbi; he told him that he wanted to learn Hebrew and study the bible. The congregation was scandalised. But, as Belousov remembers: 'The rabbi said: "Jews, *sha*! [silence]; if the young *goy* wants to study Torah, perhaps God has sent him to us."' The rabbi introduced him to an old, learned survivor, a locksmith named David Isakovich, whose family welcomed Belousov and taught him not only Hebrew, but every aspect of Jewish education they remembered. He picked up Yiddish, which was spoken in the house, 'as easily as breathing'. It was easier for him to speak Yiddish on a daily basis than Hebrew, as Yiddish was a permitted Soviet 'ethnic' language, whereas Hebrew, because of the association with religion and Zionism, was forbidden. The Jews made no effort to convert him, and Belousov, no longer an atheist, remained a Christian.

It was probably inevitable that Belousov, increasingly involved with Jews and their culture, should at the age of eighteen have met and married a young Jewess. He met his wife, daughter of a fervently Communist Jewish family, in the Pedagogic Institute where they both studied Russian language and literature. She was a member of the Communist youth movement, the Komsomol. What was ironic was that it was he who introduced her to Jewish culture. They met when he was giving lectures on Yiddish writers to the youth groups.

Belousov became a fine linguist, mastering, among other languages, English, German, Polish, old Slavic, and even Anglo-Saxon and Middle English.

In Soviet Russia he worked as a technical translator in the local radio station, translating from English and German and specialising in mobile radio communications. He also taught at the Pedagogic Institute where he had studied, teaching Russian and literature. In his spare time, he wrote poetry both in Russian and in Yiddish – in which he had become equally fluent. At the same time, Belousov wrote articles for local literary papers, studied more languages, and collected rare books, some of which he discovered in the synagogue – among them an Amsterdam Haggadah (Passover book) dating back to 1672. During the Brezhnev regime, it was easier to get hold of Yiddish books – at least those which had escaped destruction in the war and the ravages of the Soviet censors. When he arrived in Israel in 1990, Belousov brought with him 300 crates of books.

Until the era of glasnost, it had never occurred to Belousov or his wife that they might come to Israel. In 1975, he travelled to Minsk to meet a Zionist group headed by two Jewish colonels in the Red Army, distinguished veterans of the Second World War: Lev Ovsischer and Yefim Davidovich, who had been inspired after the Six Days War to seek visas to Israel. As a result, Ovsischer had been demoted and both veterans threatened with trial; only the intervention of American politicians saved them. Davidovich died the year after meeting Belousov, and was buried by his family – allowed to leave Russia after his death – in Jerusalem.

Belousov's encounter with the disgraced officers impressed him deeply. It also involved him in a clash with the Soviet authorities. Returning from Minsk with 'forbidden books' in his possession, he and his wife were detained and interrogated by the KGB, who tried to intimidate them from seeking further contact with Zionists. His wife was obliged to leave her work, and at one stage, the KGB suggested that the Belousovs leave the country within twenty-four hours. Unlike the Zionist refuseniks, however, they refused to go. Belousov still saw his task as promoting Jewish consciousness within the Soviet Union.

With the advent of glasnost, this became a legitimate activity. From 1985 onwards, he taught Hebrew, using the traditional *cheder*, or Jewish primary school, methods by which he himself had been taught. He gave lessons to hundreds of Jews leaving the Soviet Union for Israel, abandoning his work as a radio translator to work twelve hours a day as a Hebrew teacher. From 1988, he helped a Russian Jew, Ilya Liebenstern, to found a Jewish organisation called Tarbut LeAm (culture for the people), and gave lectures on the Talmud and Hebrew tradition. At the same time, Belousov still considered himself a faithful Christian. The metropolitan Archbishop of Samara blessed him as a Hebrew teacher and for his work in preserving Jewish culture. When he finally left Russia, there were three Russian bishops at his farewell party.

'In Russia I lived all my life in one place, in Samara. I never wanted to go anywhere else. Now, in Israel, I want to stay here in Ma'alei Adumim. I don't like moving around. I'm a settled character.'

From the start, Belousov said, he had felt at home in Israel; knowing fluent Hebrew obviously helped, but so had his desire to work in building, however simple the work. He wanted, he said, to imitate the Zionist pioneers, and today the main task was to build houses. After a first period as a building worker, then one in a local branch of an American steel company, he now works in Tel Aviv in the Labour backed Russian paper *Nasha Strana*. In Russia he had written in Yiddish; here, he works in Russian, writing mainly about Yiddish culture, and on the problems in Israel between the religious and secular populations.

The dichotomy between traditional, religious Jewish culture and modern nationalist Zionism, unknown in the Diaspora, disturbs him deeply. 'I know all about Judaism, and about Christianity, but that doesn't mean I have to convert.' He describes himself as a Zionist nationalist. 'Anyone who knows Jewish history has to be a Zionist.' This had not meant that he became a refusenik. Perhaps the anomalies of his situation had prevented this, but it seems more likely, though he was reluctant to speak of this, that, like many Russian Jews, he felt that perestroika threatened the Jews with the renewal of anti-semitism endemic in the Russian Orthodox Church.

In many ways his attitude to Yiddish culture was similar to that of Sandler. He felt that the Zionist revolutionaries, like Ben Gurion, had tried to destroy the rich past of Eastern European Jewry. Many great writers had been forgotten because they belonged to the Jewish Diaspora – especially those who had written in Yiddish, though 'the Russian variant of Yiddish culture had not had time to develop'. He himself had lived in two cultures, honoured both. He could not understand why Israel should reject the culture of the Diaspora. And Israeli hostility to religious Jews, he thought, was 'almost anti-semitic'.

But he reserved his real enmity for those Russian Jews in Israel who did not want to assimilate into Israeli culture and wanted to remain 'Russian'. People like that, he said, glaring, were 'traitors' and he refused to read their work.

CHAPTER SEVEN

A Month in the Country

When Mikhael and Raissa Gorbachev visited Israel in 1991, the secretariat of the kibbutz at Eyn Gedi, an oasis overlooking the Dead Sea, invited him to inspect the premises. Raissa tiptoed among the palm trees with a pink and yellow striped parasol held elegantly over her head and informed the then leader of the new Russia that this was an Israeli *kolkhoz*; Gorbachev told the new immigrants who came out to wave flags that it was he who had brought them there; and a kibbutz member retorted: 'If you're ever out of a job, we can offer you one here.'

Eyn Gedi is the perfect site for so surrealist a scenario. It nestles beneath the sand-coloured crags of the Judaean desert, chiselled vertically as if by some giant hatchet; the Dead Sea, so rich in salts that it is impossible to swim in, shimmers beneath, and the mountains of Moab, in Jordan, are just across the water. Eyn Gedi, an hour's drive from icy Jerusalem, is warm in the winter, enclosed by stockades of palms, adorned by clusters of hardy geraniums and flowering cacti. Founded in 1937 as a frontier outpost in hostile territory, it now subsists mainly from the winter tourist trade, with a guest house, a nature reserve, and a botanical garden nearby. In summer, it is one of the hottest places in the Middle East, near the lowest place on earth. A beautiful, savage and harsh environment, it is currently a temporary home to nine Russian immigrant families, who live in air-conditioned caravans somewhat apart from the members of the kibbutz. They have been taken in as part of a country-wide kibbutz-sponsored plan called 'First Home in the Motherland', by which immigrants can spend a year or so on a kibbutz. There are also fifteen Russian adolescents who came on their own; they attend the local kibbutz regional school and boarding at the kibbutz. A very few, if they conform to the rigorous standards, may eventually join as members.

Among the few fortunates are Mila and Arkady Lifschitz, from Gorki, and their five-year-old daughter. Mila is a music teacher who now takes a class twice a week in the kibbutz primary school, and also gives private lessons to kibbutz children. Arkady, a mechanical engineer, is currently working in the botanical gardens, and will soon be sent by the kibbutz to a special course for plumbers in Tel Aviv. The only real problem is that Mila has no piano of her own, though there is a good one in the kibbutz hall which she is allowed to practise on, when there is no one around. 'Anyway, the walls of the caravan are too thin – it would disturb the neighbours.'

'In Russia, we thought a kibbutz was like a *kolkhoz*, but that didn't put us off. We were brought up to believe that the capitalists were all rotten, and we expected the kibbutz to be a little version of the old Russia, before Stalin, the time when people really wanted to help one another, when there was the real collective spirit. I was a Komsomol member, of course.'

'Things started to change with glasnost, we could talk openly, without fear. But it turned out that nothing was really changing, the new people aren't making things better. We began to be afraid as Jews, because of the new nationalism; we thought there might be pogroms. So that was why we came here.'

During their probationary period, the Lifschitzes are paid salaries; when they join formally, as kibbutz members, they will cease to receive payment for their work, but will move into the kibbutz proper. Like other members, they will have well-equipped kitchens, and good educational and leisure facilities; but private property, such as cars – or a private piano for Mila – will be forbidden, and if they leave the kibbutz, they will leave empty handed. This, like other conditions of kibbutz life, has deterred many of the immigrants who spend their first year on a kibbutz from remaining. For its part, the kibbutz, while it will pay salaries to its temporary tenants, and allow them use of its facilities, has draconian standards of its own for accepting the Russian immigrants as new members.

Meira, a veteran member who handles the immigrants at Eyn

Gedi, is a typical daughter of the kibbutz. Sturdy, hard working, she is a graduate of the Israeli youth movement, served in the para-military Nahal corps in the army, and moved to Eyn Gedi after the Six Day War. Meira and her husband – son of a German-Jewish family which returned to Germany after the Second World War – have adopted a little Ethiopian girl in addition to a daughter and son of their own. The photograph of two toddlers, one very black, one very white, naked on the kibbutz lawn, is the first thing that strikes the eye in their living room.

'We don't want immigrants over thirty-five, and we want people with something to contribute to the kibbutz. Some of the families we have now have been here two years, although they're only supposed to stay one year under the project. We've got an unmarried mother, a sad case; her daughter was born in a forceps delivery in Russia, a bad job, and on one side of her head she had massive haemorrhages which have deformed her whole face – it'll take many operations to put that right. Then there's a doctor who was a cardiologist in Russia; his special qualifications aren't recognised here, but he works as a doctor at the Dead Sea hotels. We put them all in the caravans, but they don't all get on together. It turns out that the Western Russians have problems with the Asiatics, just like our Ashkenazim and Sefardim; we didn't know about that.' She also complained that they sometimes took advantage, asking to use the phone and then ringing Russia.

The kibbutz population today is Israel's equivalent of landed gentry. Once pioneering outposts when only agricultural collectives could extend frontiers for the growing Jewish community in Palestine, the kibbutzim are now beautifully landscaped, apparently idyllic communities, whose children enjoy small classes and the chance to study in university and to travel, and who are more likely to live off industries such as tourism, irrigation equipment or plastic crockery than the production of fruit and vegetables. But the danger menacing these communities is the departure of their own younger generation, attracted by the opportunities and freedom of life in the cities. Hence, apart from the declared desire to 'do something for immigration', the kibbutz interest in the immigrants and the various plans to attract their young people.

From the immigrants' viewpoint, integration into the Israeli community is much easier in a kibbutz or small town than in the big centres to which most immigrants are attracted. This is particularly visible in the northern Negev region, the semi-desert area of southern Israel, where the kibbutz movement is active both in the surrounding 'development towns' and among the immigrants who have settled there.

The population of the smaller 'development towns' in the Negev, who are overwhelmingly Sefardi, of North African extraction, are well aware that the Russians, with their technological skills, are valuable in attracting investment and new industries to these towns, which remained semi stagnant throughout the 1960s and 1970s. Naturally, and by tradition, very hospitable, many of these people have rallied round to help the immigrants. Twenty-nine per cent of recent public housing, the largest proportion of all areas in Israel, has been built in the Negev.

The small towns in the Negev – Kiryat Malachi, Shderot, Netivot – lie at the centre of kibbutz country; all resemble one another. Over the entrance to the town there is usually an arch welcoming visitors, and it is easy to locate the town hall, the community centre, and the labour exchange and health fund premises. The shopping centres have shop windows whose owners have a strictly utilitarian attitude to display. Food, or clothing, is stacked frontally, usually bearing signs of recent reductions in price (real or imaginary). There is usually a local cinema (increasingly difficult to run in the era of video libraries) and always a 'celebration hall' where barmitzvahs, weddings and circumcision parties are held; these are lavishly decorated, with black or coloured glass walls and ceilings which transform the guests into a multitude, with winking strobe lights which change the colour of the food: meat revolving on, and carved from a spit, felafel, and sticky sweet pastries, turn from green to red and purple.

For the guest who comes into the town on an ordinary day, there is no restaurant in sight, but several snack bars where you can buy hot and cold drinks and eat pitta filled with humus or techina and heavy croissants or pastries – a clear hint of the

French colonial origins of the original immigrants. The radio in the bar is tuned either to Arab stations, or to Israeli rock, and the volume is impressive, disguising the fact that in a town blessed with high employment very few people are out in the streets before the evening. The original housing blocks are grim affairs, stark concrete with tiny balconies stacked with spare bicycles and discarded washing machines, and neglected communal entrances. But in what were once the poorest quarters, where immigrants were once housed in makeshift cottages or shacks, 'Project Renewal' – with the Camp David accords the chief achievement of the Likud right-wing era – enabled many of the early settlers, with government help, to build annexes on little plots, and shape their homes into mini villas, imitations, at a modest level, of the luxurious suburbs of Tel Aviv and its satellite towns.

At first, the only sign of the Russian immigrants' presence is the notice board in the town halls advertising various courses, and the fact that many of the products in shop windows are labelled in Russian. But the eye soon picks out the Russians by their cloth caps, heavy clothing, and – among recent arrivals – a northern pallor.

In the town hall of Kiryat Malachi, the man in charge of immigrant absorption, Amnon Hadad, is an energetic, dark-skinned man, a Sefardi who came to Kiryat Malachi at the age of seven from North Africa and is a local patriot, proud of the town's success in integrating the Russian arrivals. The head of the council is now Yossi Vanunu, a Moroccan.

Between 1990 and 1992, Kiryat Malachi, a town of only 18,000 people, Hadad is proud to say, took in nearly 3,000 newcomers, and provided almost all of them with work. The unemployment rate is only three per cent, far below the national average of ten per cent.

Hadad's pride is significant of the change that has taken place among those Israelis who were immigrants from the Arab countries in the 1950s and 1960s. It is not that they identify with the new arrivals; the Russians, to them, are first-class travellers whereas they travelled steerage. The Russians can choose where they go in Israel; they themselves were taken from the port or airport in the back of lorries, to patches of wasteland which had to be settled for 'population dispersion' or security reasons. The

Russians have come to a modernised, reasonably prosperous society, while they arrived in periods of austerity, when few consumer goods were available. The 'peace process' was far in the future when the Sefardim arrived; they expected to fight, not long after arrival, in one of Israel's seemingly endless series of wars.

Perhaps most important, and initially to the Sefardis' resentment, the Russians were eagerly awaited and welcomed as highly skilled, well-educated immigrants. The Jews from Arab countries were 'the wilderness generation', few with more than a few years' schooling and many of the elders illiterate: small traders, artisans, whom Israel turned into a labour force and an instant working class long before it had the huge cheap reservoir of labour in the West Bank and Gaza. They were at the bottom of the social ladder, and they knew it.

At the same time as these people arrived in the 'development towns' which took decades to develop, so did a much smaller population of Eastern European Jews – survivors of the Holocaust or fugitives from Communist regimes. Very few of these remained in the new towns; they argued or wangled their way out fast. The Sefardim stayed behind. It was they who built up the little towns in the desert area of Israel, and they are proud of it. The former underdogs are now the immigrants' hosts, the bosses. It is they who can welcome the Russians, use 'connections' in nearby factories or hospitals to get them jobs, organise their entertainment, and patronise them in every way. For the North African Israelis, it is a satisfying metamorphosis.

Hadad stressed what Kiryat Malachi had to offer to the immigrants: work, no pollution, a small and friendly environment, and (as this is the northernmost of the Negev small towns) a forty-minute drive to Tel Aviv for those who have found work there. There were Russian workers in the town's factories, and 150 engineers. Fifty per cent of the new immigrants, he said proudly, were 'academics' (those with some form of higher education). He had used all his manifold personal connections to find them work both in factories and in local hospitals. The cultural centre of Kiryat Malachi had taken on the task of organising events of the kind Russians like, such as classical music concerts and ballet.

There was work for Russians in the supermarket, and in the local dairy industry, Tnuva. Others were training to become cashiers and sales women for Gottex, the local bathing costume factory, as well as other textile industries which had taken advantage of the tax breaks the government allows in development areas to set up factories nearby. The Jews from the Asiatic republics have a clan tradition similar to that of the Moroccans. Many of the Russian families in Kiryat Malachi are from Bukhara, Uzbekhistan and Kazakhstan. The older generation of immigrants from this group are almost indistinguishable from the older North Africans, the women in headscarves and long flowered dresses, the old men puffing at pipes over a game of *shesh besh*. Young Russians and immigrants from the Baltic republics, however, have small families and, with little or no Jewish tradition in their lives, have no use for the 'celebration halls'. There were ninety single-parent families (rare among the Sefardim), but Hadad was doing his best to bring them into local celebrations. The community centre put on parties, and at Jewish festivals they donated presents for immigrant children. Thirty children had been bussed to barmitzvahs at the Western Wall in Jerusalem: local children, Russians and Ethiopians, all in equal numbers. Housing in Kiryat Malachi was spacious by Russian standards, and there were no caravans or other temporary housing.

Most of the Russians worked in local food-producing factories, many as mechanics and mechanical engineers. They even had, Hadad said, a Russian space scientist who had a job in the municipality. This legendary figure, Lazar Chodorkowsky, turned out to be an expert not in the stratosphere but the ocean. He was a graduate of the Institute of Naval Construction from Nicolayev who had spent twenty-five years in ship construction, and had reached the position of Professor at the local university. Now he was revelling in the role of public administrator.

Chodorkowsky had made health care his special task. Ten per cent of immigrants' salaries, he said, went on various payments for health care. This was a great deal for people used to free treatment. He was making it his business to help immigrant doctors with licences to find work, and by his persistence, a whole extra floor had been added to the local health clinic. Other doctors were working, after retraining, as nurses.

While the new system of 'direct absorption' Israel adopted in

1987 was: 'find your own apartment, find your own job, get yourself fixed up', this was ill suited to the Russians who were used to
being told what to do and where to go. In Kiryat Malachi an
energetic administrator could master the local terrain in a short
time, provided that he knew, as Chodorkowsky did, his target
work-force.

In his work, Hadad had the help of one of the original inhabitants of the town. Sarina Blumenfeld was from Romania, one of
those Ashkenazim who had stayed behind when others fled the
development towns. She had worked for twenty-one years in the
bank in Kiryat Malachi, but had now turned into a general
factotum for all the Russians' problems. The Russians who
clustered round her in the town hall all praised her feverish
energy in trying to find them work and housing; she wanted
them to stay. Not only did she run around to prospective
employers; she was also trying to organise more rental housing
from government housing authorities who functioned on the
mortgage/sale principle, and she had got the mayor's support
on this. She was familiar with the problems of mothers used to
working full time, who were baffled by a school system which
sent the children home at midday. Sarina was also canvassing a
pair of adoptive families for each family of new immigrants,
to help them sort out their adjustment to the bewildering
Israeli bureaucracy, and to help the children after school hours.
Like all the officials in the town hall, Sarina worked long beyond
regular hours.

In their anxiety to keep the Russians, the leaders of Kiryat
Malachi were even bringing a Yiddish theatre to put on performances for the older immigrants. There was also a Russian immigrant newsletter whose front page addressed the newcomers and
invited responses: Are things going well for you? Are you home-
sick? Please write in and tell us your successes and failures. What
more could an immigrant want?

Kiryat Malachi seemed idyllic compared with the larger towns.
But there was one serious question mark over the Russians' per-
manence in the town; no educated Western Russian family, save
for the minority who had turned back to Jewish orthodoxy under
the influence of the proselytising Hasidim, wanted their children
educated in the state religious schools which dominated local

education, and which sent few children on to university.

Svetlana, a rosy-cheeked black-haired woman from Belarus who handled immigrants in Kiryat Malachi, had been in Israel two years and had been working for six months in the municipal offices. When she arrived, in autumn 1990, she and her husband, who was an engineer, had heard there was accommodation in Rehovot, a town further north, most of whose inhabitants were prosperous farmers, middle-class commuters, and the scientists in Israel's chief research facility, the Weizmann Institute. But Rehovot was too costly for new immigrants. Kiryat Malachi, a short drive into the northern Negev, sounded more promising. The new neighbours, who were Tunisians, could not have been kinder; they immediately lent them all the kitchen equipment and furniture they could spare, until they had enough money to buy their own. Svetlana's husband found work in Gedera, further north. Svetlana had been a teacher in general history for seven years in Kazan university (where Lenin had studied, she could not resist pointing out) and she had two sons aged eight and six. Though all her family had been born and raised in big cities, she found living in a small town, at this stage, convenient; but she thought the local schools were all of a very low standard.

This was partly because the local population was multi ethnic; the Jews from the Asiatic republics, religious and oriental, demanded little but religious studies and fitted in well; but Svetlana's sons were unsympathetic towards the Moroccans in their class in a state religious school, whom they found uncouth, and lacking in respect for the teacher. When Svetlana said in the company of other parents that she thought the children needed more discipline, she was told: 'Then go back to Russia.'

Her elder son, she said, couldn't fight back when harassed, was not sufficiently aggressive, and things were becoming problematic. She said they had chosen the state religious school because they thought the children should learn Jewish customs. They did not have to be orthodox, but this was, after all, their culture. Now she was thinking of removing them and sending them to a local cooperative village or *moshav*, where there was a better school. Finally, she admitted that if she wanted her sons to go to university, at a later stage they would probably have to leave Kiryat

Malachi, in order to find a good secondary school which would prepare them for higher education.

So, despite the welcome the Russians have received, they are ambivalent at finding themselves among 'orientals'. Shderot, further south, is a development town lying in an area thickly populated with the kibbutzim of the northern Negev. In the past, relations between the kibbutzim and the development towns were problematic. The kibbutzim took hired labour from the North African immigrant centres, but allowed them no access to their own facilities, such as regional schools, and there was little or no social contact between the kibbutz population, highly conscious of its ideological purity (there were endless discussions about the morality of hiring labour, but few about shared educational facilities) and the North Africans. Today, the kibbutzim are in a very different situation, so they are more conscious of regional problems, more involved in the economic development of the Negev, or the Galilee, as a whole.

Nitai Schreiber, a kibbutznik living in a temporary urban commune with several others from nearby kibbutzim, in Shderot, works for Shinar, a regional organisation for the absorption of immigrants, run by the American Jewish Joint Distribution Commit-tee. Its job was to act, in social work and in an advisory capacity, as interpreters between the authorities and the immigrants, during the process of acclimatisation. At first the local authorities did not like the intervention of kibbutzniks and outsiders. However, he said that by now they had been accepted. Schreiber suggested that if the Russians could staff the local schools, the danger of the others leaving would be minimised.

Among those working with him were: Maya Katznelson, Anna Gelebtin and Klara Streicher, new immigrants. All had come to Shderot after six months in Tel Aviv. Klara was a widow with two teenage daughters, a nurse from Orma in Belarus. She had decided to remain in Shderot, despite the mixed and 'oriental' population. She felt that new immigrants like herself would eventually 'raise the cultural level'.

Anna was an economist from Moscow, who had done a six-month retraining course to become an accountant. She had settled in Netivot, but seemed less satisfied with the 'oriental' town, which she said was dirty, with too many religious people. She was used to life in a big city, and to go to Tel Aviv or Beersheba on one's own was virtually impossible, as the last buses returned at 9p.m. She was divorced, with a small son, and lived with her mother and grandmother.

Maya was a computer scientist, who had become the secretary of a contractor in Netivot. She and her husband and children were among fourteen families who had come as a group to the Negev, as housing was easier to obtain, and they had been in Beersheba and Bat Yam near Tel Aviv before settling here.

Each woman had different reasons for coming to Israel. Maya said that she was tired of living with non-Jews, fearing anti-semitism. Nothing, she said, had changed under perestroika, the same people were in power. The main reason they had come was for the children. Anna said that she had little or no knowledge about how or why she was Jewish, but in Russia she was made to feel it was somehow shameful. The decision to leave had caused trouble in the Institute of Economics where she worked; her colleagues had been jealous of the Jewish option for emigration. Her parents had remained behind. Her father was a Communist who had fought in the Red Army, and he was suspicious of Israel, and thought things were bad there. Klara, a widow, said her father, on the contrary, had been the driving force behind the decision to emigrate. He was a mechanical engineer and probably would take a retraining course in Jerusalem. The Moroccans, she confirmed, had been very hospitable; but as for cultural activities, she too took every opportunity to join excursions out of town.

Nitai Schreiber was particularly proud of the integration of Sofia Lifschitz, who works as a group organiser for immigrant youth. She lived in a neat little house in a neat little suburb in Shderot, an ideal environment to any immigrants leaving the terrible state housing of the Soviet Union. It had a little garden, and the living room had a TV, a video, and a camel-coloured carpet; there was a well-equipped kitchen, a patio, and she and her husband had taken out a thirty-year mortgage. Sofia was cheerful, constantly smiling, perhaps a little highly strung. She came from Sverdlovsk, and had begun her life in Israel in Tel Aviv. Life there, she had discovered, was too expensive. She and her husband had arrived at the beginning of the mass wave of immigration. She had a master's degree in chemistry, had taught for three years, and her husband, a mechanical engineer, was now working as a mechanic in a garage.

In Sverdlovsk, she said, with a population of one and a half million, there had only been 20,000 Jews. There was no synagogue and no real Jewish community. But when they were ill, Jews wanted only Jewish doctors, and when they wanted to marry, the girls looked for Jewish husbands; the parents felt they would only be secure with Jews, who rarely beat their wives, or got drunk.

'Every immigrant feels like a baby when he arrives, with no self confidence. We felt we needed to learn how to walk.' She confided: 'My husband used to be a decisive character, but he lost the confidence as soon as we arrived, couldn't decide what to do. Our child was five and a half. We had to learn to trust people. In Russia one couldn't trust anyone.' Her husband, she said, had adjusted more slowly. His present job brought in 1,000 shekels a month, for fifty-six hours' work a week. This is a meagre salary (about £250) but at least the working hours were reasonable. When they had lived in Tel Aviv, she said, he had worked for three months for six to twelve hours a day, sometimes till 10p.m.; 'He stopped being a husband or a father.'

Sofia said that most of the time she was out of town, running around from one settlement to another: 'We are a modern family,' she said cheerfully, but with a note of sadness. Very house proud, she confessed that she did not like change. But with Lifschitz, as with the other Western Russians, the really discordant note in her life was the future of her little boy. Her husband spoke Russian to the child, she, Hebrew. At school, she said, discipline was poor, there were many petty thefts. She was clearly not very happy with the Asiatic Russian population. The Georgians, she commented, got on well with the Moroccans; this was not praise.

Sofia is employed by the Negev Regional College. Run by the kibbutz movement, it sponsors *Sela*, a training scheme for new immigrants enabling them to study in the college while living in the kibbutz. The college also runs its own *ulpan* for new immigrants.

The kibbutzim, however, are not as altruistic as appears at first sight in contributing to the immigrant problem. They have not only a drop-out problem but are in trouble financially, so encourage members to work outside the kibbutz and bring in money. Under *Sela*, they are pleased to take in immigrants in return for the 'absorption money' the immigrants contribute to the kitty. The immigrants do not leave better off than they arrived.

Among those studying in the college and living meanwhile on a kibbutz was Rivka, who arrived in May 1989. She was an English teacher from Tashkent and Moscow who said she had come to Israel out of the desire 'to rejoin the Jewish people'. In Tashkent the Jews had been courted by all kinds of Israeli emissaries, who had confused them: there were orthodox Jews, non-orthodox Jews, Americans with Sabbath candles, books on Jewish history and the rules of *kashrut*. It was a lot to absorb. Now they had to learn about the kibbutz. Not quite a *kolkhoz*, but similar. Everything provided. Several tens of families had joined the scheme, but she wasn't sure if any would remain.

Marina Livkanska was from Moldava, and was living in kibbutz Nahal Oz for a short period. She was doing a course in accountancy, but would shortly move to Beersheba. Her father was a carpenter, her mother a seamstress. At the moment she was working in the kibbutz packaging parsley for £1.70 an hour. The family paid the kibbutz most of their 'absorption basket' and in return got accommodation, food and education for their two children. They did not intend to stay in the kibbutz, but it was an interim solution to their problem of adaptation to the country.

Miriam Kalika came from Vinnitsa in the Ukraine, the frontier of the former Pale of Settlement. She was a trained economist, having studied at a local college of economics for five years. Kalika had arrived in January 1990. After six months in an *ulpan*, she had moved to Shderot with her parents and a brother, and received a three-room flat from Amigur (a government housing agency.) The Kalikas were among the first thirty families in Shderot. Firstcomers were better received than those who came later, who found that most of the work had gone, and that there were no flats for rent under £250 a month. She had done an accountancy course, and another course in Hebrew, but was offered only work as a 'simple labourer'. She heard that the

Negev Regional College provided further education which would suit her for more advanced work. To enter, she had to pass a number of exams: Hebrew to matriculation standard, maths and psychometric tests. Her case was typical of a number of families in which the parents remained in the towns, the children in the kibbutzim. The kibbutz was prepared to take young people, rarely families, but this posed special problems for Russia.

'People who go to the kibbutzim get a taste of freedom. I keep in touch with my parents and know about family problems. But at home I can't really criticise the family; here, an eighteen-year-old is already independent.' There was greater closeness among the Russian than the Israeli families, particularly that of the mothers with adult sons and daughters – a fact the immigrants attribute to the need for Jews to keep together in a hostile society.

Among the kibbutz members employed as teachers in the College is Yehudit Hermoni; she helps run a course for *metaplot*, the staff at crèches for small children below kindergarten age.

The college, she said, ran special classes for unemployed immigrants. Twenty-five of those attending now had been two years in the neighbouring town of Kiryat Gat, and seventeen were new immigrants from Shderot. There were also ten Israelis in the course, so it was an 'integrated' course. One day a week, under supervision, they were allowed to work with children in the local crèche.

But the Russians created unique dilemmas. One was the fact that some elderly women came only because they could get unemployment pay if they attended the course six hours a day. Another was that the Russians were not used to the idea that children could improvise games, that they did not have to be instructed and taught all the time, and told what to do. They were shocked if the toddlers were given a blank sheet of paper and a crayon and left on their own. In Israel, education only started at the age of five in 'compulsory' kindergarten; before that, the children were given the maximum freedom. In Russia even toddlers had been disciplined.

Chaim is from one of the oldest established kibbutzim of the region: a grizzled, hyper-energetic man of about sixty, whose schedule was hectic and who seemed continually to have to be somewhere else. He had been in the kibbutz since arriving from Yugoslavia as a young man. He said that whereas in the early days, he had never questioned the decision he had made to join a collective settlement, these days he did ask himself this question, every morning. But, if he decided to leave, where could he go, without money, without experience of working and living on his own? In many ways, therefore, the dilemma of a self-questioning kibbutznik resembles that of the Russians afraid of total freedom. In the kibbutz there are no money worries, everyone receives his or her dues in return for their share of the kibbutz labour, which is decided by committee.

Chaim was proud of the fact that the kibbutz movement had taken in 20,000 immigrants, eighty per cent of them from the USSR. Four hundred families were candidates for permanent residence. Some would inevitably work outside and bring in money, some work in temporary jobs in the kibbutzim as employees. The candidates the kibbutzim were looking for, as in Eyn Gedi, were twenty-three to thirty-five-year-old immigrants. They were not sure if they wanted professional qualifications. On the one hand, professionals might have exaggerated expectations, but they might be suited to specific jobs which the kibbutz needed. Generally, kibbutz members are rotated.

During the first, trial period, the immigrants paid the kibbutz a rental from their absorption basket, and received all the kibbutz services. If they worked overtime or on Sabbaths, they got paid. There were some scientists who worked outside, in the framework of the Ministry of Absorption's programme for the integration of scientists, and some were involved in kibbutz industry. Whatever work they found, they were paid the same salary. In some cases they lived in caravans for which they paid about £40.00 (a fraction of the usual rent in a town) and a small payment for health care.

The kibbutz had done research into the lives of 600 immigrant families. They were asked whether their kibbutz stay meant that they had to integrate twice over; but they thought not. The kibbutz *ulpan* was of easier access, nearby, and they had ample chance to talk Hebrew. The kibbutz provided the immigrants with their launching pad into Israeli society.

But one Russian immigrant at Chaim's kibbutz, Sasha, too old to be accepted, was leaving with a bitter taste in his mouth. The kibbutz, he said, was a society based on an ideology which was no longer viable in a market economy. For instance, he said, people were still rotated in jobs, so they could not acquire a permanent skill; they were provided with a marvellous education, sent to university for instance to get a doctorate in philosophy, but would never make use of it. What purpose did that serve the community? This kind of idealism, he said, reminded him in some ways of the Soviet society he had left behind, and he did not like it. He did not think the kibbutz, in the long run, could survive. Despite all this, he was clearly unhappy that the kibbutz had not accepted him as a permanent member. It had offered something of the same security to immigrants as life in the former Soviet Union, with none of the disadvantages.

CHAPTER EIGHT

The Insulted and the Injured

'In Russia, women were "work horses", men were kings. Women not only held down full-time jobs, but when they finished work were expected to clean the family apartment. I never met a woman in Moscow who had hired help. Without labour-saving appliances like washing machines, they kept the home clean and the family fed. That didn't mean ordering from the supermarket, and having a woman in once a week at least, as in Israel, but going out and searching, sometimes for hours every day, for whatever goods were on sale. In Soviet Russia, the men in the family, even if they didn't necessarily earn more than their wives, and sometimes earned less, were in far more prestigious professions and jobs. Very few helped in the home,' said Ella Zeitlin, head of the Movement for Immigrant Women.

'The men usually turned over their share of earnings to the women who were solely responsible for the purchase of food, clothes and everything else the family needed. So the women became enormously strong. They had to be.'

Eighty-four per cent of Russian women, double the number of women in the Israeli work force, were employed outside the home under the Soviet system. In Israel, few have found work in their own professions, and Zeitlin estimated that three-quarters of all immigrant women, regardless of age, and most of whom are professionally or technologically qualified, had worked either permanently or as part-time workers in domestic service to supplement their salary.

The Movement for Immigrant Women functions out of one tiny room on a floor of a building run by Forum, the Russian immigrant association. But whereas Forum is supported by the

Jewish Agency, the MIW is run entirely by unpaid volunteers, in shifts. Zeitlin has herself been through the immigrant mill since her arrival eight years ago and has shared most of the experiences of the women she deals with. She is a chemical machine engineer, who retrained in Israel, working first as a quality-control chemist in Rafa, a pharmaceutical firm, and then, later, as an insurance agent, a job she still holds part time.

Zeitlin arrived in Israel with her husband, and divorced there, like many young Russian women. She has a six-year-old child. The Zeitlins were refuseniks, one of those Zionist families who under the Soviet regime were persecuted for their desire to leave Russia. They belonged to a core group of fifty families of would-be emigrants in Moscow, and were among the first to leave, just before glasnost began, in 1985. At this period, an International Youth Festival was just about to open in Moscow, and the authorities did not want it to be spoiled by the appearance of chanting dissidents. The Zeitlins' group had persistently staged demonstrations and even marches, particularly when visiting foreign delegations were in town. They were threatened by the KGB that if they demonstrated on this occasion, they would be sent to jail, but went ahead with a march just the same. The KGB then gave a number of families three days to leave the Soviet Union, and jailed the rest. The Zeitlins were among those who left almost destitute. Three days left them no time to find portable valuables. Their apartment reverted to the state.

As so often in Israeli immigrant history, those who came earlier, and who had stood up to persecution, were those who left with little but the clothes on their backs. Once divorced, Zeitlin, like tens of thousands of other immigrant women, found that the Israeli welfare system did not favour single parents. It is estimated that about a third of all the recent Russian immigrants, about 50,000 families, are one-parent families – and most of the single parents are women.

Zeitlin and the other volunteers began organising at the beginning of 1992, sending out 1,000 questionnaires to women who qualified for help from the National Insurance Institute. Now they have branches all over the country. They try to make sure that immigrant women are informed as to the services they can apply for, help them find accommodation, and advise them on

138

questions of Jewish law where marriage and divorce are concerned. They are now looking for a lawyer, and have found a Russian psychologist qualified to practise in Israel. Almost all their work concerns single-parent families.

The Russian divorce rate was one of the highest in the world, and Zeitlin thinks that this was because marriage and divorce were so easy, because marriage took place early, and because there was no psychological counselling. But this is not the only reason for the mass of single-parent women among the immigrants. Some women left their husbands behind in Russia, hoping that they would follow. Some men, dissatisfied with life in Israel, simply abandoned their wives and returned to Russia. Many, according to Zeitlin, found that the strains of immigration and the problems in the new country exacerbated existing tensions, and couples divorced shortly after arrival. For the men who had been 'kings' in Russia, the drop in status, and the problem of finding work which was not consonant with their skills, affected their sense of self respect and often made them impossible to live with – an immigrant syndrome familiar to Israeli psychologists. 'Anyway,' says Zeitlin, 'a woman is much better off without a husband who sits around at home all day complaining.'

Zeitlin answers the telephone during her shift, but there are also reception days when women can consult her advisers, between ten and fifteen in number every day; these volunteers come after or before their working hours. The entire organisation is a complete innovation for the Russians, who are unused to the idea of voluntary work – which did not exist under the Soviet system. Zeitlin feels her organisation is new even in Israel: 'Here women over sixty, women who have retired, are those who work as volunteers. But we are all young women, with jobs and children. We just felt someone had to take charge, to lobby with the authorities, and to bring the problems to their notice. Otherwise the women are completely lost.'

As we spoke, a television crew arrived, with another Russian woman, Hanna Dashevsky, who works for the Israeli Council for the Child. Zeitlin was interviewed so briefly that only one sentence of hers survived in the five-minute item on the television news that night, and the item itself was absurdly superficial, focussing on a beautiful young woman (filmed trendily in slow motion and freeze) whose husband had gone back to Russia leaving her with two small children on her hands; as she had to go out to work to support them, neighbours had complained she was neglecting the children and she found herself in danger of having them taken into care. But, although the report admitted that the authorities are little help in such cases, the item ended cheerfully: the moment her case was made known, said the commentary, help was available and the problem solved. In other words: trust media exposure.

Things are not usually so simple. That same day, Zeitlin had tried to advise Ludmila, a wife whose husband had gone back to Russia and simply disappeared without trace. Not only had she no means of support, but she had not a single document to help her establish her claims for support from the state. Her husband had taken with him their 'immigrants certificate' indicating her status, and all the couple's other documents. Ludmila was thus an abandoned wife, in Jewish law an *Aguna* or 'anchored' woman who is not free to marry unless her husband signs a document (the *get*) releasing her from her marriage, or until seven years have passed and there is evidence that he may be dead.

Dozens of other Israeli women are in this predicament, but in Ludmila's case there is an added complication. Like most Russian immigrants, she was married – to another Jew – in a civil ceremony. Although the state of Israel recognises such marriages as valid – an act intended to simplify matters for immigrants from countries where civil ceremonies are standard – this very liberalism has proved disastrous for many Russian immigrants. As Ludmila is a Jewish married woman, the only body entitled to authorise her divorce is the rabbinate, and their conditions for divorce are often draconian. The fight to get alimony, or some form of state welfare, can go on for years. 'They've opened a file,' says Zeitlin laconically.

'For most women with such problems, there is very little we can do,' said Zeitlin. 'We've applied to the Ministry of Education and the Ministry of Labour for special allocations, and to Forum, which has promised help, but so far we're on our own.' Where the problem of single-parent families is concerned, Zeitlin had registered two successes, however, in recent weeks. The authorities had finally agreed to regard single-parent immigrants as 'social cases' entitled to larger benefits from the National Insurance Institute; and a rabbi influential in the rabbinical administration in Jerusalem had promised her that special rulings would be drawn up regarding alimony for women caught between civil and rabbinical law, left either without alimony or with payments totally inadequate to support their families. These are important achievements, but where the second is concerned, only valid when the husband is in Israel and under the rabbi's jurisdiction. If this is so, and he is willing to divorce, the minimum waiting period is six months.

Furthermore, the entire question of alimony in Israel is a nightmare of conflicting claims by the civil and religious courts. Here the state can intervene. But the rabbinical courts, although they alone can grant a divorce to Jews, in many cases will not press men to pay alimony if the marriage was not carried out according to Jewish law, and the woman has no *ketuba*, the marriage contract which specifies the sum to be paid over to the woman if the man wishes to divorce her. According to civil law, a husband who leaves his wife must only pay her maintenance if she does not work; according to Jewish law, he need only pay her maintenance if there is a child of the marriage. In any event, the woman is inevitably the victim, and, as Zeitlin says drily 'the law favours the man at every turn.'

But all this is nothing compared to the particular problems of women and children caused by the conflict between the Law of Return, under which the immigrants claim the right to be Israeli citizens, and rabbinical law, which determines who is defined as 'Jewish' by the Ministry of the Interior – a Ministry which has always been controlled by members of Israel's religious political parties. According to the Law of Return, the right to enter Israel as an immigrant, and to become a citizen of the state, extends through three generations: to any Jew, his or her children, and his or her grandchildren. It also applies to the immigrant's husband or wife, whether Jewish or not – hence, the possibility of becoming a citizen of the state of Israel without being Jewish. In the case of the new immigrants, such partners are registered as 'Russian' rather than 'Jewish' or 'Muslim'.

However, among Russian Jews who have intermarried steadily since the Revolution, there are myriad anomalies. For instance, a woman whose father was Jewish, but not her mother, is enabled to become a citizen; but if she does not go through a conversion ceremony, and even if she is married to a Jew, her child is not Jewish (because Jews are defined according to the mother's religion). Nor is the child of a non-Jewish mother married to a Jew. Such a child will be entitled, as a citizen, to health care if the mother is registered under a health fund scheme; and to free schooling; but he or she cannot marry another Jewish Israeli; cannot serve in the army; and cannot work in any security-linked industry. In other words, their situation is very similar to that of Israeli Arabs, who, as most civil rights activists would agree, are second-class citizens, since having served in the army entitles citizens to many privileges.

Another problem is that legally, the son born to a non-Jewish woman cannot be ritually circumcised, even though the child is born in Israel. There are Conservative or Reform rabbis who would arrange this privately, the cost being 1,200 shekels, or £300. This is a lot of money for a new immigrant. Medical circumcision alone does not constitute conversion.

Moreover: should an immigrant, non-Jewish husband or wife of Jews have children by a previous marriage to a non-Jew in Russia, and have brought the children of such a marriage to Israel, such children are neither citizens nor, of course, Jews. The only status they can receive is that of 'permanent residents' of the state, and at the age of eighteen, this status may be revoked.

Hanna Dashevsky says that the only solution to such a problem, where women are concerned, is for the new husband to adopt the children of the previous husband. This procedure is simple and enables the children to acquire Israeli nationality. 'But is this ethical?' she asks. 'Supposing a man does not want to adopt his precedessor's children? And supposing the children do not want to be adopted? What then?'

Perhaps if the feminist movement were stronger in Israel, the Russian women would find it easier to lobby. In Israel there is a women's section in the trades union movement, the General Council of Women Workers in Israel, but this protects and supports only those women within the framework of organised labour. The fledgling Israeli women's organisation is the Israel

Women's Network, led by a vigorous campaigner of British origin, Professor Alice Shalvi.

The Women's Network does employ a Russian woman, Lena Gravetz, to deal with the specific problems of the women immigrants. Gravetz agreed that the anomalies of the Russian women's legal situation, somewhere between the secular and religious spheres, often made their economic situation a nightmare.

Those women who separated in Israel from their husbands were not prepared for the complex procedures of the rabbinical courts. Divorce was a simple matter in the Soviet Union, taking only three to four hours. The Russian bureaucracy, said Gravetz, was much easier on such matters. She had had a case here, in Kfar Saba, where a woman had been abandoned by her husband for a friend, leaving her with an eight-year-old child. She had opened a joint account with her husband, which he had emptied; the car was his, and she was now doing housework for 50 to 70 pence a day – slave labour.

Even the elderly could face similar problems. Gravetz was also trying to help a seventy-year-old woman, defined as eighty per cent crippled by the National Insurance Institute, whose husband had gone back to Russia to open a business, and disappeared. To get an injunction preventing him from leaving Israel had taken too long. It would take seven years for her to be officially pronounced as an abandoned wife and get a divorce. Property was usually divided in half in an Israeli divorce, but most immigrant women had no property, and if the husband left, there was no alimony.

Rich women could be blackmailed into granting a divorce. Childless women who had never worked could not manage, as there was no obligation on the husband to support them. One woman whom she was helping had two daughters aged seventeen and twelve. She was worried what would happen when the elder reached the age of eighteen, when support from the state would stop. As, at this age, the child usually enters the army and therefore cannot earn, this is a serious problem for the single-parent family.

It was absurd, said Gravetz, that women who had married non-Jews, were legally accepted as married by the Ministry of Absorption but not married according to the Ministry of the

Interior. Some had come to Israel ahead of their husbands hoping that they would follow. If they had not, there was no way that, here, the wives could get a divorce and alimony. Many such women shared flats, on the Russian pattern in the old country: 'It's better to share with strangers than with your parents, as so many do; that really makes for friction.' Very few had the kind of collateral which would enable them to take out a mortgage.

Apart from the legal problems of single parents, almost all immigrant women struggled to be paid a living wage. Women were frequently paid below the minimum rates; some women were earning as little as 5.7 shekels (about £1.20) per day. The minimum wage is 30 shekels a day. They could get twenty-five to fifty per cent overtime pay if they worked more than eight hours, but in the USSR overtime had always been paid double.

'Immigrant women are often like slave labour. Because they don't know the law, they are often sacked without compensation, and employers often don't pay National Insurance. That is again against the law, but many immigrant women don't complain because they are afraid of losing their jobs. I even had a case of a Russian woman employing another immigrant and failing to pay her after a month, saying she was "on trial". The law says that pregnant women cannot be fired, but I had one case in which the woman was simply moved to a more difficult job, to force her out of her own free will. There are all kinds of ways of getting round the law without actually breaking it.'

Gravetz told a harrowing story of a girl employed by a hotel as a chambermaid who had been ordered to lift a heavy bed. She had damaged her spine and was one hundred per cent disabled as she was paralysed. The National Insurance Institute had at first not paid compensation, as the employers denied the accident had happened at work. After legal action, and medical evidence, the compensation was paid over. To get a medical certificate, incidentally, cost 500 shekels (over £100).

In many cases, as Zeitlin said, despite all the problems, immigrant women were better off without their husbands. On the same day that the television crews visited her, Zeitlin had tried to find alternative accommodation for 'Vera' who, since her arrival in Israel, has been systematically ill treated and even beaten by her husband who had also attacked their children. The Russians are getting a reputation for violence in Israel, but Zeitlin thinks a great deal of the violence is the result of the trauma of immigration and the inability of the husband to find work and feel himself the man he was before he arrived. Many men, in this predicament, she said, begin drinking and beating their wives.

This was confirmed by Ruth Reznick, the director of the shelter for battered women in Herzliya, near Tel Aviv. It is a small building surrounded by high walls, with an iron gate guarded by an intercom – a brave effort by a beleaguered organisation devoted to dealing with a problem Israel, clinging to the stereotype of the protective Jewish family, would like to pretend does not exist.

Reznick strikes one as being a large woman. Perhaps she has to appear so to face down angry men besieging her office, but she is not actually tall. A woman in vigorous and handsome middle age, she has been the pioneer in this field of women's right's for many years.

'It began ten years ago, in 1982. I had a phone call from a welfare officer about a woman from the Caucasus with three children. She was divorced, but the man had reappeared and torn her home to pieces. She stayed in the shelter for a full year, with the children. It was no good her moving, because he found her each time. Once he broke all her front teeth, and that was the state in which she arrived; she didn't care in the least about her appearance, all she wanted was protection. She was an exceptional case, in that we found her a sponsor to replace all her household equipment, to the value of £750, and she got help from the housing ministry to find a flat in Afula [a provincial town in the central part of Israel]. We thought the problem was solved. She started working, the children were in school. But then the probation officer in charge of the family found out where she was living, and supported the husband's right to see the children. So he followed her there, and smashed up her flat again. She came back to the shelter with the children, changed her name, and got an injunction forbidding the husband to go near her.'

This turned out to be only the first of Reznick's many cases involving women from the former Soviet Union. Some reached the headlines, like a recent case of murder in Beersheba in which a young man from one of the Asiatic republics waylaid a girl who had turned him down and murdered her and her entire family. A woman had recently come to the shelter from Uzbekhistan, twenty-five years old, with three children, the smallest of whom was five. She had been married at fifteen, and had been beaten regularly from the outset of the marriage. When they arrived in Israel, the family lived in Haifa. Neighbours, Bukharan Jews, explained that she did not have to put up with this, that she had rights, that she could complain. In the end, however, she went back to her husband.

But the problem of battered women was not just that of the women from the Eastern Soviet Union. Only the causes were different. 'With the Asians, beating their wives is a part of the culture. The girls marry at fourteen or fifteen, and the boy's mother teaches the wife how to look after her son, and children. The only purpose of women in most of those societies is to serve men.' In such families, said Reznick, there was complicity between mother and son faced with a passive or helpless wife. The plight of such women has been intensified with their arrival in Israel.

'The problem is,' said Reznick, 'that in Israel the police usually identify with the man in the family. It's a violent society and one in which men try to dominate.' What Reznick did not say, but was understood, is that the rank and file of the police force are Israelis of North African and Middle East origin, whose social norms are similar to those of the Russians from the Asian republics.

The situation with women from European Russia was quite different; there, a husband who abused his wife could be sent to Siberia for five years. Public order was much more important than the family values of Muslim-dominated society in the eastern republics. Violence and drunkenness were severely punished, and so to some extent the women were protected. But on the other hand, this extreme reaction boomeranged. Women did not dare to go to the police to protest in Russia, as the result would be the loss – temporarily at least – of the father of the family and main breadwinner. Violence against women, in European Russia, was not part of the local culture but the result, usually, of alcoholism.

'At least, that was the excuse,' says Reznick angrily. 'Men come to the shelter and say "I didn't know what I was doing, I was so

146

drunk." Some of them just slap the women around. Ninety-nine per cent of the women don't want to go to the police. They're afraid for the children, for their livelihood. But legally, in Israel, all that happens, if a man knocks his wife about, is that he is remanded in custody for a fortnight.

'The Russian women who come to the shelter are in a state of terror, abused by their husbands, and alone in a strange place. From the very beginning of the mass immigration we had women coming to us as soon as they found out we were here. Some of them spoke English, with others I had to manage with sign language.

'We don't have enough social workers in Israel to handle the typhoon of problems in the Russian immigration. Three times as many at least are necessary. We're swamped. They don't know the laws, they don't know the language. There weren't any shelters in Russia. We put stickers up everywhere, but the information isn't always available. Many women just think they have to put up with violent husbands.'

The numbers of battered women in the two countries, it emerged, weren't very different: twenty to thirty per cent of all women in Israel get beaten at some time, according to Reznick, and twenty-five per cent of women in the USSR. 'The syndrome is the same. It starts with verbal violence, develops into a kind of psychological terror, with the men controlling the family income and thus the whole family, and then comes physical violence. The first slap in the face is like the first kiss. It doesn't stop there. Many women have told me that they think it is a sign of passion, that all men are violent. They blame themselves.'

The Jewish marriage laws are especially problematic where battered women are concerned. 'The rabbinical courts disapprove of beating: if the couple are Jewish, it is recognised as a reason for divorce. But the rabbis always try to patch things up for a while, as long as the violence is minimal. However, no woman need live with a man who beats her, and the rabbis don't explain this. The main problem is that the immigrants don't understand the option of appeal to the civil courts. The rabbis fix the sum of alimony as low as possible, say £2,000 a month, where a civil court would award a woman £5,000. The idea is to prevent divorce by keeping the woman dependent. When the women are on their own, with children, they can't afford the rents in Israel. The government ought to step in and freeze rents for families who have social problems.'

If Israeli and immigrant Russians both suffer from beating, the worst violence is among the Russians. To drive her point home, Reznick looked for the latest statistics. In 1992, she had eighteen battered Russian women in the shelter. Nine out of seventeen murders of women that year had been carried out by Russians, all in the family and by husbands or male partners.

Dr Ina Palin, a gentle, softly spoken woman, a paediatrician from Leningrad who works in the Herzliya shelter, sighed as she opened the handwritten register in which she had noted all the cases which had passed through her hands recently. Between March and October, in just one year, she had received 328 phone calls. The shelter published ads in the newspapers, on Russian television and on the Russian radio programme. There was a serious problem of outreach, as advertising in the newspapers was expensive.

Palin had been two years in Israel. Although she had practised medicine for twelve years, she had as yet no licence to work in Israel, which would take further training and two examinations. Meanwhile, she worked part time, four hours a day, at the shelter. Palin, like all Russians, contended that in the big cities in Russia, in Jewish families, there had rarely been any violence. Alcoholism, widespread in non-Jewish families, was unusual for Jews.

Tatiana, from Bat Yam, who was divorced and lived with her mother and a boy of seven, had suffered sexual harassment from her landlord, who had threatened to kill her. She had gone to the police, who arrested him. But she was afraid he would return, and kept in touch with Palin. A probation officer was in charge of the case. Maria, a religious woman, aged forty, was regularly beaten by her husband. She had been ten months in Israel. The social welfare people had referred her to Reznick's shelter where she had spent a month. Fathers who beat their wives, said Palin, still wanted to see their children. The visits had to be arranged through the police.

Yelena, a Russian non-Jewess married to a Jew, with a son of thirteen by a previous marriage and two sons by this one, was being beaten; so was the thirteen-year-old. Both husband and wife were employed at a florist's shop, and her husband had attacked her there too. He was not drinking. The employer had fired the husband and phoned the social worker, who had been unable to help. Nor had the police. The wife was desperate and had threatened suicide. Eventually the courts had issued an injunction forbidding the husband to approach the wife.

The hot line which Palin operated was anonymous, but many immigrants had no money even for the phone calls. Tatiana, a year in Israel, had arrived at the shelter with a child of three. The husband was an alcoholic and sometimes on drugs. He had beaten her though she was pregnant. She had given birth, but had no milk, and had no money to buy powdered milk. She had spent eight months in the shelter.

Palin had never encountered such cases, she said, in St Petersburg. Only the non-Jews, she was convinced, beat their wives in Russia.

'New girls recently arrived from Russia!'

An entire column of advertisements in Tuesday's edition of Israel's largest mass circulation evening paper, *Yediot Aharonot*, is devoted to the notorious 'massage parlours' of Tel Aviv, most of them in the HaYarkon and Ben Yehuda streets' red-light district. Russian girls were most in demand.

In the winter of 1992–93 the Ministry of the Interior deported some eighty Russian prostitutes back to Russia, claiming that they had entered the country illegally. *Maariv*, the second evening paper, carried a two-page illustrated spread at the end of 1992 under the heading 'The War on the Russian Flesh Market', giving the number of Russian prostitutes currently working in the 'massage parlours' on an organised basis as about 300, a figure confirmed to me by a working prostitute in Tel Aviv. *Vestiye*, the Russian newspaper, gave details of gang warfare and murder against the background of the Russian underworld and the import of and trade in Russian prostitutes to Israel. 'Jerusalem', a supplement distributed with the evening weekend papers, ran an article in September 1992 about two Russian teenagers 'Vicki and Tali', high-school students who worked for an eighteen-year-old Russian friend and pimp, 'Grisha', who all spoke freely to the paper's correspondent about their after-school 'work'. 'All we want is pocket money and a bit of love,' they told the journalist, claiming that they 'enjoyed their work'. Dr Itzhak Kadman, the director of the Israel Association for the Child, commented that these were not exceptional cases, but 'difficult problems of social deviation of immigrant children from the Soviet Union', which should not be allowed to tarnish the image of the entire current wave of immigration. The solution, to his mind, was a greater effort to 'absorb' the children, both educationally and socially. He too attributed the phenomenon to poverty and overcrowding at home.

No social problem has preoccupied the Russians so obsessively as the incidence of prostitution among the new immigrants – whether professionally organised or 'amateur'. Educationists complain that immigrant prostitution has been inflated by the Israeli press to absurd dimensions, or that it is very largely the creation of the sensation-thirsty 'Western style' press. Russian-born psychologists and sociologists, particularly those who have been in Israel twenty years or more, see teenage prostitution as the result of the permissive atmosphere of Israel operating on young people previously subject to excessive restraints. Julia Mirsky, a leading psychologist, says: 'They see freedom as licence and don't recognise that there are any boundaries.'

Like Dr Palin, who argued that in Russia Jews did not beat their wives, immigrants contend that teenage prostitution did not exist in Russia. But Israeli research reports maintain that casual sex was common, that Russian youth did not see that sex involved any emotional commitment, and that even prostitution was not socially condemned. Psychologists link this with the lack of sex education in the Soviet Union and overcrowded living conditions, though this seems a partial explanation, at best.

Lena Gravetz of the Women's Network put the stigma of pros-titution first on the list of the ordeals of the immigrant women. Gravetz did not deny that there was a problem: immigrant women were occasionally driven to prostitution by poverty. She said that there were indeed many promiscuous girls who were charging for sex but she saw this as part of the economic prob-lems of the immigrants. In one Jerusalem suburb she knew that there were a number of brothels in immigrant apartments. But this was quite a different question to that of the organised prostitution racket in Tel Aviv, with the import of professional non-Jewish prostitutes from Russia. Because of the existence of what she termed an 'epidemic' of teenage prostitution, there was a problem with Russian rape victims, she said, as their stories were often not believed.

Talking to Russian prostitutes in Tel Aviv about organised crime in the winter of 1992 was like trying to interview the prisoners of Alcatraz. Most are incarcerated by their pimps. The Tel Aviv prostitutes were not only angry; they were clearly terrorised, and the accounts in the Russian-language press made it clear why.

There were two sensational murders in Tel Aviv in the autumn and winter of 1992 and all those involved were Russians. In September, Ludmila Uziganova was killed in Kazachov restaurant in Ben Yehuda Street. Vlatislav Ilychayev was accused of premeditated murder. On the night of 3/4 December in the same street, near the Russian restaurant Kalinka, Yevgeni Moldvinov, alias Yevgeni Dan, a twenty-eight-year-old new immigrant from the former Soviet Union and only seven months in Israel, was stabbed to death. Witnesses from the restaurant said Dan was murdered in a fight between the heads of two 'massage parlours'. The murderers had escaped in an Audi.

According to the Russian language press, during his brief stay in the country, Dan had acquired ninety-nine per cent of the shares in Top Man, a firm importing Russian prostitutes. But, he had complained, a colleague had forged his signature and stolen his money. Beaten badly not long before his death, he had been told this was his last warning. He might have been threatened by those immigrant 'investors' whose money he had lost, and it was said that he was more scared of his fellow countrymen than of the Israeli police.

'Anna', a Russian prostitute who worked independently, who was understandably terrified that she might be murdered in her turn, was prepared to talk on condition that no detail would betray her identity. Her story matched, in every respect, those details which have emerged since the murders.

A blonde girl in jeans and with no make-up, not in her 'work clothes', she was suspicious, aggressive and nervy. She confirmed indignantly that 300 Russian girls were being kept prisoner in brothels and terrorised. Most girls, she said, were professionals

151

trying to make a few thousand dollars. They arrived 'with protectors' who dominate them. Some had been smuggled in as immigrants with the pimps pretending to be their husbands. Once in Tel Aviv, they became virtual slaves, frightened of going to the police for fear of deportation, bullied by violent men who managed the brothels.

'Anna' worked alone, did not want a 'protector' and worked out of her own home. This was unusual as most Israeli prostitutes prefer to keep their clients out of their homes, both for safety's sake and because of the clement climate of Tel Aviv at night. She said that those who worked with pimps or in brothels were robbed of most of their earnings. She personally had seen girls who had been locked up taken out on to a beach road near Tel Aviv (the favourite haunt of prostitutes at night) and that they had a man on either side who did not leave them alone for a moment save when they were alone in the car with a client.

From her experience on the streets, said Anna, she had seen it was true that many Russian married women from the Galilee came to Tel Aviv to earn some money from prostitution and then went home in the evening, pretending to have been on a shopping expedition. Their clients included Arabs from conservative village society and orthodox Jewish youths who are not allowed any sexual life until they marry.

The existence of a few hundred Russian prostitutes, many of them imported for a limited time from the ex-Soviet Union, on the Tel Aviv streets, says nothing about the mass of immigrant women. The incidence of teenage prostitution, whose dimensions are unknown, is more significant and may be linked with the complex attitudes to sex among the young Russian women, a curious blend of public prudery and private licentiousness which perhaps has no equivalent in the West – and certainly not in Israel.

Natasha, a young woman who emigrated on her own, described in these terms her sex life and that of her friends, back in St Petersburg:

'However romantic you are, there's a huge gap between what you dream of and what you actually experience. In places like Leningrad, where housing was scarce, the whole family lived in one room so your first idea of sex was your father and mother grappling under the blankets when the lights were turned off. When you grew up, there was nowhere you could really go to be alone with your boyfriend, if you lived in the city. Maybe in the countryside it was easier, but how many Jews lived in the country?

'In the towns you couldn't have sex in the open, in a park or somewhere, you'd be arrested. And where could you go otherwise? There was no real courtship. So for most kids it was the top landing of the big apartment blocks. It's dirty, it's squalid, but that was the only place that was really safe, near the roof. If you came back late at night, when you came in on to the stairwell you'd hear cries and groaning.

'Of course, if you had enough money, you could go to a hotel in some other town where no one knew you. But that was expensive, and we didn't have money to spare. So it was the top landing.

'About money; you were really dependent on your parents for handouts till you started working, and any girl likes to have some little thing of her own apart from clothes, some little trinket, or a new handbag, those new jeans when they started coming in. Where could you get the money? Lots of girls I knew had sex with older men who bought them things they wanted, it wasn't such a big deal. It wasn't prostitution, it wasn't regular, it just happened. No one made a fuss about a girl having sex in her teens. But if you got pregnant, that was another matter, then it was a public disgrace, it was shocking, there'd be an uproar. Plenty of girls got pregnant, because we didn't have sex education in schools, we got all our information from other girls, and we were pretty ignorant on the whole. The men usually left the precautions to the girls, and it was better that way, because the Russian condoms were dreadful; I had a friend who worked in a tyre factory and he said that they made the condoms out of what was left over from the tyres.

'We didn't know anything about the pill, except that it was dangerous. The pills they sold in the Soviet Union wouldn't have been allowed in the West, too powerful chemically, and everyone said they gave you cancer. Some married women had IUDs fitted, but there were no checkups so sometimes they stayed in for years and caused bleeding.

'So it was abortion. No problem getting one, in and out in a few hours – no anaesthetic – and the only catch was that if you were working, you had to have a doctor's certificate to explain the reason for absence from work; they'd write 'abortion', and the whole thing was public knowledge.'

Natasha, from a family which included both western and eastern Russian members, said that in the Asiatic republics, 'oriental' harassment of women, and open approaches coexisted with a conventional pattern of early marriage and sexual secrecy. To accept an invitation to a drink in Bukhara or Georgia meant that the woman accepted that sex would follow. This wasn't so in Western Russia, where comradeship and friendship of young people was established early in life, at schools, and in the youth movements. But that didn't make the transition to an adult sex life any easier.

Hardly any Russian immigrant families have more than two children. One child is usual, especially in the one-parent families. Most women have had several, possibly as many as eight or nine, abortions. In Israel, however, the girls are gradually learning about efficient contraception. Yet ironically, in Israel too there is a wide gap between official attitudes and actual practice. Except for the religious orthodox, sex life begins in adolescence, and there are sex education lessons at school. There is no Pro-Life lobby as in the United States. On the other hand, abortion in hospitals is hard to get. Women, and although parental consent is not required, girls, have to receive the sanction of committees including two doctors, a social worker and a psychologist. The law was tightened up in 1977, when economic hardship was no longer recognised as a reason for a married woman to ask for an abortion. There is no official Family Planning service in Israel. All this is because of the political power of orthodox Jewry – about fifteen per cent of the population. The official policy of the government (influenced no doubt by the religious parties) is to encourage population growth and to make it difficult for married women to get legal abortions. But girls under seventeen and women over forty can have abortions, as can an unmarried woman. Pregnancies dangerous to the mother or occurring in a mentally disturbed woman can also be terminated.

Shilo, a privately funded birth control organisation, has scored at least one victory over the ostrich policy of the authorities. The Ministry of Education has agreed to Shilo's proposals of a counselling service, given the high rate of abortions in Israel (an estimated 16,000 legal abortions a year and probably another 2–3,000 more illegally).

Some socio-medical committees are rigid, others liberal, depending on the part of the country. Policy depended on the hospitals involved, many of which do not like performing abortions. The law cannot be forced on the hospitals. Jerusalem, the religious centre of the country, only has two committees, though it is the largest city in Israel with half a million people.

A pamphlet in Russian distributed in all the absorption centres, labour exchanges and other places where immigrants gather points out that it is difficult to get a legal abortion in Israel, and that an illegal abortion is extremely expensive (certainly for an immigrant). The pamphlets are distributed by Shilo, which is supported by various funds set up by Western Jewry. Its director, Joanna Zak-Pakes, comes from America.

The office of Shilo is hard to locate, and would be particularly so for a desperate immigrant. It is situated at a main crossroads in downtown commercial West Jerusalem, in an old building, but the signs outside advertise only law offices and a design firm. In the hall, too, there was no indication of a birth control centre, and the only sign was on the actual office door. Even this did not actually say what the organisation was – its name, Shilo, tells nothing. 'Each time we put a sign up outside,' said Zak-Pakes, 'it's either defaced or removed, so we stopped bothering. It was costing too much money.' The office is not far from the orthodox quarter of Jerusalem.

Shilo has functioned in Jerusalem since 1976, and Zak-Pakes has headed it since 1984. It is an educational programme, which sends trained representatives to secondary and vocational schools. Sex education lessons in schools diffuse basic information but do not give practical advice and help. Shilo reaches young people mainly through ads in *Ma'ariv LeNoar* (a paper put out for adolescents by one of the main mass-circulation evening papers). The most important aspect of Shilo's success, thought Zak-Pakes, was having got Russian girls to abandon abortion as a means of birth control and use the pill. She now has a separate, all-Russian clinic serving 200 women, and is writing a training programme specially for the Russians. Zak-Pakes feels 'she has something to sell'. Altogether about 2,500 women and girls from the former Soviet Union have passed through the clinic.

The girls who arrive at Shilo come from all socio-economic groups, she said. There is a special department for immigrant girls. 'The Russian girls definitely want to learn the methods of birth control, most of which were new to them. I think about fifty per cent of immigrant girls apply for contraceptive advice. They can now see that abortion, especially repeated abortion, can do damage, though there was no alternative in the USSR.'

But most of Shilo's clients are in their twenties and thirties, many married women. They are contacted in the *ulpanim*, in hotels, on the campuses and in workshops. Shilo goes out to look for them and a major part of the budget is spent on outreach pro-grammes. Shilo has a Russian-speaking paid staff, and thirty-five volunteers, many of them social workers.

'It's difficult to talk to the young people still living with their parents about the emotional side of their sex life, but if it is kept clinical and physical they can communicate. They have a big problem with their parents, they just can't talk to them about it at all.'

Soviet-born parents, say the psychologists, who controlled their children in Russia by holding the purse strings, often lose their authority over children in Israel, especially between the ages of fourteen and sixteen. The current permissiveness over sex cer-tainly began in Russia, but has become intensified in Israel.

'Once a girl goes on the pill,' said Zak-Pakes, 'it's clear that there is some relationship going on, so she and her parents start talking about her future sex life. But this brings in emotional fac-tors which the girl does not want to discuss with her mother, whom she sees as belonging completely to the past.

'Russian and Israeli young people have a completely different attitude to responsibility for contraception. Israeli boys know about condoms, and Israeli (or imported) condoms are of good quality. Russian men think contraception is entirely the woman's responsibility, and the women agree that it is 'their job'. Israeli men and boys are more likely attend the clinic than the Russians;

it is rare even for Russian husbands to accompany their wives to the clinic.

'Their view of sex was totally different, on the one hand permissive, on the other far more puritanical and secretive. It is very difficult to talk to Russians about their sex lives, and for them it is unthinkable to discuss sex as openly as we do.' Russian men rarely harassed women in other groups, and even in cases of rape, it was Russians and Russian women who were involved. However, Israeli men often harass Russian women, as they do any strangers, or newcomers – particularly blondes.

'The young women are picking up new contraceptive habits very fast. They realise the effectiveness of the pill. They also realise the importance of follow up, and come back for check-ups. The Israelis don't. However, for the Russians, a regular appearance at the birth control clinic, for adolescents, is an acknowledgement of regular sexual activity; so where parents and children are very close, tensions arise.'

'The problem for Israelis,' says Joanna Zak-Pakes, 'is not to impose our own cultural patterns and fears on the immigrants too fast. We shouldn't judge them; we haven't enough knowledge of their background.'

CHAPTER NINE

A Raw Youth

'The most difficult thing for me was language. When I began, I didn't know a word of Hebrew. I still can't understand why, if I want to be an electronic engineer, I have to learn so much bible!'

Vadim Gechtman is an only child. He is also remarkably successful, well integrated into the comprehensive school in Jerusalem where he is studying, has many Israeli as well as Russian friends, and is fortunate in having two parents at home, both of whom are working. His mother is a mathematics teacher, his father works as an electrician.

Fifteen years old, Vadim lives with his parents in one of the older blocks in an area of town which middle-class Israelis no longer patronise; like many of the Russians, the Gechtmans have brought their dog with them, and he makes the living room seem smaller.

The Gechtmans have been two years in Israel. Vadim wants to do well in his school-leaving exams, to be taken in three years time. His Hebrew is now fluent. He looks rather delicate and sensitive, with the shadow of a new moustache on his upper lip, but the conversation reveals a steely determination to succeed. It was not altogether a surprise to learn that he had a black belt in judo, which had immediately earned him the respect of his classmates.

'The toughest subjects for me are bible, Hebrew language, and English. The scientific subjects are no problem.' Vadim's difficulties with languages was typical; his success is far less so. Russian adolescents arriving in Israel in their mid teens face such formidable obstacles to passing their school-leaving examinations with marks high enough to enter university that numbers of them have been sent back to Russia by their families to take their examinations in Russia and then re-emigrate. Those who stay on at school in Israel have had to learn not only two new languages (only the best schools in the big cities of Russia taught English efficiently) but two new alphabets. Bible studies, a compulsory subject for high school students in their final examinations, take up only three hours of the weekly curriculum at Vadim's age, but involve more work at home for the Russians. Biblical Hebrew (not a different language, as with classical and modern Greek, but possessed of a totally archaic style and vocabulary) was, Vadim said, terribly difficult, and there was so much of it! He liked the historical portions of the bible, when he felt he was learning something about Jewish history, but not the legalistic part; the textual criticism learned at high school he thought belonged rightly to university studies.

Had there not been parts of the Soviet curriculum he regarded as irrelevant? Oh yes, said Vadim: 'Communism and Marxist theory included in history lessons was often boring and incomprehensible and yet it was compulsory.' He thought there were ideological reasons, too, behind the inclusion of so much bible in the curriculum.

It is not easy being an adolescent Russian in an Israeli comprehensive; Vadim was one of half a dozen Russians in a class of forty. 'At first I had trouble with a group of very hostile North Africans in a parallel class. They lay in wait for me outside the school and attacked me. In Russia we fought one against one, not twenty against one like here.' A friend of his had his face scarred by a boy wielding a stick with nails. Vadim's mother proudly intervened to say that although he looks so slender and delicate, Vadim was more than able to defend himself; his judo skills had been useful, and won the admiration of the girls.

Vadim had no free time to speak of, as he was studying so hard. The school provided six hours a week remedial lessons, and there were also Russian teachers there, who helped. His mother had begun work in an Israeli school without a word of Hebrew, teaching maths in Russian to sixteen–seventeen-year-old immigrants who had school-leaving exams coming up. Now, still at work, she is doing a retraining course in order to get tenure. She, too, complains about the compulsory bible classes and was annoyed that one of the questions she was asked during a class test was : 'Why do the Israelis dislike the Russian immigrants so much?'

Vadim had made his own way, asking little of his parents. He has his own personal computer which he bought himself, and, unlike most Israeli boys of his age, works his way through all his school holidays – most recently in a flower-packing factory at the nearby Youth Farm. In one month, working from 6a.m. to 2p.m. he earned nearly £225 – a lot for a Russian immigrant. With this, he paid for extra remedial lessons, and for his computer.

Vadim would join up, of course, but was not enthusiastic about army service. He was intensely critical of the Israeli system of recruitment. 'Mobilising kids at eighteen is all wrong, because there should not be a break in education, it should continue until the completion of your studies. It's difficult, I think, to get back into the habit of studying after the army.'

Israeli adolescents never voice such criticisms, and in Israel, once a norm is established it is rarely changed. When the current Director-General of the Ministry of Education once suggested postponing army service, he was accused of élitism. In fact, there is already a small élite (dentists, some doctors and others) who join what is called the 'academic reserve' and are able to study before army service on condition that they serve, using their skills, afterwards, for slightly longer. Vadim said that he had been told, like other immigrants who had been five years or less in the country, that when he reached army age, if he got high marks (over eighty per cent) in his school-leaving examinations, he would be able to go straight on to university, and then serve in the army as an electronics engineer. This of course motivates him to work far harder than he otherwise would have done. He said he thought the army would profit by extending this system further.

'Seventy per cent of the kids in my class agree with this system,' he said confidently. 'I'm quite prepared to serve a longer term in the army if I can work in my own profession. So are they, wherever they come from.'

Who, then, was most highly motivated to go into the army immediately on leaving school? 'The weaker students,' he said with no hesitation. 'The kids who do badly want to prove themselves in the army by becoming fighters. Either you have it up

161

here (pointing to his head) or you have it down there (pointing to his arm). The second sort like the idea of the army best.'

Vadim is, by Israeli sociologists' standards, an almost ideal immigrant adolescent. But few young Israelis would voice such statements openly. It is accepted in Israel that all boys are burning to go into the army, and that combat units are the finest: 'the best to the airforce' (in itself very élitist, as only those who get high marks at school get into this crack force), or to combat units like 'Golani' where the training is particularly tough. Anyone in a clerical job, or in a maintenance unit, is defined as a 'plug' or a 'screw' and despised, openly or secretly. Very few young people can be indifferent to these social pressures. Vadim's scorn of those who 'had it down there' was very unusual.

Maria Sokolinsky is the daughter of a single parent, a chemical engineer working at the Technion in Haifa; she is a student at the same institution, having, fortunately for her, finished high school just before emigrating.

Maria studies computer sciences, and won entrance to the Technion (which is highly competitive) via psychometric tests, and an examination in mathematics. Though she now speaks Hebrew, some of the textbooks she uses are in Russian.

Maria left Russia with her mother two and a half years ago. She did not remember experiencing anti-semitism at school in Russia. She still kept up contacts with her school friends, and a little while ago visited Leningrad and met her friends there. In this respect, the Russian immigrants are somewhere between the immigrants from the West, who come and go freely, and the mass immigration of previous generations, from Eastern Europe or North Africa, who were fleeing persecution and could not go back. As young people, in particular, miss their schoolfriends, this mobility is important for the Russians. To earn her passage, Maria had worked for a telecommunications firm.

Maria is a blonde, shy, delicate-looking girl. 'I have no Israeli friends at all at the Technion. The Israelis are always busy; they live away from their families and only go home at weekends or on holiday. They're all army veterans, and not interested in anyone who has not shared in that experience. It is much easier to be befriended by an English or Canadian student than an Israeli. So I have French, Russian and Swedish friends.'

'I wanted to serve in the army at first, but they told me that I'd come too late.' Did she think she would eventually make Israeli, sabra friends? Maria said wistfully that she hoped so. But there was a large Russian immigrant community in Haifa, and it was much easier to stay inside it.

The Russians would not campaign, or protest, she thought, against social norms which made life difficult for them, because they wanted to show one another that they belonged to Israeli society. Families kept together, however, because of economic problems. Russian kids could not afford, like Israeli students, to rent flats on their own. The parents helped the children, and there was usually a grandmother or grandfather at home too. Old age homes for what Israelis call 'the Golden Age' were distinctly unpopular with the Russians. 'Such places, in Russia, were terrible,' Maria said with a shudder. Grandma would stay with them, at home.

So at exactly that time of life when most adolescents start to break away from their parents, Vadim and Maria are far more attached to their families, in the physical and perhaps also the emotional sense, than their Israeli counterparts.

Vadim himself had no leisure time to speak of. But he thought it was much better to try to attract immigrant kids to activities like computers, sports, pop and rock music ('anything but classical music' he said with a grin), in which they were interested, than to give them Zionist lectures or even educational trips round the country; all this smacked of their previous indoctrination and compulsory leisure time activities under Communism.

All over the country, youth leaders are trying to organise Russian youth, to 'integrate' them, to get them to join youth movements, and are racking their brains to try to find something that will bring these rather withdrawn, overworked young people into the boisterous world of the Israeli adolescent. Most of these activities now centre on community centres – a relatively new development in Israel, and one which is most involved with new immigrants.

Varda Eitan, the young immigration coordinator at Pisgat Ze'ev, one of the new housing developments in east Jerusalem, is a former schoolteacher who acts as a kind of informal labour adviser, social worker and information centre. There are between

163

1,500 and 1,600 Russian families in Pisgat Ze'ev, one of the largest of the new suburbs built like a wall around Jerusalem after 1967. Eighty Russian families have already bought homes here, and many of the others are in the process of paying off long-term, subsidised mortgages on their apartments. The immigrants make up twenty per cent of the local population, double that of a year earlier. The word had gone round the Russian grapevine that this was a good place to live.

As in all Russian groups, there was a high rate of unemployment, but many had managed to find work in the local industrial centre of Atarot, where there are factories which pay £350 a month. Immigrants over fifty-five, who normally would find it difficult to get work in the city, have an advantage in being nearer to this source of labour, and former engineers have found work, making chocolate matzoth and textiles.

Pisgat Ze'ev is reached by one of the new ring roads which allows Jews to skirt the Arab areas of east Jerusalem. It is perched on the very edge of the Judaean desert and the standard of building, compared with that of government housing in previous years, is extremely high. The apartments are spacious, in elegant blocks, the roads wide, and there are shopping arcades and gardens; but as in most of these suburbs, there is no place of entertainment, no restaurant or cinema. After work or school hours, the streets are deserted, and the place looks like a vast dormitory.

For those who have cars, central Jerusalem with its many amenities is a twenty-minute drive away; the others stay home, unless they want to go to a lecture, or a study group, at the local community centre, which is the nearest thing to a social meeting place which the suburb can provide. As in the other ring suburbs, only the community centre is alive at night. Its activities are serious enough to attract the most earnest Russians. The centre provides, apart from the usual Hebrew classes, remedial classes in English, history and bible, for children who are finding these subjects hard at school, given by volunteers, and there are also courses in Jewish education. In the Soviet Union, enrichment courses of this kind were for children; here, it is the adults who attend.

Hundreds of adolescents live in Pisgat Ze'ev, members of the group between twelve and eighteen – an age all psychologists say is the most difficult immigrant age of all. These are kids who very often were high achievers in the USSR, now suddenly 'disadvantaged' because of problems with the language and the Israeli curriculum, and who find it difficult, unlike primary school children, to form friendships with Israeli children. In a suburb like Pisgat Ze'ev, moreover, with no real amenities, cooped up at home with parents and usually grandparents as well, adolescents often drift into the town centre and, sometimes, become delinquents.

Varda Eitan said that the community centre had organised exploratory trips round the country – projects together with the cadet corps, the Gadna, and sometimes with the local scout movement. All had been notably discouraging. On the trips the Russians had clung together and sometimes come to blows with the Israelis. The cadet corps reminded them of the loathed Komsomol Communist youth movements; the other Israeli youth movements, which in any case attracted far fewer young sabras than they had done thirty or forty years ago, were equally unappealing. The Russian kids did not want to be organised, directed, told what to do. The youth instructors were at their wits' end.

There were six schools in Pisgat Ze'ev, said Varda Eitan, but not a single psychologist working there who spoke Russian. There had also been cuts in extra school hours for the immigrants, who needed remedial help desperately. Social workers too had been laid off. There was no ambulance system working in the suburb, no local health centre, and no financial assistance with bus tickets, though the suburb was so far from the centre of town. The dental clinic functioned only six months in the year.

Both Varda and Haggai Atiya, the local youth instructor, had cogitated on how to draw the immigrant kids into the social life of the suburb.

Summer camps had not attracted many Russians. Teachers complained that the parents did not take an active interest in the schools, and did not attend parent-teacher meetings, a regular feature of Israeli school life. But when children came for remedial lessons, they were almost inevitably accompanied by their parents. The kind of child-parent dependence the Israelis were witnessing was alien to the child-orientated, permissive Israeli society, where children come home early from school only to rush out again to play in the street or in local playgrounds with friends.

Atiya, an eager, worried-looking young man, was very disturbed by the self segregation of the Russian young people. 'The problem is whether the two groups should really be kept separate or not. We started out determined to integrate them, but perhaps it's better to organise them on their own. The Russian kids always say they are "busy" when we approach them. They have to study harder, some of them work after school hours, it's difficult.

'So what we thought was that instead of just trying to recruit them for courses or youth movements, maybe we ought to set up clubs for activities they could choose on their own. On questionnaires they said they were interested in motorcycles and archaeology.'

At the first meeting of the club, about ten youngsters turned up, between the ages of twelve and fifteen, many of the girls accompanied by their mothers. They were all rather hesitant and timid, reluctant to take the biscuits and soft drinks which had been provided.

Haggai asked about their hobbies and what sort of clubs they would like to join. Most wanted singing, music and religious classes (three of the boys already were wearing skullcaps). Haggai explained painstakingly that attendance in these clubs was not compulsory, that it was up to them. The atmosphere warmed up a little and one boy suggested computer classes, another, guitar sessions. Most of the boys repeated that they had no time for such frivolous activities; the only youth movement that had found recruits, among the children who had become religious, was B'nei Akiva, the orthodox youth movement.

The Israeli youth leaders Haggai had invited tried to explain that these activities – trips, youth movements and so on – were something which was a part of Israeli society, that if the immigrants wanted to feel that they belonged, they should come along. The more courageous Russian kids said no; 'friends' should be made on a basis of individual choice, not in groups. Not even sport interested them.

At the other end of the country, in the Jewish-Arab city of Acre, another youth leader, Moshe Hovav is also struggling to create a club for Russian youth, culled from the 8,000 immigrants living in the city.

Hovav is an Arabist by profession, one of those dedicated public workers who is fascinated by the challenge of the new immigrants; he, like Gelbart, wants to start a job workshop in the nearby, far more sedate town of Nahariya. 'We've got Ethiopians and Russians. Many of the Ethiopians have distinguished military records from their old country and volunteer for combat units in the army.' The Russians were harder to integrate.

The community centre caters for Moroccans and seventy Ethiopian youngsters. Hovav was hoping to eventually get some of them to help with the new Russian immigrants, but the mix was a difficult one. Meanwhile, he had managed to get a Russian group together – forty kids, aged fifteen to eighteen. Like all the Israeli youth instructors, he found that persuading them to do things for themselves was difficult. The most popular event of the week was the club's disco, to which young people flocked every Saturday night. The other activities were formidably serious.

A very pretty, extremely prim Russian girl called Vicki, quite clearly the 'group leader', complained to Hovav that there were too many Russians in the 'club' who came to the centre only to dance. She thought this was uncultured of them. Hovav, rather diffidently, asked if she would like to try and get more Israelis to join. No, she said, it was better to keep the club for Russians, as it was going so well. They didn't want undesirable elements.

The group was varied. All the boys looked as if they had come straight from a demo in Red Square; they wore jeans and leather jackets, while the girls teetered in on high heels, wearing the kind of make-up worn in the West in the 1950s – very red lipstick, mascara, and even a spot of rouge on the cheekbones which gave their very young and innocent faces a hard look. One fair-haired boy sported a punk hairstyle and a leather jacket with *Wehrmacht* on the sleeve. Most of them had probably come to the club to get away from crowded apartments and worried parents, but they certainly could not go far astray with the immigrant teacher brought specially from Haifa, Marina Blumberg, who quizzed them earnestly on whether man was created in the image of God, and if so, how. First she read a poem whose symbolism, the young people recognised, had to do with belief in God and rejection of

167

secular ideologies. Most of them, as might be expected of adolescents in their free time faced with such cosmic matters, were
clearly bored – whispering, giggling and kidding. But Vicki, a
schoolmarm, or Komsomol leader, to the tip of her elegant nose,
frowned and called for silence and respect for the teacher; in a
Pavlovian way, it worked.

When they did talk, what they said was not very different from
the criticism often voiced by their parents' generation. Israel was
an 'oriental' country with dirty streets and rude behaviour.
People did not know how to drive, overtook on the roads, tail-
gated. They were hurt by the image of Russian immigrants, particularly the women, in the papers. Why were all the Russian
women thought to be sexually loose, or actually prostitutes? Only
one boy present was clearly Israeli, and popular, as he kept the
Russians giggling. 'I spent two years in Austria, I like people from
other places,' he said, 'and the behaviour there was much better
than here.' Everyone slapped him on the back.

The blond young man in the *Wehrmacht* leather jacket was
called Yigal Chernchenko (not a Jewish name) and came from
Vitebsk. He was a driver in the army and he was pleased that this
left him enough time for his real interest, which was painting. His
idol was Salvador Dali, whose work he had spotted in a Russian
gallery. He knew of no more recent Western painter.

Why was it necessary to have a separate club for Russians? The
mood became more serious. Because the Israeli kids were more
childish, they said, had easier lives, they hadn't grown up with
problems. The sabras were more self confident. The Russian
youngsters spoke sadly of how they had hoped to have come to
their own country, but they were made to feel like strangers. All
of them were wrestling with what they saw as the 'religious' content of the school curriculum. Coming from a totally atheistic
school system, from homes where there was no bible, they hadn't
made the connection between history, literature and bible study
which non-observant Israeli children accept naturally. On the
other hand, they complained that the maths was too easy, that
they were learning all over again what they had already mastered
in Russia.

Vicki summed up: 'Do you know,' she said, 'our teacher won't
let us write the *real* date on the blackboard, just the *Hebrew* date.

But no one uses that in everyday life.' The double calendar familiar to Jews in every Jewish community in the world, for as long as they attend synagogues, or observe festivals, a calendar whose dates are recorded only on birth, marriage and death certificates, or marking the anniversary of parents' deaths, and used in Israeli schools, is the reminder of a separate history. To the Russians it is something totally artificial; the suspicion of ideology, of indoctrination, had made these young people hyper conscious of anomalies even in the most innocent folk traditions of their own people.

'They have real problems showing emotion. They're far too controlled, compared with my own girls. When Grisha can't get a passage on the cello right, he doesn't yell or carry on, but he goes outside and breaks a bamboo stick to pieces. Quietly.'

'Vicki doesn't really know what to do with fantasy. If she sees UFOs on Russian TV she believes it. She looked at a picture of Anubis, the Egyptian god with the head of a wolf and the body of the man, and she told me she thought he really did exist. How could his picture be in a book if it wasn't true?

'When I took them to the Martha Graham ballet, they complained there was no story. Everything has to be realistic. Or idealised . . .'

Marilyn, the foster mother of Grisha and Vicki, is a forthright and sophisticated American woman in her early forties, divorced with two little girls of her own; she has cared for Grisha, now sixteen, and his younger sister Victoria, now eleven, since their mother died. In Israel twenty-seven years, and often involved in volunteer work, Marilyn is concerned with the Russians; (her own family, five or six generations back, came from the Pale of Settlement). Moreover, as she lives in a spacious house (most Israelis live in flats just big enough for their own family) and has a generous nature – together with a salty sense of humour – she did what few Israelis would do, which was to take a series of lonely young Russians into her own home and cope with all their problems. 'Thank heavens', she said with a laugh, 'taking on Grisha and Victoria for an indefinite time means that social workers have finally stopped foisting unhappy loners on me. I was getting a reputation.'

Marilyn's involvement with the young Russians began a couple of years ago. She is one of the mothers at a school belonging to the American Reform Judaism movement which, from the outset, has been at the forefront of work for the immigrants. 'The parents' committee has always been involved in social issues. At first we tried to get more children from disadvantaged homes, most of them North Africans of course, into the school, without patronising them, but trying to get the parents involved. When the Russians started coming, we canvassed them at the absorption centres. The parents want some kind of teaching of Judaism, but not the orthodox kind, so we were hopeful. Of course we went about it the wrong way. The Western way is to find a reason to celebrate, get hold of people's phone numbers, and send out printed invitations. Well, that didn't work, of course, they have no idea of this kind of thing, they keep to themselves. Then we had the idea of getting them all together for Chanuka [the Jewish celebration of the Maccabean victory, with candles lit every evening for a week] and having a torchlight procession. They were a bit baffled. I mean, in Russia when you move into a new flat the neighbours don't come out and say "Welcome to the new complex, here's a cake."

'So we thought the separate approach would be better. Lots of Israelis have "adopted" families. We got the names of people at an absorption centre and set out to find a family that needed a sponsor. Quite a job. One family had twenty-two sponsors already.

'I decided that I wanted a single Russian student as an *au pair*. Not that they know what an *au pair* is, but still. So I took on Sveta.' Marilyn brushed her dark fringe away from her forehead and sighed again. 'Oh, Sveta.'

'Sveta had come from Russia all on her own. She had a boyfriend who was an actor, he didn't want to come, so she came by herself. I think she was waiting for him to propose, but no go, so she left. Her job was designing tunnels, she was from that railway institute where so many of them studied.

'Anyway, the moment she got here, at the airport, in the middle of the night, a girl on her own, they told her your name is Liora now, that's Svetlana in Hebrew. Took away her identity. They sent her to the religious girls' boarding school, Bet Ya'akov. She didn't put up with that for long, and she ran away, in the direction of the nearest university, which was the Hebrew University at Scopus. Just walked in. You see, her mother had died when she was sixteen, and her father had looked after everything – sick mother, a nephew or cousin who acted as a brother. Father had a full-time job as a chemical engineer but he cooked and cleaned and did the lot – Sveta was spoiled rotten. He'd told her: go to university! So that was what she did, literally.

'She walked in and enrolled for the foundation course. No Hebrew, nothing; she put herself down for an *ulpan*. Then she found two American girls and agreed to share with them. She paid several months' rent in advance from her "absorption basket".' It was incredibly expensive, the most expensive part of Jerusalem, but what did she know? She'd no idea of the value of money. She didn't think about food, or fees, or anything. The American girls had a great time, there were beer cans all over the living room.

'I met Sveta through the supervisor at the university, an acquaintance of mine. Warned me off her. She thought she was a con-woman, because she stopped turning up for classes. She'd enrolled for Jewish history, with no background, and no Hebrew. The Hebrew classes were much too advanced for her, and the maths course was far beyond her. The supervisor wanted to send her to a kibbutz. Sveta was petrified; thought it was some kind of punishment camp.

'The first thing to do was to save her from that flat before all her money went down the drain. The landlord made a fuss. I sorted it out. Took her out of the foundation course and sent her to learn Hebrew. *Ulpan* starts early, though, and she had this problem getting up. In Russia, it seems, you had to get up early to stand in line – queues for bread, queues for shoes, anything. So here she didn't want to get up. I had the same problem when I took on the children. Finally Vicki got up to watch breakfast television.'

'Sveta stayed with me eight months. She had this problem with a mother image. She needed parenting, mothering. Not much of an *au pair*, she didn't know how to relate to children, and the girls lost interest in her. You know what's the sign of a Russian in the house? A coffee cup with a spoon in it. They think it's a good conductor of heat. And they never wash it up. Like they don't clean the loo. I told them, look, your excreta is yours, right, you take care of it, there's a brush. But in their communal apartments the loo down the corridor was just the place you went into holding your nose and got out of as soon as possible. No one was responsible for keeping it clean.

'Then there was Sasha.' Marilyn sighed again. 'Friends in the Foreign Ministry sent me Sasha. Look, the thing to do is *not* to come Wednesday or Thursday. They pay for three nights in a hotel, but everything is closed Saturday, and then you're on your own. Nowhere to stay. Sunday is decision day.

'Sasha had nowhere to go, nothing. Twenty-one years old. He threatened to demonstrate in the city centre. Sasha was odd man out. Gay, I'd say. Still not out of the closet, of course. *Are* there any gays in Russia? [Until recently repealed, a Soviet law enabled the courts to send homosexuals to jail for up to five years.] I'd never heard of it. His potential is going to flourish in Israel, that's sure. He stayed four months. He told me some of his problems, but he didn't really like talking to a woman. I got a clear picture of how the young live in Russia from Sveta and Sasha. Sasha's been through everything. One day he wears Pierre Cardin clothes and the next he's dressed as an American hippie. One day he gets religion and puts on a skullcap, and the next he's joined the Jewish Defence League.

'Manners. Yes, they've got formal manners, but it doesn't mean anything. They lie like mad. I have this thing with Grisha, he lies all the time to get out of trouble. You tell people what they want to hear, there's the mask of propriety and nothing underneath.

'I got Grisha and Vicki because a social worker rang me and said: there are these two children all alone in a flat, wandering around, the neighbours don't know what to do. Their mother, Natalya, was a piano teacher, arrived here in a state of advanced cancer. October 1991. She came because she thought they'd help her in an Israeli hospital. Riddled with it, but denying all the way, said it was these polyps she'd suffered from for years. She got chemotherapy here and had to stay in hospital. The kids had nowhere to go.

'Her ex-husband was a film director from the Ukraine, she'd

inherited an apartment from her parents, in Leningrad. There was no love, the way she told it, he wanted somewhere to live. They had these two kids, and then fought all the time. Divorced. But he wouldn't leave. Nowhere to go, he wasn't going to share a communal apartment with strangers. And she wouldn't throw him out, apparently. So there was this divorced couple, living together in conflict for *eleven years*. He knocked her about. The children talk about it all the time. She came to Israel to escape. And when she was dying, she was afraid all the time that he would come and take them back, that was an obsession with her.

'She needn't have worried. He came on a visit three months after she died. Said he wanted to do the right thing. I took the children down to the airport to meet him, and do you know what happened? For once, El Al was early, ahead of schedule. He got to the airport, he knew we were coming to meet him, but he went off with a friend who lived somewhere else. Didn't even wait to see his own children. He was here seven weeks and saw the children exactly seven times. Vicki, his daughter mind you, warned me about him. She said "don't leave things lying around or he'll take them."

'You know what his farewell to the kids was? They saw him on *television*. He appeared in an interview, must have known someone who got him on. Talked about the coup and the counter revolution and how he was there when it happened. Great hero. That was the last they saw of their father. He calls once a month from Russia, he has a fictitious marriage with some woman so that he can keep the flat. He told me that he publishes some kind of pornographic magazine, under the new dispensation. Pornography educates people, he said.

'Grisha is changing, slowly. He needs guidance. He can't stand all the Israeli permissiveness. Every moment, at the beginning, had to be controlled. He wanted to be told what to do, absolutely all the time, every second. I'd say look Grisha, you've got spare time, just go out and mooch around. That was terrible. He'd say, what do I do when I finish my homework? *Tell me what to do!* The teachers at school said he was a pathological liar. Written off at fifteen. They don't understand the background. With Vicki it's a different matter. She doesn't read. She's forgotten her Russian and doesn't yet know enough Hebrew to read, totally non-intellectual. And they're living in my house with kids who have a story read at bedtime every night. Something new for them. I was brought up in a house full of books, so are my kids.

'They could never make up their own minds about anything. Even standing in line was delegated. They got sent out. The Russian kids think the Israeli kids are more childish, but they're not more adult themselves. They're just more streetwise.

'I got the impression that there was no real relationship towards children in Russia. But there was a hierarchy, a terrific hierarchy in the family. Authority. Grisha was appalled when I said I was sorry one day. I wasn't supposed to say that, *I'm* the authority. I told him I made a mistake, so I'm sorry.

'They're sentimental about their Jewishness because they don't know much about it. I found Sasha crying his heart out at 4a.m. in the kitchen because he'd found a recording of the Andrews Sisters singing *Bei Mir Bist Du Scheine*. Kitsch, pure kitsch. The Andrews Sisters! The young activists in Russia sat round singing *My Yiddishe Mamma*.'

Vladimir is seventeen, and comes from an excellent family; no divorce, everyone working. In Russia he worked, had friends, was a paragon of all the virtues. But he could not cope with the past, or as psychologists say, 'internalise' it. He thought he could continue to be successful, a good mixer, and failed; the gap between expectations and reality was too great. He could not manage to call the teacher by her first name; when he did not understand the content of lessons, he would not ask, show he didn't understand. He could neither accept the lack of discipline nor the fact that he himself was not part of the crowd. He went to extremes, and to curry favour, became the clown of the class, making jokes frantically all the time. The jokes were mostly in Russian, and won him the support of other kids, so he had a ready audience in the special classes arranged for immigrants.

Vladimir broke down when he was sixteen. Before school-leaving exams, he dropped out of school. At one time Vladimir was in the streets. Then he worked in a private business under good conditions, but his spare time went in playing the automatic machines. He disguised himself as an Israeli, with locally made clothes, earrings, and a punk haircut. He stopped learning Hebrew, and the army did not want him.

Anya had arrived in Israel aged fourteen. She left behind a serious boyfriend in Russia. For a time they corresponded, then the letters stopped. He survived the parting; she could not. Her parents were divorced and her mother had remarried. Anya, whose sexual life had started young, became promiscuous. She modelled her sex life on that of her mother, who did not stay with her second husband. She made no Israeli friends. Soon, she started drinking. She had become a lost girl at the age of fifteen who made men leave her by getting drunk all the time. But she glamorised herself and her freedom in order to escape reality.

Both Vladimir and Anya now take part in the group therapy sessions run by Irina Metelitsa, formerly a lecturer in psychology in the Pedagogical Institute in Minsk, and now a therapist employed in a downtown Jerusalem centre for what Israelis call 'marginal youth'. Vladimir is studying externally for his school-leaving exams. But he has, says Metelitsa, no sense of the future. Everything is in the past. Nevertheless, he intends to join the army and is trying to rebuild his life. His parents, said Metelitsa, did not even know that he was receiving treatment. Anya had made some progress, however, had started to write and to express herself. At the age of seventeen, she now wanted to marry. This would mean, of course, that she would not serve in the army.

Metelitsa works in a spacious office in an old building in the very centre of West Jerusalem, the 'triangle' where most of the older shops and the main pedestrian precinct are situated. This is still the real heart of Jerusalem, particularly since the *intifada*, and this is where everyone congregates: in the day shoppers, at night (as the more innocent activities like night clubs and pubs have mostly moved to a warehouse and garage area to the south) after the cinema goers (a dwindling public since videos and cable TV) go home, a meeting place for drug pushers and prostitutes; all too often, young immigrants on the loose get involved with them.

Metelitsa is a gentle, graceful young woman with a charming smile. No one could look less like the matron at a school of correction or a psychiatric institute, to which 'wayward' youth were consigned in the Soviet Union. By profession an academic

175

psychologist, in the Soviet Union she would not have worked with problem youth. Her present job carries nothing like academic status. She has 200 registered clients, sixteen of whom are pupils in an Eyn Karem boarding school for problem children.

In Soviet Russia there had been no psychological therapy of young people in trouble – only psychiatric treatment. In Israel, when adolescents play truant, take drugs, or go wrong in other ways short of actual criminal activity, they are given help. In the Soviet Union, young 'trouble makers' were sent straight to psychiatrists – if not to the police.

In Israel, said Metelitsa, the family, society and culture were supposed to provide the kids with examples of normative behaviour; in the Soviet Union, education and discipline were synonymous. If a teacher had a problematic pupil, it was primarily the teacher's job to cope. The teacher would visit the pupil's home to warn the parents. In Israel, parents are summoned to the school if the children misbehave, but the teachers have very little authority.

In Israel, there is a 'parents' committee' in every class, which is extremely articulate and voluble. Teachers know they are under scrutiny. Parents may also, on occasion, be involved in questions regarding textbooks, the cost of various courses for the children, and even the way the curriculum is taught.

The question of parents' involvement was not uniform in the Soviet Union, Metelitsa said. In some schools, for instance in Moscow or another big Russian city, there were parents' committees. But these dealt with things like the maintenance of the classroom, graduation parties, and presents for the teacher, who enjoyed absolute authority and commanded respect, not only from the pupils but also from their parents.

Parents, said Metelitsa, handed over the child to the school at the age of six or seven and, thenceforth, the school took over education in all senses. There were excellent extra-curricular facilities to keep the children busy – possibly because their parents were both likely to work long hours. There were clubs for drama, sport, and music. All these were didactic and educational, and the fees were minimal. But there had been only one psycho-analytical clinic, in her time, in all Russia. It was, she said, connected to a school which specialised in experimental education.

But when problems in the family affected children, there were no social workers or psychologists to help. (Like accountants or brokers, those who form a screen between administrative or industrial powers and the public, social workers, who have the same kind of role, had no place. People who worked in the social services, dealing with cripples, pensions, children in boarding schools – state officials, highly specialised – were representatives of authority, not trusted to *help* the individual. Having a criminal file, or a file in a corrective institution, was something which could follow young people for their whole life. Boarding schools of this type have practically disappeared in the West. But young Russian emigrants find it difficult to believe that any kind of institution exists to help them, for their good, and not to punish them.

In Israel there is a psychologist, a 'counsellor' in each school – sometimes more than one. Such people, who are trusted by Israeli parents, are feared by the Russians. They are seen as representatives of authority, instruments of punishment. Parents would never seek 'help' from authority, because it was dangerous.

This did not mean that Western psychology had not penetrated the Soviet Union. Freud's theories had been known since 1924. Gestalt psychology, Metelitsa said, and Rogers, had been accepted but not necessarily implemented. Where children were concerned, Williams and Piaget were the latest authorities.

In the Soviet Union, Metelitsa said, young people with mental problems, or handicaps which became obvious at school, were often neglected. They were simply kept for three years in the same class, left alone to fend for themselves, given a fail mark. Children with dyslexia, dysgraphia, hyperactivity or other learning problems were only diagnosed and treated in the large cities. More often they were criticised as 'lazy'. Again, because the institutions to which such children were confined were often primitive, merely grouping such children together without treatment, parents did all they could to hide or deny any learning problem, in case the children became stigmatised for life.

To have a 'neurological', organic problem, was less of a stigma than to have a psychiatric problem. In such cases, medication was suggested. But it was more difficult to be referred to a neurologist than to a psychiatrist.

Jewish families worried more about their children's education than other Russians, and so tried to conceal their deficiencies even harder. But they were no better informed about psychological problems. They pressured their children more, but also spoiled them more: a bad combination. With the advent of perestroika, said Metelitsa, a fashion had evolved for psychological clinics. These were not expensive, but they had as yet little experience.

'One girl said to me: "In Moscow, I lived; here I merely exist." That was what many feel. The young people who come to me for help badly need to improve their self image; they need prestige. They will not be satisfied with anything less than a university education. They are worried about their future, and suffer from nostalgia for Russia. The result of the migration for young people like this is despair, and apathy. Those who had been outstanding students are in more trouble, as the fall is further. The talented suffer most.'

The punitive system in the Soviet Union had not been entirely negative, however, Metelitsa insisted. Despite the dislike of the totalitarian regime, despite a latent contempt for politics, young people had clear criteria for behaviour, which was reassuring psychologically. Even fear could be productive. Metelista was treating a girl who went on to drugs, in Russia, at the age of thirteen. But she was prevented, by fear of punishment, from becoming an addict, and stayed on soft drugs; hashish and marijuana. In Russia, drug addicts were sent to a psychiatric ward and forcibly weaned. Here, with drug clinics and help available, the girl had run wild.

'Prostitution in Russia was illegal and could be punished by imprisonment. Here it is legal – only pimps can be prosecuted. Moreover, here you can get drugs immediately in exchange for sexual services, so it is far more difficult to check addiction. Even stealing is punished less severely, thus more tempting. In Israel a juvenile offender is out of jail in forty-eight hours. Even a fourteen-year-old, in Russia, was afraid to steal. There was no juvenile court, no probation service.'

Most Russian youths were out of school by sixteen plus. Metelitsa saw those who had finished school in Russia. In Israel they were put back to school again, usually into the ninth grade (of twelve Israeli school years). Most of these young people would

178

prefer not to go to school again. The Israeli school system was not geared to this age group at all.

But perhaps, in the long run, the greatest obstacle to assimilation into Israeli society, she said, was that the Russian youth did not want to go into the army – neither boys nor girls. They do not, said Metelitsa, feel that the state needs defending. They bring the image of the Russian army with them, one which was totally negative. It was the epitome of Soviet nationalism, of brutality, of the sacrifice of youth in Afghanistan, of militarism, of the waste of valuable years. In order to serve on the Lebanese border, moreover, or in the occupied territories, the Russian recruits must feel an allegiance to the state of Israel which they have not yet acquired.

'These youngsters do not feel that they belong and prefer to opt out of military service, and the army lets them do so fairly willingly. There is a glut of manpower just now, resulting from the baby boom of the years following the Six Days War; the army does not want the trouble of possibly recalcitrant Russians. Thus the Russian youth is excluded from the one genuinely egalitarian (and not very militaristic) organisation which exists in Israel, and they will not carry the Reserves Duty booklet which entitles them, as demobbed soldiers, to many social privileges.'

The one factor, Metelitsa insisted, that made the difference between success or failure in assimilating to Israel, if you were young, was the family, which had to understand the crisis the young person was going through and help him or her. That was hard if the parents themselves were in trouble.

Experts maintain that fifty-seven to eighty per cent of such adolescents were leaving Israel already. What was needed was more parent participation at school, and for Israeli kids to 'adopt' the newcomers. The volunteers should be organised into one group. As for the army, it is claimed, if it continues to reject ill-adjusted immigrants under 'Clause 21' [psychologically unfit] those who don't serve will be finished for good in Israeli society.

CHAPTER TEN

Notes from Underground

Anyone visiting Israel today would be justified in thinking that Russian, not Arabic, is the country's second language. In the local supermarket most basic foodstuffs carried Cyrillic lettering, with an explanation of ingredients, from 1989. The arrival of half a million new consumers, all of them without possessions, but with government grants in their pockets, meant that hardware and electric shops swiftly followed suit. On television, during the Gulf War, instructions about gas masks and protective equipment for babies were translated into Russian, and mindful that the new arrivals were going to account for two crucial Knesset seats, all the election broadcasts had Russian subtitles. The main commercial banks spent hundreds of thousands of dollars advertising for Russian customers in their own language.

The Russians soon started providing their own information services, some with government help, some by finding Israeli backers. A radio programme, *Reka* – 'Background', broadcasts round the clock and the state television has a Russian service. Those linked up to cable television can get news from the motherland straight from Moscow. On the newsstands there are three serious Russian dailies, a dozen or so weeklies, and a few heavyweight literary journals. One of the dailies is the Israeli trade-union backed *Nasha Strana*, founded in the 1970s; at the other extreme is a lively magazine on arts and fashions, *Portrait*. Scenting profits, the mass circulation Israeli evening paper *Ma'ariv* launched a new paper, *Vremya*, but made the mistake of underpaying the Russian journalists. The second mistake was not renewing their formal contract. By this time, the Russians had contacted the competition, and when *Ma'ariv*'s rival, *Yediot*, set up yet another paper, *Vestiye*, offering higher salaries and job security, *Vremya*'s brightest talents defected en masse.

Forum has set up advisory bureaux and cultural centres where visiting actors, singers and celebrities from Russia, can collect hard currency, a mere four hours' flight from Moscow, and perform before a large and appreciative Russian public. Russians of all ages will trudge out to the remotest hall or community centre to listen to lectures in their own language; small children will listen to talks on kabbala and grandparents to instructions on contraception.

The Russian intellectual élite meets regularly in the larger cities to discuss contemporary trends in Russian literature, and Russian writers and poets have established an exile salon, headed by the critic and essayist Maya Kaganskaya, with distinguished figures like the poet Mikhael Gendelev. Within a few years, they have established a lively Russian sub culture which has only the most tenuous relationship to Israeli political and cultural controversies; many of these people define themselves as exiles and have only a nodding acquaintance with the Hebrew language.

Nothing like this has been seen in Israel since the arrival of the German intellectuals in the 1930s, who were notably slow to speak Hebrew and convinced of the superiority of their own culture. But the Germans were outcasts from their own country; by comparison, those Russians who can afford it revisit post-Soviet Russia, where they are welcome often under the new regime. The documentary film maker Leonid Kelbert, struggling unhappily to find his way through the monopolist maze of Israeli state television, found that his films condemning Soviet anti-semitism were not only shown at Russian film festivals, but reached an audience of millions on television there.

The Russian press provides information on world and Israeli news, with advertisements for every service, from cheap housing to singles clubs, English lessons, and advice, for a fee, on applications to Germany for compensation for Holocaust victims. Horoscopes, until recently forbidden in the Soviet Union, are prominent, as they are now in Russia, where ESP centres, group therapy and mystic cults have burst into flower. Lonely hearts columns, which existed only in the newspapers in the Baltic republics, list the needs of solitary Russians: 'Music teacher, broad minded [referring to a broad educational background and not to sexual permissiveness], from a good family, very feminine, slightly handicapped in her legs, seeks gentleman' etc. A delivery service is advertised for sending presents to relations in Russia: items most in demand are coffee, tea, chocolate, and even flowers.

Many features describe the plight of unemployed Russians struggling with Israeli red tape. Prominence was given to a new Russian commission set up to restore citizenship to those emigrants who had lost it automatically when leaving the country. *Portrait* ran a description of 'Divorce Israeli Style', the ordeal of a secular Russian couple at the rabbinate. The rabbis having asked for four witnesses who knew the couple well, they roped in chance acquaintances who couldn't even remember their names, and one, attesting to the Judaism of the wife, insisted 'Of course she's a good Jew, she observes the Sabbath every single day of the week.'

More seriously, in a recent number of the daily *Vestiye*, a lawyer called Anatoly Victorov wrote an article under the title: 'Immigration is not needed'. Victorov argued that Israel had exhausted both its economic and moral potential for absorption. Neither the right nor the left wing in politics were really interested in the immigrants, and were tired of the problems they presented. This was the time of crisis for the Zionist ideal. Israel was well established. The union of all Jews was a formal, impractical ideal, possible only on paper. A quota should be introduced now, wrote Victorov, for immigrants, to enable Israel to extract more funds for their settlement from the United States.

Maya Kaganskaya is uncrowned queen of the Russo–Israeli literati, who gather regularly to listen to poetry readings – such as a recent one by Mikhael Gendelev – and discussions among writers who continue to write in Russian.

Gendelev, the most celebrated of the Russian Israeli poets, is translated occasionally into Hebrew but most educated Israelis know nothing of his work. He has been in Israel thirteen years, representative of the entire sub-culture of the Russian Jewish intelligentsia which has grown up in Israel quite apart from the Hebrew literary world. He has described himself as writing 'in a vacuum'.

The Russians have formed what is in essence an exile salon, and it is difficult not to see, in this, an imitation, conscious or unconscious, of the great exile (external or internal) figures of modern Russian literature, from Tsvetaeva and Mandelstam through Solzhenitsyn to Brodsky. However, unlike these giant figures, they have not been recognised by the outside world and Israel does not welcome them. It is too young a culture to accept 'exile writers'.

All educated Russian immigrants, from the adolescents onward, will claim that what remains of their cultural luggage is Russian literature, by which they mean essentially the great novels of the nineteenth century and the poetry of the early twentieth century – much of it written by Jews. This is their cultural heritage, one that Jews have detached from their Russian background – since they no longer identify themselves, if they ever did, with the Russian people – and have carried with them to their new country. Inevitably, those who write in Russian must look back on, draw on, that tradition. This is particularly true if they continue to write in Russian.

But the comparison many Israelis make between the German and Russian adherence to their mother tongue is misleading. Although a very few established German writers (Else Lasker Scheuler and Arnold Zweig are the best known) continued to write in German, and only those who came as children (like Yehuda Amichai) were able to write in Hebrew, the political circumstances made it impossible for them to maintain links with the country whose language they loved. The Russians in Israel today, on the contrary, did not leave primarily because of anti-semitism, were not persecuted like the German Jews, can revisit Russia, and can find intellectual stimulus in the new writing appearing in Russia today. To that extent their exile status is a pose.

Kaganskaya lives in a basement flat in an outlying suburb of southern Jerusalem. Her consciousness of belonging to an élite triumphs over her recent rejection by the Israeli literary world after a political controversy; she gives the impression of a grande dame living in reduced circumstances. Later, when she makes her entry, suitably late, at a literary evening, in a gallery which earlier that day has hosted an international poetry conference at which the Israeli Russians were conspicuous by their absence, her eyes shine as she is greeted with deference by her compatriots.

Kaganskaya comes from Kiev, the third generation of Jews in that city. Her ancestors were Hasidim, pietists and mystics. Beyond that, like most intellectual Russian Jews, she knows little of her Jewish background. Her grandfather, fighting in the Red Army, was killed by White Russian forces in the battles following the Revolution at the age of twenty-four.

The young Kaganskaya studied Russian philology and spent four years in Moscow and Leningrad writing on music and the theatre. She was uninvolved in politics, but waited two years to receive her exit visa, arriving in Israel in 1976. There she swiftly realised that Israelis and Russian Jews did not understand one another despite – or perhaps because of – their common origins.

'The Israeli establishment thought that the Russian immigrants were going to be the heirs to the Second Aliya [those Zionists with a revolutionary background in Russia who arrived in Palestine after 1905]. They didn't accept that we were not the children of the *shtetl* and that we were no longer socialists.

'The Russian Jews who came in the 1970s are still on the margins of Israeli society. And we are all classed together, which is a mistake. The Israelis think of all the Soviet Jews as belonging to one people. But we who came from European Russia didn't know anything about the Georgian or Bukharan Jews; we were in shock. They belong to a different culture altogether, they know nothing of Russian culture. We Jews from Western Russia are Europeans.

'The new immigrants from Russia have fled the new national-ism, but here they find no security, there is no earth under their feet. Some of them feel that Israel is their homeland. Others are alienated, so they fall back on Russian culture, work out a sym-biosis between Russians here and the Russian mainland. There must be some sort of continuity.'

Kaganskaya kept stressing how exciting the new intellectual life in post-Soviet Russia was becoming. But she was also enthusias-tic about the intellectual currents of the West which she was now experiencing for the first time. What she did not seem to realise was that the writers she found so exciting – Foucault, Levi-Strauss, and the ideas of 'post modernism', were now the subject of debate and controversy in the West and that the glitter of these 'new' ideas had of late tarnished.

Israel, which had only recently picked up some of these ideas, she termed 'provincial'. It was in Russia that deconstruction was being eagerly adopted. 'The novel is finished. Russian writers are discovering prose, the new philosophy. Many young people want to return to Russia where intellectual life is more exciting. Here everything is politicised, even culture. The writers here are all left wing. But culture should be independent, a value of its own. Jews hung on to their culture even in Auschwitz.'

She reacted promptly to the suggestion that the only really Jewish culture was religious tradition, and that this was a problem for a secular society; for instance there was no anthropological analysis of the Talmud. Kaganskaya seized on this eagerly: 'Exactly: why do I have to learn about Jewish mysticism from Borges? In post modernism it's the importance of reinterpreting the early texts that matters, but who is interested in that in Israel? Instead, we have realistic novels. But Amoz Oz isn't Tolstoy.'

'My theatre will be now the Theatre of Exodus. I will write about the drama of emigration to "another planet", about people without roots,' said Semon Zelodnikow, one of Soviet Russia's better-known playwrights, three years in Israel. He acknowledged that he was taking a risk, but he felt that Israel was a good place for a dramatist, a place with so many conflicts, religious, social, all focussed in one place. In the 'evening of his life', said this youthful-looking forty-five-year-old, he would write about expulsion, about 2,000 years of Jewry, of the need of a man to understand himself and his place in history.

Everything Zelodnikow was saying was somehow at odds with his plays; naturalistic comedies about ordinary Russians leading ordinary lives, in which there is no reference whatever to politics; he said that in Russia he was called a 'Western' playwright because his plays have no message and were neither Soviet nor anti-Soviet. Their first interest, for a Western audience, would be the characterisation of the sexes – the women are almost invariably strong and wily, the men hesitant, awkward, essentially spoiled and weak – and the portrayal of the drabness of Soviet city life, of lost and alienated people on their own. The translation of one of his most popular Russian plays, *A Man Comes to a Woman* is being produced by the Israeli National Theatre, Habima.

Zelodnikow was born immediately after the war's end in Europe. The awareness of anti-semitism is deep in his consciousness, and, perhaps, the strains of a lifetime of defensiveness. Zelodnikow's Ukrainian parents spoke Yiddish; when, as a child, he asked them what they were speaking they told him: 'Uzhbek'. As a young man, he wrote poetry, and his first play was produced when he was thirty. He accosted a famous Jewish actor, Sergei Yusky, in the street, thrust his play into his hands, and had his talent recognised immediately. On several occasions negative reviews in the state press, which he thought were aimed against him as a Jew, led to the closure of a play. Eventually he decided, he said, that the only place for a Jew to live was Israel. Others in the Russian theatre world in Israel say that what he really wanted was to run his own show, to direct his own plays, without interference by any outside authority.

Whatever the reason, in 1990 Zelodnikow took a little group of actors, renamed them Noah's Ark, and drove across Eastern Europe to Germany, and thence to Israel. He says optimistically, that he thinks his profession can be practised anywhere, though he has no illusion that he could write in any language but Russian.

But can a playwright, taken away from the society he portrays so skilfully and amusingly, go on writing? Zelodnikow believes so, and a play he wrote partly in Russia and partly in Israel has also found a producer. *The Mutants* is a play in total contrast to those he wrote in Russia. While his 'Russian' plays are naturalistic, artful, and humorous, *The Mutants* staggers under the weight of symbolism, makes its points with sledgehammers, and in its use of sexual symbols, seems to be nudging a 'Western' audience into recognising his liberation from Soviet prudery.

Amazingly enough, given the problems of language, Russian directors, actors and even drama teachers and choreographers are making their mark in Israel very fast. This is history repeating itself with a vengeance. Habima, was originally, in the 1920s, a

187

troupe established entirely by Russian actors and directors, disciples of the famous Russian director Vakhtangov. For years, the chief Israeli actors, like the leading Israeli politicians from Ben Gurion downwards, all spoke Hebrew with heavy Russian accents. Even in the 1950s, many of the most famous actors and actresses, like Meskin, Finkel and Rovina, were Russians, and they left their mark on Israeli theatre. Their style of acting, to anyone coming from Europe, was very old fashioned, even melodramatic, with too many attitudes struck, eyes rolled, and dramatic points heavily underlined. On the other hand, they moved well on stage, they had a good grounding in classical theatre, and their voices were audible even in the cheapest seats.

As this generation died off, they were succeeded by young Israelis; new generations of Israeli playwrights emerged who wrote controversial and vigorous plays about political issues (as compared with the 'biblical' dramas and translations of Yiddish classics in the earliest Russo–Hebrew theatre). But most young actors looked uncomfortable in costume drama, delivered verse badly, and – more familiar with film than with theatre acting – were much happier with contemporary plays. The Russian tradition – which was the only theatrical tradition in Israel save for Yiddish theatre, which only the older generation understood or patronised – expired. Almost miraculously, it has now been revived by a new company of immigrants.

Despite intervention by politicians and bureaucrats, the Russian theatre, which, with its sound classical base, survived the Stalin era, over recent years has produced a number of brilliant directors, of whom only Lyubimov and Efros were well known in the West. The most exciting productions in Israel today are being given on alternate nights in Russian and in Hebrew by a company of actors who have barely been in Israel two years, who do not speak Hebrew offstage, and whose talent has already been recognised internationally, with performances scheduled in New York, Vienna and Avignon.

The *Gesher* (Bridge) theatre was formed by a group from Moscow's Mayakowsky Theatre, headed by their director, Yevgeny Arieh. *Gesher* began its career in Israel in April 1991 with a scintillating production of Stoppard's *Rosencrantz and*

188

Guildenstern are Dead – in Russian with a Hebrew translation provided over earphones for the Israeli audience.

The company continued with Bulgakov's *Molière*; but meanwhile, realising that if they continued to perform only for their fellow immigrants they would never attract Israeli audiences, they made the risky decision to perform in Hebrew. Their adaptation of Dostoevsky's *The Idiot*, in Hebrew, was immediately acclaimed by Israel's theatre critics and won the Margalit Theatre prize for the best production of 1992–93.

The acrobatic skill with which this company overcame a series of apparently impossible barriers to success augurs well for its future. Dostoevsky's lumbering masterpiece was alchemised, by Arieh and Katya Sasonsky, into a brilliant, fast-moving drama; their names did not appear on the programme, for the company's teamwork extends even to shared credit for the adaptation. The *Gesher* actors had never acted before in Hebrew, spoke Russian to one another, and were forced to speak Hebrew only to their public relations officer.

But after a bare two and a half weeks coaching by Mark Ivanir (an actor fluent in both languages) and Alona Minokovska, they were performing with scarcely an accent, having had every word and phrase made clear to them. After two months' rehearsals *The Idiot* was playing to packed houses: in Russian to the immigrants, in Hebrew to delighted local theatre goers, among them many who had reserved theatre-going for visits abroad.

Gesher began by rehearsing in a cellar obligingly lent them by Habima, and for nearly two years they had no premises of their own. The Tel Aviv municipality has now presented them with an old, crumbling theatre – the Nahmani – which is icy in winter and suffocating in summer. But the company now has its own home, recognition by Israeli audiences who pack every performance, and is already appearing at festivals abroad. Its newest production, to be performed in a circus tent, is an adaptation of the Israeli writer Yoram Kaniuk's novel *Adam Resurrected*. The old Russian founders of Habima must be jigging in their graves.

'Gorbachev was a passionate theatregoer, but no mere observer. He visited both rehearsals and performances, gave his opinions as to repertoire and acting, and his visits, sometimes planned but often unannounced, threw the bureaucrats who ran the local theatre, and the producers and actors, into a frenzy. One local director had a heart attack after a Gorbachev visit, and another was fined for inefficiency. When he arrived with his retinue, rehearsals had to stop for a dialogue with the party bosses. Command performances were given for Gorbachev and Raissa, who studied the actresses' deportment attentively. No one who watches Raissa in public can fail to see, keeping this in mind, that she models herself on the heroines of nineteenth-century Russian plays.' Her performance at Eyn Gedi suddenly became clearer.

Mikhael Luria, teacher at the Tel Aviv theatre school Bet Zvi, was for years producer at the Rostov state theatre, the centre of the Stavropol *krai* or Soviet region which was Gorbachev's power base before he became Party Secretary. Luria is a bearded, greying man in his fifties with a cloth cap tipped over his eyes and leather jacket slung over his shoulders, looking like a character in a Strindberg play. He spent years as a producer in the Baltic republics and Russia, and now he teaches in several Israeli schools. Like Zelodnikow, he refers to himself as 'ageing'.

Gorbachev's interest in the theatre was not exceptional. In every theatre in the Soviet Union, said Luria, there was an ideological commissar who was responsible for checking the repertoire. Only in the big cities were the classics popular. In the republics, they wanted easier entertainment but also sat through political dramas glorifying Communism. The level in most local theatres was so low, said Luria, that for sheer entertainment you'd have been better off going to get a drink. But whether in the provinces or the main theatres, theatres were heavily subsidised and tickets were distributed in schools and factories. So acting and directing was far from being the precarious living it is in the West.

Until well into the Brezhnev era, the repertoire was weighted heavily in favour of educational plays about Communist history. But, in Luria's experience in Tallinn and Tbilisi, from 1976 onwards, the repertoire became wider, including many foreign dramatists like Pirandello and even Françoise Sagan, as well as plays by controversial writers like Bulgakov, and by younger Soviet dramatists like Zelodnikow. From the 1980s, a new wave in Russian theatre produced plays which had little or no political content and were naturalistic portraits of life in the Soviet Union.

Nevertheless, he said, Tallinn was under Russian rule, and was a 'Russian ghetto' in the cultural sense. No play about Estonia which suggested that it had an independent history could be produced. As a student, Luria himself had been expelled from the theatre school in 1968 for 'faulty ideology'.

Once glasnost got under way, from 1985, Luria decided that he wanted to leave. His chance came when he visited Israel with an Estonian company which appeared at one of the Israel Festivals. Luria feared the consequences of perestroika, of a coming 'earthquake'. He had considered emigrating to the United States, as he had friends in Hollywood, but at the age of forty-five, he said, he felt it was too late to begin a career from scratch, and he realised that he would have more of a chance in a less competitive, smaller, more welcoming society. He came to Israel just before the attempted *putsch* against Gorbachev. He was now trying, he said, to instil some of the discipline of Russian theatre tradition into his Israeli students.

'What you can't do in real life, you can do on the stage,' said Binyamin (Venya) Smehov, one of Russia's best-known actors, to a local reporter. He was talking about working with Arab and Jewish actors together in Haifa, but his words could apply, too, to the success of Russian actors and producers in Israel, both with the Russian audiences who mobbed them and with the Israeli theatre-going public. Smehov, on a visit to Israel, has worked for years with the famous Taganka theatre in Moscow.

Like all those born into Communism, Smehov got some sense and pride from his Jewish past through his grandparents, with whom he spent his holidays as a child, and who he said were 'very theatrical'. He still has an interest in children's theatre (his own version of Ali Baba was produced as a record which sold three million copies, a play and a film in Russia). Smehov was now in Jerusalem directing what one sensed could be a marvellously paced production of Bulgakov's *Don Quixote* at the tiny Khan theatre in Jerusalem. At least, that was what he was trying to do, but the Israeli actors were having a hard time with his instructions (given through an interpreter) while Smehov and Marina Beldova, the Israeli Russian choreographer, had established a perfect rapport from the first moment. Beldova behaved to him with enormous deference, all the more striking because her own talent was so evident. The actors found Beldova's elegant demonstrations of stylised movements, in time with the music of Slava Ganelin, a Russian jazz composer, almost impossible to copy. After the seventh or eighth try they achieved a passable imitation.

Beldova is a single parent with two boys of school age. To be a young working mother in Russia, she said, had been difficult. The diapers available for babies were of such coarse cloth that they had to be washed by hand and ironed on both sides. There was no baby food, and everything had to be specially ground and prepared freshly. All her salary, as a graduate of the Moscow Theatre School, had gone on reliable child minders.

Beldova had fled Russia out of disillusionment with perestroika. Like so many Russian intellectuals and artists, she said quite frankly that the Brezhnev era had at least sketched exact boundaries, that standards were clearer. Gorbachev had promised the earth, but Russian tradition and the crippling Russian bureaucracy had triumphed over change. Many theatre people were seeking to get out, and most of them had wanted to go to the United States, but with the closure of that option in October 1991, they had come, as she had, to Israel.

Beldova's grandparents had been the 'Jewish' generation, still linked with that Yiddish culture which constituted, for the first Communist Jews, an ethnic identity. Her parents, however, born in the 1930s, and both engineers by profession, were brought up without any knowledge of Judaism, save, perhaps the Passover Seder, which celebrates the Exodus from Egypt. She herself had only encountered anti-semitism once, at school, when she had been called a Jew and kicked during a game. She had enjoyed, she said, a happy childhood in the Brezhnev period, received a good education. Her parents had been sceptical about the claims of Communism, as who had not, but accepted it passively. As an adult, however, her view had changed.

What she said about Russia also did much to explain the profusion of talent in the Russian theatre, the hunger for theatre, the preservation of tradition, which prevailed even during Communism, and which was never suppressed by the authorities. 'Life in Russia is grey, miserable. The whole place is in a state of dissolution. Perestroika doesn't offer hope, because Russian suffering always drives the people into the arms of a "strong leader". That is always the illusion.'

Beldova's pervasive sadness had good cause. Her parents had stayed behind, and now her father was gravely ill; she visited Russia as often as she could. She was not a Zionist, but she had become integrated very fast into Israeli theatre life, dashing from one theatre school to another, lending her talents to several different theatre groups, hopeful that her sons would become thorough Israelis. She separated from her husband, a journalist on a Russian paper, in Israel; he, she said sadly, was 'still living in Russia'.

In the 1970s, Israel's existing orchestras were enriched by the first Soviet immigrants, and many new ensembles were created. Leonty Wolf, formerly of the Novosibirsk opera house (capacity 2,000, between twenty and thirty operas in the repertoire in any one month) is in Israel head of the Idit choir in Haifa, and is also directing a production of *The Mikado* at the Beersheba Operetta, which is an amateur group funded by wealthy Israelis.

Wolf said he had been the director of the Novosibirsk opera for three years but his association with the house went back twenty years, starting at the age of fifteen as an extra in the chorus. His family came from Novosibirsk, but he had spent five years in the Urals. He was born in 1956, at the beginning of the Khruschev era, and studied at the conservatory. In every Jewish family he knew, he said, there was someone who had studied music.

Wolf is a fat young man, swarthy, bearded, and a former prodigy. By the age of nineteen, he said, he was the Novosibirsk Kappelmeister. Also, he said on occasion, the prompter. He had been assistant conductor at twenty-two and sang in the chorus for eight years – in a repertoire ranging from Tchaikovsky through Gilbert and Sullivan to Gershwin and Ravel. The repertoire of the average provincial opera house in the Soviet Union would strike terror into the heart of most Western musicians.

Wolf referred to the Novosibirsk opera as 'my opera house' but did not really give an explanation of why he had left at the peak of his career other than that 'he had always felt a Jew'. He said that at first, he had been enthusiastic about Gorbachev, but that his conscience troubled him. The revolution had disillusioned him; there were the same people, no new ideas. The administrative director and deputy director were Communists and they still remained in their posts. Wolf was not convinced that change was imminent and that he could influence policy in the opera house (also the home of ballet). This, rather than his Jewishness, appeared to be the reason for his emigration.

Both Alona Daniel and Maxim Leonidov are top of the pops in Israel. The Israelis like them, the Russian immigrants don't, though they like Western pop music and what they still call rock 'n' roll: in the eyes of neo-Communists and nationalists, a corrupting foreign influence. But singers like Leonidov are already old hat in Russia, the TV programme *Vzglyad* having presented satiric songs by 'heavy metal' groups as far back as 1987–88. Western rock stars like Pink Floyd and Bon Jovi were familiar. Conservative Russians, of course, see these as the ultimate in decadence.

Alona Daniel, who came to Israel seventeen years ago as a small child, has converted the subject of immigration into pure kitsch. Both singers trade on a certain nostalgia for Russia, and merge this with an 'exotic' colour in their lyrics, with explicit images of their past. Daniel's group is called 'Wolves' and Israeli television screened them recently on a return visit to Russia. In this film, made by a Russian documentary director immigrant, Daniel, a cropped-haired blonde with a well-developed resemblance to the American pop star Madonna, wearing an ankle-length mink coat, strolls through Moscow and St Petersburg against a background of snow-covered pine trees, jackbooted soldiers changing the guard at Lenin's tomb in the Red Square – the old Russian flag having replaced the familiar red flag with hammer and sickle.

It would be difficult to imagine anything in worse taste than this film, in particular Daniel's opulent presence against the background of beggars and gypsies in Moscow squares, or gazing from the windows of a train at the birch trees beside the tracks 'awake like a cat all night'. The obvious prosperity of the pop group compares blatantly, and perhaps deliberately, with the shots of the poor Russians left behind, treading on one another's threadbare heels in endless queues for their meagre provisions. 'We can begin to forget,' Daniel intones. Lucky her. To wear a full length mink when revisiting a country even more poverty stricken than it had been under Communist rule looks insensitive. It is perhaps stranger to revisit Kishinev, a town notorious in Jewish history for the pogrom of 1903, on a note of sentimental yearning. Daniel puts roses on her father's grave, and revisits her former home which the current tenants have filled with Christian relics and icons. Smiles are exchanged. The theme tune is 'Moscow Doesn't believe in Tears'.

Maxim Leonidov (known in Israel just as Maxim), is a much more recent immigrant, and arrived in Israel at the beginning of his career. Married to well-known actress Irina Selzniyova, Maxim's tunes and lyrics are much harsher and more compelling than those of Daniel. He, too, exploits his Russian background.

His first cassette, MAXIM, produced in 1992, obviously on too low a budget (one song is cropped from an Israeli Russian radio programme, and some of the tape is left empty) is labelled 'my first cassette in the new country'. Most Hebrew songs on the cassette are rock, and the theme of rock 'n' roll as the salvation of Russian youth, gives way to the weariness of the emigrant. '*I was born in Leningrad*', Leonidov shouts defiantly in one lyric, '*rock 'n' roll opens a door to me, it opens doors to everyone.*' But another song states '*Rock 'n' roll is dead, now it's a one-way street – I've burnt all my bridges, there's a dirty road before me.*' Other songs are wilfully 'Israeli', angrily macho, aggressive towards women, playing with the theme of sex, guns and violence. All this has a certain plausibility in the way it reflects the confusion of a Russian singer trying hard to hit the right key for a new audience. One song is pure propaganda – 'Only One Way' – a tear jerker about the Russian immigrants on their journey, with their cheap suitcases, and no money in their pockets, the women weeping, the men smoking, going into the unknown. '*They don't know what a cantor is, they don't know a muezzin, They don't know the Passover Haggadah, All they want is to be people.*'

'Anything but the classics,' Vadim had said. The little girls and boys going off to class with their violin or cello cases may be giving way to the boys with electric guitars, a more visible part of

Russian luggage today than the thousands of Volga uprights imported at the beginning. But the Russians in their thirties or over still cannot do without music, whether on a professional or an amateur basis.

On a cold night at the Association of Americans and Canadians in Israel, Jay Shir, a musicologist, voice teacher and bass baritone, rehearses an immigrant choir called *Zemer Oleh*, which means in Hebrew both Immigrant Song and A Song goes Up, an elegant play on words. The choir was first made up of immigrants from the West, a pleasant communal endeavour for people used to making music in their spare time. It became a largely Russian choir, providing perhaps the only moments of relief for immigrants going through a painful transition.

Shir is a genial, bearded man of Canadian origin in his early forties, a polymath who has published articles on literature in internationally renowned journals, studied singing with Hans Hotter, the German bass baritone, and is well known to music lovers in Israel, particularly for his master classes and his appearances on the concert platform as a *lieder* singer. The choir functions sporadically. Sometimes the singers join while still looking for work, and, when they find it, discover they have no time, or strength, to sing. One evening, at rehearsal, Shir says, he noticed how 'down' they all were, how lacking in energy. 'You've got to sing as if you were all princes and princesses,' he told them, and one answered: 'How can we, when we're all out of work?' But somehow they have sung at the Jerusalem Theatre, at hotels, at parties for visiting Jewish dignitaries from abroad, at receptions for volunteers. It doesn't matter. The main thing is to make music together.

Most of the immigrants, some professional musicians and others simply music lovers, arrive after a day's work. There are among the Russians several music teachers (one of whom has just had a baby and hands round photographs), the ex-first violinist in the Tashkent opera, a student at the conservatory; a mathematician and identical twin engineers from St Petersburg, slight young men who demonstrate impressive and similar bass voices.

Shir looks round urgently for the missing link in the choir and sighs with relief when a sole tenor finally appears. There are a few

Americans (North and South) but teacher and choir communicate in Hebrew – for some of the Russians the only chance they get to practise the language and, on this evening, to learn some Latin and Italian. The choir is rehearsing two works, *Salve Regina* by the young Schubert, and Verdi's *Laude Alla Vergine Maria*.

At first the sound is rather thin, polite. 'It's too Catholic,' Shir frets, 'Make it more Russian Orthodox.' That works. Many of these immigrants had recently visited the newly reopened Pravoslav churches in Russia to listen to the singing. But the cry of the penitents '*Gementes, et flentes*' doesn't come over, and Shir lapses into Yiddish: 'more *kishkes*' (guts). That works better.

Shir coaxes a pure, cohesive sound out of these weary-looking immigrants by the end of the evening. Everything is forgotten – rent, guarantors, work prospects, families left behind in Russia – in the sheer joy of making music.

'I came from a country which was a superpower – a country full of talented people – scientists, writers, poets, to a very small, provincial place. I had a sense of Jewish history which was a huge, unknown world, and I thought of Israel as a great achievement. In fact it is a very small country.'

Leonid Kelbert is a Russian film maker who, though of Western Russian origin, was born and brought up in Tashkent. He has three degrees from Tashkent University, in scientific subjects. Kelbert was destined, according to the Soviet system, for military research, because of his distinction in physics, but he did not want to go into this field – though recognising that it was Russia's achievements in military technology and science that made it into a superpower. When Kelbert speaks of Russia, it is always with both pride and loathing.

Kelbert's scientific training stood him in good stead when he later became a skilled film director, a graduate of the All Union Film Institute in Moscow specialising in popular scientific films, spreading knowledge to the masses. 'This was a field which was free of censorship, and I could use it for my own speculations about the history of science. The first film I made was about solar energy, the symbol of creativity in which I saw, too, how I could make my way out of the ideological system, from the inside.'

197

His decision to leave Russia was taken when he made a film about the great Russian Jewish physicist Lev Davidovich Landau, imprisoned in the late thirties for two years under the trumped-up charge of being a German spy.

This was in 1976. At first he was more attracted to the United States than to Israel. 'I knew America from the writers we could read – Hemingway, Salinger, and Faulkner influenced me most. We all idealised the United States; jazz music, for instance, gave us a feeling of freedom.'

At this time, Kelbert knew nothing about Jewish tradition. Even the Six Day War, when anti-Jewish propaganda in Russia made many Jews conscious of their allegiance to the Jewish state, had no effect on him. He says he is not a Zionist and identifies with Jews everywhere, not just in Israel. But when he was refused an exit visa, he began to meet other Jews in the same predicament, and step by step, became involved in studying Jewish history. He was, by now, thirty-five years old. 'Until then I had always been successful. I was the first Jew from Tashkent admitted to the Film Institute, and I was very successful in the Scientific Department of films.

'As a refusenik, I began to understand better what it was I wanted to express. My job became less important than a return to my heritage. I began to feel my place in the chain of Jewish history. It was certainly a matter of history, not of religion. Eisenstein said that the best way to study a subject was to teach it, so I started to teach Jewish history, from the basis of total ignorance. It was almost impossible to find books which could help me, but people brought books from abroad, and I found many hidden away by old people. In the Soviet Union, there were many underground libraries for Jewish books, both the current sort and rare old books. Many had disappeared from the public libraries.' It was such habits that impelled the Russian intellectuals in Jerusalem to create a Society of Bibliophiles, this time collecting Russian Jewish books in Israel, in January 1993. 'That is what is unique about this immigration, that it brought nothing at all but books. No money, no possessions, but hundreds of books.'

Kelbert's experience as a refusenik and Jewish educator led him to a new career as a director of amateur theatricals on 'forbidden'

Jewish topics – plays performed in private rooms, by no more than three people. He wrote and produced plays about the Purim story (Esther and Mordechai), and the far more controversial story of Masada, the mass Jewish suicide of the Zealots, the last resistance to Roman rule in Palestine. These plays were performed at the time when Israel was under constant attack by Soviet propaganda as aggressors in the Middle East conflict.

'The plays encouraged pride in Jewish underground existence. They were generally performed in darkness, by the light of a candle or with me holding a lamp so that the actors were seen in silhouette. Sometimes, by the end of the performance, my hands were blistered. When we played by candlelight, Yair, the last man to commit suicide, blew out the candle.'

It was when Kelbert was on his way to organise performances in Riga, Latvia, that he was arrested in the street. 'I was informed on. People had been threatened that their children would be taken away and put in orphanages if they did not give information.' Kelbert's wife was eight months pregnant and did not know where they had taken him that night, but on the next day, he was taken to court and sentenced to two weeks' imprisonment for 'hooliganism'. He was badly beaten by the KGB.

In 1987 Kelbert was given permission to leave for Israel. 'At first, I felt at home here. It was the oriental atmosphere – after all, my youth had been spent in Tashkent. I spoke no Hebrew so I had no way of understanding what was going on.' But before long Kelbert began to face difficulties.

Kelbert is perhaps the classic example of a Russian immigrant who came to Israel with great expectations of the Jewish state, nurtured during his years as a refusenik, and whose encounter with reality has led him to identify many things in Israel with the hated regime he abandoned. He can spot, more easily than most Israelis or foreign observers, those elements of Russian socialism which still characterise aspects of the Israeli economy; government monopolies of key industries, a top heavy bureaucracy, and the propagandist ideal of an intellectualised proletariat which never existed in Russia and has long since ceased to exist in Israel. He is, like so many Russian immigrants, intensely hostile to Labour and its policies and admires only a handful of politicians on the right.

'The things I see as positive in Israel are that it is a country where people can feel at home, where their existence is safe, where there is opportunity for the children. The fact that there are so many people from different countries, which also interact, is interesting, and there is the opportunity to travel.'

But at worst, Kelbert attributes the many difficulties he has encountered as a film maker in Israel to left-wing nepotism and 'censorship'. His most painful experiences have been with Israeli television, where until recently there was only one channel, controlled by the government – whose administrative appointments were often political, whether right or left parties were in control. The hothouse world of Israeli television does not welcome outsiders. But Kelbert sees all the rebuffs he has suffered as the work of 'leftists'.

Increasingly, Kelbert is seeking his backers among Jewish and other organisations outside Israel. Kelbert's 'sponsors' will probably not be in the Israeli film industry, where everything depends on old established contacts and a closed shop atmosphere, but among the emissaries of world Jewry, the people who channel funds coming from abroad. Inevitably, the basic lesson creative Russians are learning in Israel is the art of courting foreign patrons – 'sponsors'.

'The word the Russians hear all the time here is "sponsor". All the immigrants are looking for "sponsors" without really knowing what that means. In Russia everyone lived on a salary and no one had money left over for philanthropy. When it is explained to Russians that money has been obtained for a project from a "donor" or "sponsor" from a private fund, earmarked for a special purpose, they are totally at sea. What is a "private fund" and how can the "sponsor" (assuming that they have grasped what this person is) stipulate what is to be done with the money?'

Masha Bouman runs an agency called SAMA – a 'multilingual institute for languages and communication'. Shock haired, humorous, she chain smokes while talking non stop with a kind of defiant lucidity. SAMA, she explains, translates not texts but concepts – Russian ideas to Israelis, Israeli or Western ideas to Russians. Her institute is much in demand, and is unique in Israel.

'Twenty per cent of the Russian vocabulary was adapted from other languages. This has been going on since the time of Peter the Great, together with the fact that the Russians often did not understand the meaning of the words they used. The word chauffeur, for instance, went on being used after the Revolution as interchangeable with driver.'

Like Kaganskaya, Bouman has been in Israel since 1976. She studied at the Institute for Railway Engineers in Leningrad but did not complete her studies as she came to Israel, and after getting a degree in Russian literature at the Hebrew University, studied literature at UCLA. When she first arrived, she went to live in Kibbutz Hatsor in the Galilee. At first it seemed a paradise, but the snake appeared quite soon. Each week she worked in a different job as a volunteer, and she was amazed to note that the people she had worked with the previous week ignored her greeting on the paths of the kibbutz. She found it far easier to communicate with volunteers from the West than with Israelis.

Eventually she managed to meet a few survivors of the golden age of the kibbutz – the original collectivist revolutionaries. To her surprise, they still spoke of Russian Communism as an ideal (Stalinism survived only in China and in the Israeli left-wing kibbutzim, a tiny enclave, well after the Twentieth Party Congress.) They were not at all prepared for a meeting with young Russians who had broken free of the Communist regime. They did not want to hear what had happened to their dream of equality, 'which was beautiful, even if utopian'.

The misunderstandings between Israelis and Russians, said Bouman, were not only linguistic and abstract. There were even problems with numbers. If the Russians were told that fifty jobs were being provided somewhere, regardless of the context, they thought this a very small number – in Russia all numbers were large. If you told the Russians that half a million immigrants meant power, meant that they could influence politics, they were sceptical; in Russia, half a million was a paltry number.

Even when Israelis were sympathetic, their institutions were incomprehensible. Social workers' well-meaning intervention is often resented. If the Israelis said that single-parent families were 'groups at risk', the Russians found this insulting. In Russia, they were almost a norm, certainly not a problem or 'risk'.

Bouman does not like the suggestion that culturally speaking the Russians are years out of date, though she knows that the breach with European thought and art during the Stalinist period was tragic. She insists that during the 1920s, Russia was in the European vanguard (as anyone who saw the Paris–Moscow exhibition at the Beaubourg some years ago will remember). In 1929, the doors had slammed shut, not to open until the Khruschev era. Only the Sinayevsky–Daniel trail in 1956 had revealed to the West the degree of persecution of Russian writers who had to resort to smuggling their work out of the Soviet Union. But Soviet psychologists like Vigotsky and Luria had recently been rediscovered and aroused interest. The West, said Bouman, had been cut off from knowing what was going on in Russia just as Russia had been cut off from the West. Even though it would take years of reassessment for the Russians to reorientate themselves, they were right to feel that they had a modern cultural history as rich as that of the West.

Evgeny Steiner, professor of Japanese culture and art, now teaching at the Hebrew University, has been in Israel about a year, and is deeply disappointed, distressed, displaced. More fortunate than most Russian immigrants, he has work in his own profession. Yet he feels, he says, like 'an emigrant and an exile'.

Steiner is a man about forty, youthful looking, bland: depressively bland. He walks so lightly that he seems scarcely to be there, and indeed, he is somewhere else. In limbo.

Steiner's work at the Hebrew University is teaching an introductory course on Japanese culture. He was disappointed in the students who, he said, were only interested in accumulating facts and not in acquiring knowledge of a distant culture. He said they would have preferred learning about Japanese politics or economics as that might have helped them earn money. They had also complained that his accented English was 'not like that on the television'. He said he felt like a preparatory school teacher. The only two students who showed any real interest, he said with biting irony, were an American with a pigtail and hippie propensities, sent by his parents to Israel, and a wealthy elderly woman with time on her hands. The following year, however, he would teach post-graduates in a speciality course. In Russia, he insisted, students were interested in the history of ideas; there, no one expected to make a living out of Japanese poetry. Many students spent years on menial work, street cleaning, after graduating. But their love of pure learning was great.

Russians like Steiner irritate many Israeli intellectuals who have attempted to help them integrate into life in the country. Lydia Aran, an Israeli lecturer on Buddhism whose Hebrew book on the subject for the general public became a best seller, contests Steiner's arguments from her double experience in the Soviet Union and Israel. Born in Vilna, she and her twin sister were rescued from the Nazis by their high school teacher. A sergeant in the Red Army at the age of eighteen after the war, Aran came to Israel in 1948 when the state was founded. She had helped many Russian intellectuals, including Steiner, adjust to Israel, but she had spent sufficient time in the Soviet Union to understand, and deplore, the effect of what she saw as their conditioning. Aran shared Steiner's interest in Far Eastern culture; she also knew the origins and character of the Russo–Jewish intelligentsia to which he had belonged. Aran's response to Steiner's complaints about Israel was both significant and more informed than the testy dismissal by many Israelis of the Russians as 'arrogant' and 'ungrateful'.

In Steiner's view, the Russian intelligentsia was a 'monastic order', dedicated to pure learning, and an élite to which he had been proud to belong. He had found no equivalent in Israel. The Hebrew University campus had not provided the 'escape' from the outside world he thought a university should provide. The Israelis, he complained, did not want to hold discussions on abstract subjects. They were earthbound and dull minded, hostile to the Russians. The Russian intelligentsia, he feared, would die in Israel, as it could not contribute to the life of the country.

After weeks of argument, and when Kaganskaya too had written in praise of the 'culture of alienation', Aran summed up the roots of her private controversy with Steiner, excerpts of which are printed here with her consent:

A Letter to a Russian Intellectual who does not wish to belong:

Dear Friend: both you and Mrs Kaganskaya speak in your articles about alienation as characterising the contemporary

Russian intellectual, and I am sure that anybody who knows
the Soviet regime and the kind of society in which you spent
your formative years will agree that alienation was one of the
ways for a decent person to protect his or her dignity and
integrity . . . But I feel that it is wrong to raise this alienation
and the attitudes which follow from it to the status of an
absolute value . . . To decide on one's stand vis à vis a culture, a society, a cause, one should at least learn something
about it. To judge a new environment by criteria derived
from a totally alien reality is like using one's sense of smell
to evaluate a symphony.

Steiner had deplored the fact that this alienated intelligentsia
was dying out. Aran reminded him that it was almost uniquely a
Russian phenomenon which had evolved in response to the
Russian history of continuous tyranny. When Steiner both cultivated 'alienation' but complained of a loss of status after emigration, she wrote,

if one chooses to opt out of the competition and remain an
outsider it is fine, except that this choice does not go together
with your concern for status. May I remind you that whereas in Russia your status was based not on your professional
or creative achievements but on your belonging to the prestigious alienated élite, this is totally irrelevant to your status
in any country you choose to immigrate to. . . .
    When you and I agreed the other day that this massive
Russian immigration could be dangerous for the future
nature of Israeli society, we had, each of us, I am afraid, a
different danger in mind. While both of us referred to the
corrupt norms of Soviet society, I also had in mind the
dangers inherent in the mental attitudes of people like yourself. I refer to those who – temporarily disorientated . . .
frightened by the unfamiliar need to compete for one's place
in society, and discouraged by a temporary decline in status
– remain émigrés rather than expose themselves to the adver-
sities and challenges of the new.

Aran pointed out that the public exchange of views, so alien to
the Soviet regime, was the main medium of discourse in the
West – and nowhere more than in the university.

We are paid to criticise, to attack, to question and to test accepted truths and to fight, if necessary, for what seems to us right. I realise that this is something very hard for you to grasp because your experience has been different, but you will have to recognise and bear in mind the difference if you wish to understand the Western cultural scene.

Finally, Aran told Steiner passionately

not to be so damned condescending! Israel has been involved with Western culture from its establishment. Whatever its faults, whatever the shortcomings of our absorption of the recent immigration, let me remind you that in the course of its short history this country has accepted without selection, and rehabilitated, millions of refugees – holocaust survivors and the sick, the old and illiterate – people whom no one else wanted . . . irrespective of their ability to contribute. So why should you not be committed to it? Why would you not give it a chance? Good luck!

The letter went unanswered.

What, Then, is to Be Done?

On 4 May 1993, the largest demonstration ever of dissatisfied immigrants, organised by Forum, was held on the hillside opposite the Knesset building, the Israeli Parliament. One hundred and seventy-seven buses had brought what the police assessed as between 12–15,000 Russian immigrants from all over the country to complain about unemployment, inadequate housing and poverty. Natan (Anatoly) Sharansky, head of Forum and the most heroic refusenik of them all, who had spent twelve years in Soviet prisons before finally arriving in Israel in 1986, addressed the crowds over a loudhailer. He alleged that a third of all Soviet immigrants who had arrived in the last three years were unemployed; that 100,000 immigrants (nearly a quarter of all the Russians in the latest immigration) were living below the poverty line in Israeli terms, among them forty-three per cent of Russian immigrant children. He asserted that the present Labour government had come to power with the help of the Russian immigrants, but that it had done no more to help them than the right-wing government which had preceded it. This, he told journalists, had made many of them disillusioned with Israeli democracy, and was causing others to leave the country.

Yair Tsaban, the Minister of Absorption, who came out of the Knesset to address the demonstrators from beyond the vast plaza and ironwork fence which separates Israel's legislature from its electorate, expressed sympathy with the immigrants' problems but contested Sharansky's statistics. He argued that immigrant unemployment had been sinking steadily over the past few years and was now slightly over twenty per cent; that a third of the immigrants were involved in government mortgage housing schemes; that the present government had increased the 'absorption basket', was planning more relief schemes, and that his office was battling to increase extra teaching hours for immigrant children. Many immigrant scientists were working in their fields, but there was no way that Israel could provide work for the large numbers of doctors arriving, said Tsaban. He was received with scepticism, and his reference to Prime Minister Rabin's concern was greeted with boos and derisive whistles.

The atmosphere in Israel at the time of the demonstration was itself indicative of the fact that the Russians are scarcely at the top of the list of the government's priorities. Far more attention was paid by the media, and by the country at large, to a concurrent teachers' strike which had left children roaming the streets for days, and another strike by government nurses, with the wretched sight of whole families in hospitals feeding immobilised patients.

For the Russians, the demonstration was an unprecedented event, a break with their usual passivity; for other Israelis, it was an everyday occurrence. Demonstrators are continually out on the streets in Israel: against withdrawal from various parts of the occupied territories; in favour of the deportation of more Palestinian extremists; against corruption; women against the occupation. The streets are a crossword puzzle of protest, decipherable only to those who know the clues provided by the Israeli political system. The Russians are just one more reason for the police barriers to go up and the overcrowded roads of central Jerusalem to be blocked to irritated motorists.

'I didn't realise that to enter democratic elections as the head of a party, I needed so much money,' said Yuli Kosharovsky, the head of the Russian immigrant party at the 1992 elections. 'Our whole campaign – mine, Sharansky's and all our other organisers – was run on loans we took out ourselves. We had no backers. We Russians came with no political experience, we didn't realise that a voluntary organisation also needs funds. We only had four months to prepare our election campaign.'

Kosharovsky, like Sharansky, is one of the veteran refuseniks who during the 1970s gathered many young Zionists around him in Moscow. His party only gained 12,000 votes, as against ten times as many, or sixty per cent of the Russian vote, for the

Labour party, and some Russians argue that the veteran leadership has, today, only the most tenuous links with the newcomers.

Kosharovsky agrees that the Russian vote was, in the main, a protest vote against the Likud right-wing government, not on national policy, but because the Likud had systematically ignored the problems of the Russian immigrants. The fact that, during the elections, there was a huge Russian media network, from the newspapers to radio and television, open to those appealing to the immigrant public, did not help Kosharovsky's party. 'That cost money too; the newspapers wanted us to pay them to publish our articles; *Reka* [the Russian radio programme] was closed to us on political grounds, and on television they told us we could not talk politics except on the party political broadcasts allotted us by the national television.'

'We were attacked as a "Russian party", though both Sharansky and myself made it clear that we wanted to represent all the immigrants, including the Ethiopians and the Argentinians. But the Russians were in such a huge majority that no one took that seriously. People were afraid that "Russians" would have political interests which went beyond immigrant problems. We weren't helped by other Russians in the media because they were all in the pay of the bigger parties, all committed to existing Israeli political interests. In the end it was all a matter of money.'

There are two conflicting issues at stake here. On the one hand, the Russians want to become part of the country, not to be a separate population; on the other, only as a powerful pressure group, a lobby, can they explain to the country's leadership the very particular problems facing the Russian immigrants. 'The politicians just don't want to know. When we [the leaders] went to demonstrate outside the Prime Minister's office no one came out to talk to us. The Ethiopians get far more consideration, because no one is afraid that they are going to take over the country; with us, it's different.'

The 'particular problems' of the Russians were, in Kosharovsky's view, first and foremost, employment; then accommodation; then the large number of immigrants who were already social cases, not only the old and the disabled, but those over fifty years old who could not find employment despite their undisputed skills, because no one wanted to guarantee them permanent work involving pension rights: people who sat at home, made their families' lives a misery, and would drag the others down with them. Kosharovsky put the numbers of these 'problem cases' at between 150,000 and 200,000 people, or about a third of all the Russian immigrants who had arrived over the past twenty years. He did not differentiate between the seventies and the nineties immigration, though on the whole the early comers were well integrated into the population. He used the Israeli jargon in terming unemployed Russians a 'social time bomb'. Other problems, in order of importance, were the youngsters who had trouble finishing their education, the issue of mixed marriages, and cross-cultural misunderstandings.

Dina Brodsky, a lecturer in political science in the Russian Studies Department of the Hebrew University, who has been in Israel since 1976, thinks it would have been possible *theoretically* for the Russians to have constituted a separate political party, and is still possible today. Firstly, because of their numbers. Secondly, because they were resentful at their treatment by the previous government. But she said that it would be impossible for the Russians to form a party with a positive, rather than a protest, platform. If they formed a separate party, they would be putting themselves into a political ghetto.

Kosharovsky's party had failed in '92, she thought, for several reasons. Firstly, it was headed by people from the 1970s immigration who did not represent the 1990s. Forum already had formed links with the Israeli establishment – the Jewish Agency, the Zionist Movement, etc. – and thus was not seen as independent. The second reason, she thought, was the inability of Kosharovsky's circle to evolve an actual programme. He had not realised that the post-glasnost Russian immigrants understood the free economy already, better than he did. Kosharovsky had hovered between proposals for privatisation and links with the monopolist government. He had suggested, on the one hand, that medical care should be privatised and, on the other, asked the government to provide work for the immigrants as the largest employer. He could not, she said, have it both ways.

'No free enterprise can cope with *all* the Russians in Israel,' Kosharovsky retorted. He denied that he was identified with the establishment, saying that no one wanted to listen, that no one in the establishment was interested in the Russians. Given the extent of the problem, did he agree with the high official in the Ministry of Labour who had said that Israel did not need all the sick, old people who were coming and that the Agency should not encourage them? 'The Law of Return should be honoured: I'm a Zionist to my bones'; though it was the young who should get more encouragement, families could not be separated. One third of his own salary, Kosharovsky said, went to his old mother, who lived with his family.

The 'absorption basket' was a good arrangement, he thought, but the Ministry of Absorption subsidies to employers which enabled them to employ Russian scientists and engineers, and so on – the system at the Technion and the Wingate Institution, for instance – for two years, was very bad. What it meant was 'Use the immigrants' skills, exploit them cheaply, and then throw them out.' The kibbutzim were doing the same thing, he said.

'What, then, should be done?' The grand plan of Kosharovsky and his colleagues was that he had found a group of foreign investors, sponsors who were prepared to invest two billion dollars in a DFI (direct financial investment) plan which would be based on the idea of employing immigrants in specially designated geographical areas near the main towns, where they would enjoy reduction in taxation, export incentives, and which would constitute almost autonomous free-trade areas, without the intervention of government bureaucracy. It would call for special legislation, however. There were precedents for this (but on a much more modest scale – for instance the southern port town of Eilat which enjoys a number of tax benefits, and development towns, where investors also have special conditions). But economic observers like the former governor of the Bank of Israel, Michael Bruno, have suggested that nothing less than economic changes on a national scale would solve the problem of immigrant unemployment. Kosharovsky, however, believed that the 'immigrant enclave' idea would benefit the whole country; meanwhile, it would give priority to the employment of skilled immigrants who had no place in the existing structure. It would also bring to Israel the other potential Russian immigrants who, at the moment, were hesitating because of the lack of work for them in Israel.

★   ★   ★

Not all the immigrant élite agree with the politicians that Israel's security and economic problems are the chief obstacle to the immigrants' absorption.

Marina Solodkina, an economist and Russian studies expert, thought that the Israeli economy had been damaged more badly by the use of cheap Arab labour than by Russian immigration. 'I'm continually being told that Israel is a small country surrounded by enemies and thus that its economic potential is limited.' Her answer to this is 'What about Taiwan?', a successful economy though menaced continually by the shadow of mainland China and, as she pointed out, running a better economy than Communist China.

Solodkina, who was close to the circles advising Gorbachev on economic policies during the first period of perestroika, comes from a Jewish family in Kiev, with a strong sense of its identity and history. Her husband, a metallurgist, had immediately found work in Israel. Solodkina, who is a political commentator for the Russian television and radio programmes in Israel, and who looks forward to writing soon in Hebrew, is a matronly, softly spoken woman in her early forties whose views are all the more pungent for being gently presented.

'There were great hopes during the Gorbachev era that there would now be a new existence for the Jews in Russia. Normalisation was hoped for, as it was during the October Revolution. But the roots of anti-semitism are too deep among the Russian people. In 1917, too, the *shtetl* Jews hoped the revolution would bring them equality. Yet the post Second World War period saw the revival of anti-semitism under Stalin. Nationalism and chauvinism prevailed, as indeed it might today.'

The reason that the Russian immigration appears so haphazard in character is that Communism had destroyed the Jewish communities of Russia. 'There's no "Jewish community escaping", because there are no more communities, but rather a conglomeration of families. Each family makes its own decision.'

She thought the way Israeli politicians and political scientists related to Israel's geopolitical problems was 'melodramatic' and that the influence of its enemies on its economy was overestimated. Economists should look at other small countries with large populations, or at cities like, for instance, Singapore or

Hong Kong. The Israeli economy is stagnant, like that of Russia in the 1970s. In the 1960s, she says, Israel and Japan were level on the degree of technological competence. Yet Japan had surged ahead economically. She thought that Israel was 'moving towards the use of Russian expertise', and like all thinking Israelis involved in absorption, that the answer to immigrant unrest was closely bound up with an overhaul of the entire Israeli economy.

Paradoxically, she thought that Russia, however monolithic, had been more flexible in managing supply and demand of qualified personnel than Israel. For instance, when it was clear that health services were poorest in outlying districts, a travelling surgical service was set up. Russian physicians could be used to service outlying districts in Israel. But this too would mean a radical reform of Israel's health services, which are heavily centralised and subsidised by the government.

If the challenge the Russians pose is taken seriously, then a partial overhaul of Israel's economic and social system looks inevitable. Efficient use of skilled manpower could lead to the proliferation of science-based industries – some of which are even now among Israel's biggest foreign currency earners. If all the Russian construction engineers in the country, some Russians have suggested, devoted themselves to improving building methods and perhaps even took over building for immigrants, then the building industry, which is years out of date because of the availability of cheap Arab labour might be modernised. In the social context, the introduction of civil marriage would solve the problem of the tens of thousands of young Russian immigrants who will not be able to marry, when the time comes, according to rabbinical law.

Paradoxically, Israel, though a young country, is still chained to political, economic and social concepts evolved during the years of state building and which today hobble Israel's capacity to use the skills the Russians bring with them to the best advantage.

Government monopolies, the slow pace of privatisation and liberalisation of the economy over recent years is reminiscent of the system the Russians have left behind them, though few recognise it. One dramatic example took place at a five-month retraining course for teachers at Bet Berl, the Labour Party training college where a group of Russian teachers of English were being introduced to the Israeli system. Typically, the Russians wanted more 'pedagogical training' and revision of the rules of syntax; what they got was 'relaxation and visualisation methods' for use in the classroom. Suddenly the director of the course appeared and announced that during the coming week there would be a visit to Kibbutz Sde Boker in the Negev, to the grave of David Ben Gurion, first Prime Minister of the State of Israel.

'It will be a whole day's outing,' he said. 'We leave at eight in the morning and arrive back about twelve hours later. You'll be given a trip through the Negev and we'll show you the kibbutz college, which is a centre for desert studies. Marvellous scenery.'

One teacher looked dismayed. She was a single parent, and her little boy of eight would return from school and find no one at home. She didn't think she could come unless she could find someone to look after him.

'Attendance on the outing is compulsory,' said the director severely. 'Anyone who fails to turn up will not receive their diploma and will have to repeat the course all over again.'

There were no more protests. It was all dismally familiar.

While the Russians detect such strange echoes of Israel's semi-Bolshevik origins in this ostensibly Western state, Israelis search for the Jews behind the Russians. No one wants to revoke the Law of Return, the moral foundation for Israel's existence, but the consequences of the law have suggested that difficult as it is to define a Jew in purely religious terms, it is even more difficult, in the Russians' case, to do so historically.

During the Soviet era, many Jews tried to escape the ethnic label which could make their lives and careers more difficult, to shed the title of *Evrei* and acquire that of 'Russian' in their 'passports'. Many paid to have new documents made out as Russians, and were undetected. But with the advent of perestroika, and with the sole option of escape from the crumbling Soviet empire emigration to Israel, these people found that their 'Russian' documents were now an embarrassment. Only those who could claim Jewish parentage were eligible for the coveted entry permit. So they unearthed their original, incriminating documents, and presented them to the Israeli authorities.

It was not long before checks revealed that these Soviet citizens had double and contradictory ethnic identities. The problem for the Israeli emissaries was: which set of documents was the forgery, the new or the old? Were these people Jews masquerading as Russians, or Russians masquerading as Jews? What made matters still more difficult was that numbers of non-Jewish Russians had learned the importance of finding (or manufacturing) a Jewish grandmother in order to leave the country, and were besieging the synagogue records in order to locate a grandmother who was safely dead and whose identity had not yet been exploited. This new version of Gogol's *Dead Souls* soon became known to the Israelis, who swiftly despatched their own experts to the scene and are now trying to sort out the real from the phoney Jews.

Historically this is amazing: throughout the long centuries of persecution and flight, Jews had adopted Christian identity in order to flee their countries of birth for safer havens. Most recently, in pre-war Germany, thousands of Jews bought documents of Catholic parentage to escape Nazi persecution. This must be the first time in history that non-Jews have claimed Jewish origins in order to flee their homeland.

But there are further-reaching implications for the state of Israel than mere bureaucratic tangles. The Law of Return, with its liberal provisions unparalleled in modern immigration legislation, was actually framed with the notorious 1935 Nuremberg Laws in mind. Under these racist laws, Jews singled out for discriminatory treatment were identified through parentage reaching back three generations – even though they might meanwhile have abandoned Judaism and Jewry and even converted to Christianity. The Law of Return aimed at redressing this wrong. It remains of importance as a charter of Israel's claim to legitimacy in the 'family of nations' in what is still a hostile environment. But Israel has now reached the stage in which, its identity firmly established, it can afford new blood – even that which is not ancestrally Jewish.

So this extraordinary exodus, posing the question of whether Gogol or the biblical Valley of Bones is more relevant to the identity of the Russian Jews in Israel, suggests that Israel is becoming not only a country of refuge but a genuinely pluralist

215

state. Perhaps it does not matter whether all the immigrants are Jews. With Ezekiel's 'exceeding great army' of revived Jews standing on their feet, the 'shaking bones' of the Russian Diaspora put together, the Jewish state is indubitably strengthened, and – whatever the difficulties – intact.

Index